CURRENCY

DOUBLEDAY

MAGIC AT WORK

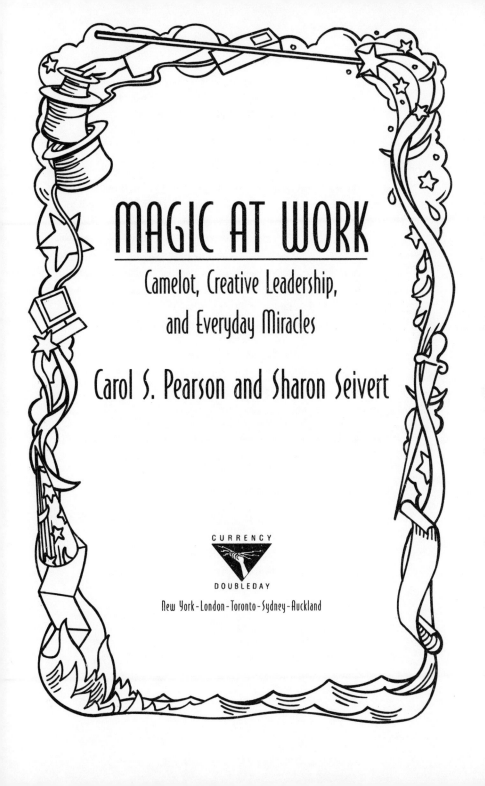

MAGIC AT WORK

Camelot, Creative Leadership,
and Everyday Miracles

Carol S. Pearson and Sharon Seivert

CURRENCY

DOUBLEDAY

New York · London · Toronto · Sydney · Auckland

A Currency Book

PUBLISHED BY DOUBLEDAY

a division of Bantam Doubleday Dell Publishing Group, Inc.

1540 Broadway, New York, New York 10036

Currency and Doubleday are trademarks of Doubleday, a division of
Bantam Doubleday Dell Publishing Group, Inc.

Grateful acknowledgment for permission to reprint "The Faces at Braga" from the
work *Many Rivers Meet*, by David Whyte, copyright by David Whyte, reprinted with
kind permission from Many Rivers Company, P. W. Box 868, Langley, WA 98260; and
excerpts from *Meditations with Julian of Norwich*, by Brendan Doyle, copyright 1983
by Brendan Doyle, reprinted by permission from Bear and Company, P. O. Box 2860,
Santa Fe, NM 87504. In addition, appreciation to Meristem, 4307 Underwood Street,
University Park, MD 20782, for permission to use the service mark "Magic at Work."

Library of Congress Cataloging-in-Publication Data

Pearson, Carol, 1944–
Magic at work : Camelot, creative leadership, and everyday miracles / Carol S.
Pearson and Sharon Seivert. — 1st ed.
p.   cm.
Includes bibliographical references (p.   ).
1. Archetype (Psychology)   2. Self-actualization (Psychology)   3. Magic.
4. Leadership.   5. Success.   6. Success in business.   I. Seivert, Sharon.
II. Title.
BF175.5.A72P44   1995
155.2′64—dc20   95-19058
CIP

ISBN 0-385-41729-2

To my children, Jeff, Steve, and Shanna
—Carol S. Pearson

To the Siddha and Reiki Masters who have guided me on my
own Magician's journey.
—Sharon Seivert

If civilization is ever going to be anything but a grandiose pratfall . . . then statesmen are going to have to concern themselves with magic and poetry. Bankers are going to have to concern themselves with magic and poetry. Time magazine is going to have to write about magic and poetry. Factory workers and housewives are going to have to get their lives entangled in magic and poetry.

—*Tom Robbins,* Even Cowgirls Get the Blues

Contents

Acknowledgments

I am grateful to Adele Ellis, who typed drafts of this manuscript too numerous to mention and who good-naturedly
warned me when the language was getting too esoteric.

I very much appreciate the contributions of Betsy Polk,
coordinator of the Mount Vernon Institute. She typed correc-
tions in the final stages of the manuscript, but over and above
that, she called on her own expertise as a writer to edit certain
passages, or called to my attention others that were either
unclear or obscure. She was wonderfully supportive as I struggled to balance the demands of administration and public
speaking with writing. To Sylvia Benatti, many thanks for stepping in in the copyediting stage of this manuscript to see that
deadlines were met while Betsy was on vacation. Without your
competent and nurturing help, I could not have finished the
book on time.

I cannot thank Angela Miller, my agent, enough for her
time and support during what can be characterized only as a
very long and difficult labor. I am grateful to Arthur Levine,
for his integrity, his expertise, and his sage advice. I also
appreciate the contributions of my editors at Doubleday, Har-
riet Rubin and Janet Coleman, and copy editor Bob Daniels,
all of whose comments were often challenging but invariably
right. Doubleday hung in with this project, even when the
writing took longer than any of us had planned.

I am grateful as well to Charmaine Lee, whose polarity
training program and ongoing synergy classes gave me a foundation for understanding how the five polarity energies—
earth, fire, water, air, and ether—work in our bodies and
psyches.

Additional thanks go to Lee Knefelkamp for the phrase "the

In-Between"; to Starhawk's workshop for teaching me about ritual and how archetypal elements can be invoked to form a magic circle; and to the Cozi for practice in creating everyday miracles.

I also must thank my husband, David R. Merkowitz, for editorial suggestions—but more than that, for unfailing emotional support. Moreover, both he and my daughter, Shanna, gave me practical help when I ran into nearly insurmountable computer problems in the final months of writing. Shanna not only lent me her Macintosh but took the time to teach me how to use it. To David, Shanna, Jeff, and Steve, my appreciation for your tolerance of the abstractedness that creeps into my life when I am writing. It made it easier to persist, knowing that you understood.

Of course, this book would not have come alive in the same way without the help of all the people I surveyed or interviewed, both the ones I cite and the ones whose stories served as deep background. I so appreciate their time and wisdom.

Finally, I cannot say enough about the support for this project I received from Mount Vernon College, especially President LucyAnn Geiselman. Without her encouragement to make the book a priority in my critical first year as dean of the Mount Vernon Institute, it could not have been completed.

—Carol S. Pearson

In addition, I would like to thank my beloved Jeremiah Cole and my wonderful family, community, and associates, and especially Donna Sherry, for their unflagging support in this long effort.

—Sharon Seivert

Preface: From Warrior to Magician

Society today is experiencing a major shift in consciousness as people switch from thinking like Warriors to thinking like Magicians. The Magician is that part of us that manifests the highest and greatest potential in any situation. But the Warriors in and around us often misunderstand magic, misinterpreting it as a means for focusing their will in order to control their destiny, which is why magic has gotten a bad name during the thousands of years in which the Warrior archetype has prevailed. Today most people think of magic as trickery, done as sleight of hand or with mirrors. Worse, people see magic as a way to gain control over others. Clients who heard I was studying magic in the workplace sometimes assumed I would be able to teach them to use communications skills to manipulate others into doing what they wanted, create advertising and sales approaches to get people to buy products they did not need, or predict the future so as to best the competition.

True magic is not a means of control or manipulation or evil sorcery. It is about cooperating with the most positive energy arising in any situation to create the best outcome for all concerned. It is less about getting your way than about expressing your best self. The Lord's Prayer, for example, invokes the highest form of magic, saying, "Thy Kingdom come, Thy will be done, on earth as it is in heaven." In more secular terms, Magicians invoke the most beautiful and noble outcome possible for themselves and others.

In our everyday world, most of us are oblivious to how ingrained Warrior thinking is in our lives and organizations. Warriors take for granted that war is inevitable, even noble. They value competition, tough-mindedness, and things they

---

A MAGICIAN BY ANY OTHER NAME

Names for those assuming the role of Magician include sha-man, medicine man or woman, and wizard. They also include witch and sorcerer, which often—although not always—are used in a pejorative fashion.

---

can touch, taste, and measure. There is nothing inherently wrong with the Warrior archetype. It has given us great gifts of analysis, resolve, and strength. But the Warrior myth can be so consuming, we forget that alternative behavior is possible. As Albert Einstein put it, "No problem can be solved from the same consciousness that created it."[1]

The Warrior archetype has been necessary to our survival as a species: It teaches how to use a military, hierarchical model to organize large numbers of people. It shows the neces-sity of establishing strong boundaries to prevent our efforts from dissipating and to protect us from real enemies. It helps us set priorities for the use of scarce resources. It gives us the courage to risk our safety for our beliefs. It helps us to make fine distinctions and set goals.

In the post–Cold War era, however, the Warrior's us/them mentality and need to win at others' expense can be a liability if we do not complement and balance it with other archetypal approaches. The Magician archetype is emerging today be-cause it can help us thrive in a world without superpowers, stable borders, or right/wrong answers. In a time of global interdependence, it may, in fact, take miracles to help us learn to balance conflicting needs and attitudes, and be willing to learn from those different from ourselves.

WHAT IS AN ARCHETYPE?

The psychologist C. G. Jung made the contemporary world aware of the power of archetypes—personages, like the Great Mother or the Great Father; and symbols, like the cross or the mandala. He became fascinated by apparently esoteric images —which he recognized from the myths, art, and spiritual belief systems of ancient times—that appeared in his patients' dreams. Jung's patients had no knowledge of these ancient sources, so how was it that they would dream such symbols? Archetypal symbols often held the key to both understanding the patients' complexes and to finding the way out, into healing. A dream of a mandala, for example, indicated a struggle to achieve wholeness.

Archetypal images are natural to the human psyche. Arising from what Jung calls the "collective unconscious," they inform not only our dreams but often our waking lives as well. Neo-Jungian analyst Robert Johnson stresses how archetypes provide structure for experience, just as a river bed gives form to a river.[2] For example, when we project the Great Mother archetype on a female boss, we unconsciously expect that she will take care of us, providing unconditional love and support. If she fails to do so, she is the Bad Mother, the reason for all our troubles. The sign that an archetype is being projected is that a regular, limited human being seems filled with awesome power over us. To work with that person, we need to learn to withdraw the projection. We also can use a knowledge of archetypes to understand how an individual or a whole culture makes meaning of the world. That is, archetypes help define different paradigms for interpreting what is happening to us. Moreover, every archetype has within it a power that, once gained, gives us an enhanced ability to express parts of ourselves in the world.[3]

The Magician Seeks:	The Warrior Emphasizes:
• Vision	• Tough either/or choices
• Consensus	• Majority rule
• Systemic, contextual thinking	• Specialized, disciplinary thinking
• Utilization of individual talents	• Meritocracy, competition
• Covenantal relationships	• Hierarchical and adversarial relationships

Magic at Work builds on three prior books about the application of archetypal psychology to everyday life: *The Hero Within: Six Archetypes We Live By* and *Awakening the Heroes Within: Twelve Archetypes to Help Us Find Ourselves and Transform Our World* and *Heroes at Work.*[4] *Magic at Work* develops theories about the Magician and Warrior archetypes contained in these books and applies them to the contemporary workplace. Throughout, archetypal theory is augmented by interviews with, and composite examples of, contemporary magical workplace leaders.

My hope is that readers will be inspired by this book as I was by the people I interviewed. Workplace leaders who took the time to share their stories with me reinforced my belief that magic is all around us today. We only have to notice.

In fact, magic may be brewing in your life right now. Read on.

MAGIC AT WORK

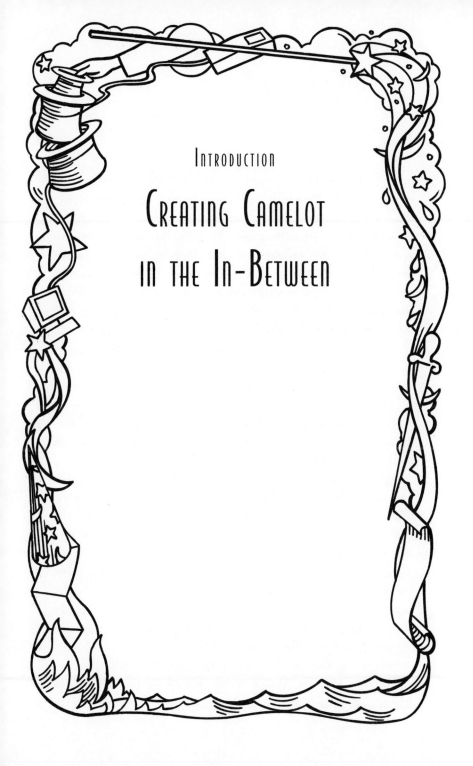

CREATING CAMELOT
IN THE IN-BETWEEN

Success in the 1990s requires us to understand that we are living in the In-Between. With the industrial age giving way to the information age, and nationalism giving way to global interdependence, something new is about to be born. As we approach the next millennium, and emerging possibilities coexist with the demise of business as usual, life can seem chaotic. *Magic at Work* is written to invite you to grasp the golden ring hidden in all the surrounding confusion—a golden ring that offers you the keys to finding magic in your life and work.

In fact, the time between two eras is inherently magical because in it new potential rises like the Phoenix out of the ashes of the world we have known. This means that the future is being born in you right now. You may feel this as a sense of infinite choice or potential, as a nameless yearning for something different, or even as an acute sense of dissatisfaction readying you to try something different.

Author Charles Handy (in *The Age of Unreason*) argues that now is not the time for linear projections or rational answers. Change today is "discontinuous." "We are now entering the Age of Unreason . . . a time when the only prediction that will hold true is that no predictions will hold true: a time, therefore, for bold imaginings in private life as well as public, for thinking the unlikely and doing the unreasonable."[1] The magic required in the workplace today is not a simple matter of learning a few new tools; it requires genuine personal and organizational transformation.

"Magic" is the art of releasing the highest and best potential in any situation. "Work" is the means for contributing to others and ideally to the greater good of society. You have

CREATING CAMELOT IN THE IN-BETWEEN

We are living in a time between two eras when the Magician archetype is reemerging in human consciousness. The Camelot stories, written in another time of massive social transformation, illustrate the stages of the Magician's journey. When interpreted metaphorically, they show us how the magic of the human imagination can help us thrive in challenging times.

Five basic stages to awakening our creative potential help us gain the gifts associated with five archetypal elements (and directions) and five magical objects:

Stage One: Initiation
   Element: Air (East)
   Object: Crystal Ball
Stage Two: Trial by Fire
   Element: Fire (South)
   Object: Magic Sword
Stage Three: Call
   Element: Ether (Center)
   Object: Grail
Stage Four: Illumination
   Element: Water (West)
   Object: Round Table
Stage Five: Mastery
   Element: Earth (North)
   Object: Grail Temple

magic in your work when you enjoy what you do, know that it makes a difference to others, and are successful enough at it to support a balanced and prosperous life. Magic also is "at work" in your life right now because you have a Magician within you. We all do. This magical part of you knows that imagination is the key to success, prosperity, and freedom.

Magic at Work provides a technology—both ancient and very contemporary—for creating or transforming your world.

Magic at Work can be read straight through like any other book, or it can be experienced as a course with readings and exercises for every weekday over a five-week span. If experienced in this intense way, it will help move you through the stages of the Magician's journey so that you can experience more magic in your life immediately. The lessons also are designed to expose you to techniques and perspectives that deepen with use. Accordingly, although you may see marked results during the next five weeks, changes in your life should intensify over time if you continue to use magical principles in your life and work.

This Introduction provides a context for understanding the rest of the book. "Living in the In-Between" describes the cultural context of our world today. We cannot be magical unless we are willing to be realistic about the forces at work around us. Then, "Creating Camelot" describes a utopian dream that emerged in another time of massive social transformation. First expressed in poetic form in the Middle Ages, that dream is now poised to guide us in the real and often prosaic world of earning a living. Finally, "The Education of the Magician" describes stages for becoming magical enough to create your own personal version of Camelot.

Living in the In-Between

Many of us have heard it said that when one door closes, another opens, but no one warns us that the hall between can be hell! If you feel somewhat disoriented and overwhelmed today, you are not alone. You can be doing your level best, working as hard as you can in ways that once were successful, and your business still may not thrive. These are not the times for business as usual; they are times for magic.

Magicians always have been masters of the space between —times like sunrise and sunset, when the boundaries between the worlds are not firm, when gods can walk the earth and humans can touch the sky, and when the line between life and death is permeable.

In the In-Between, we are challenged constantly to come alive by letting go of old habits, old methods. To progress we must, metaphorically speaking, die and be reborn into new experience. If we fail to rise to this challenge, we begin to feel like the walking dead, going through the motions of life without intensity or joy.

We get caught in the hallway of the In-Between until we heal whatever traumas or limitations are holding us back from being truly authentic and alive. After this is accomplished, we move into the next world. For example, an executive who has grown up protecting a fragile and childlike mother may waste much of his valuable energy protecting his employees and limit the company's potential by an unconscious tendency to hire employees who are like his mother. If the executive comes to understand this pattern, he can let the past be the past. As he lets go of this old pattern, his personal creativity and energy are greatly enhanced. He begins to expect employees to perform as responsible adults—and when he does so, they either rise to the occasion or leave. Gradually, his business improves, realizing a potential he had only dreamed of before.

The In-Between is a time of miracles, and a time when our deepest truths show through. If you ever have been present as a baby is born or someone you love is dying, you know the awe, the transcendent quality of such transitional moments. And if you have been through puberty or midlife, or have left a marriage or a job, you know how vulnerable you can become as you simultaneously grieve for what you have left behind and face the infinite possibilities of choices not yet made. Various spiritual and psychological traditions warn us that when our egos give way to allow our deeper soul realities to come forth, we can experience a similar kind of vulnerability —which is both exciting and terrifying.

Even if we are not aware of any inner need for transformation, our outer world is changing so dramatically that we will not be able to remain as we have been. Today our workplaces are in transition. We are "reinventing" government. Most of the organizations we work for are in the process either of metamorphosis or of dying. Often employees in organizations that are undergoing change—or actually going under—continue with business as usual or defuse their anxiety by arguing with each other and blaming management. Their behavior is not unlike that of family members who sit at the bedside of a dying relative and act as if nothing major were happening, or distract themselves from their grief by fighting or planning to sue the doctor. However, when the enormity of the transition is faced, people often do break through to their potential for greater authenticity, intimacy, wisdom, and spiritual depth.

Transitional moments are dangerous, disorienting, and full of opportunities for magic. That is why it is natural to feel alternately euphoric and powerless. Buckminster Fuller once said that from the time we are born into this world (because we have outgrown the womb), we are ever after constantly being born from realities that have become too small for us into greater and greater realities. The magic of the In-Between holds the potential for exponential growth. The pain we feel is a result of our attachment to the old ways, even though the old world is too small and limited for what we are becoming. Magic emerges when we let go of that to which we are accustomed so that we can grow into a world large enough to accommodate who we can be.

In the In-Between, we all are inherently magical because we cannot help being catalytic agents in the transformation of the culture. To put it a different way, because the old ways are dead or dying, the choices we make today, for good or ill, help shape the new era. In transitional moments, things are fluid, not set. Our current behavior establishes the new patterns.

Perhaps this is why so many people we encounter identify themselves as change agents. They understand that nothing is predetermined about the shape of that new world. We can be evil sorcerers, creating antiutopian havoc as easily as, or perhaps even more easily, than we can create utopian visions. To make a better world, we have to live consciously. To create a world of war, injustice, and environmental catastrophe, all we have to do is allow things to drift without making choices. Despair and cynicism are the enemies of magic. They cause us to contract, and in doing so, to limit what is possible in the future we are creating collectively.

So many people today worry about how they can create change, assuming that change will not occur unless they make a great effort. The truth is that change is the only constant of life, especially in the In-Between. When we think of causing change, we move into Newtonian thinking, as if reality were a heavy boulder and to move it along we must exert great force. Contemporary scientific thinking recognizes that we do not need to cause change; we just need to influence its direction a bit. A better metaphor than moving a boulder is sailing, where we use the force of the wind to take us where we want to go. The gift of the In-Between is change. We are in the process of creating our future world, whether we are aware of it or not, so we might as well create a society filled with wonder, awe—and magic. We can re-envision Camelot for our own time.

Creating Camelot

Once upon a time, long, long ago, there was another In-Between, much like our own . . .

Medieval Britain is in disarray. In a forest cave Merlin, the great Magician, has a vision of a utopian age that will bring Britain together with more peace, prosperity, and harmony than it has ever known before, and of the man who will make such a dream possible. Merlin engineers a tryst between King Uther Pendragon and Igraine, the wife of the Duke of Tintagel, thus producing a royal offspring—Arthur, the man destined to reunite all of Britain and create the kingdom of Camelot.

As a young king, Arthur is an accomplished Warrior, routing the Saxons, the Picts, the Scots, and the Irish, and finally also adding Norway and Denmark to Britain's domain. With the help of Merlin, his court Magician and advisor, Arthur becomes, over time, such a just, wise, and able ruler that the very name King Arthur calls up the image of the ideal Ruler.

Arthur is especially gifted at recruiting talent, including the great knights of the Round Table—Percival, Gawain, Lancelot, and others. His knights and ladies swear to uphold the standards of chivalry: to act nobly, be fair and kind, rescue those in distress, and be loyal not only to Arthur but to God. This high-minded and principled reign produces a prosperous and happy Golden Age.

Perhaps the best-known event in the Camelot legend occurs on the evening of the Feast of Pentecost, when the Holy Grail appears above the Round Table. The knights swear to go in search of the Grail, each taking a different and untrammeled path. Mythologist Joseph Campbell thus sees the appearance of the Grail as announcing the birth of individualism, marking the triumph of Western civilization.[2]

The Grail myth and the Camelot legend are teaching stories. Scholar R. J. Stewart calls them the Western mysteries, encoding ancient myths for modern edification.[3] Some stories tell how Joseph of Arimathea brought the Grail and Christ's secret mystic teachings to Britain, where they were combined with ancient Celtic and other magical traditions. The resulting wisdom texts teach the secrets of expressing spirit in the active world of enterprise through the intermediary force of the human imagination.

Passing wisdom on to the next generation is an important part of these legends. Taliesin taught Merlin, who in turn taught Arthur, who taught the knights. In a parallel female magical line, the priestesses of Avalon taught the sorceress Morgan le Fay and others. Today the Camelot legend makes ancient esoteric lore available to all of us. It challenges us to allow ourselves to be transformed, so that we may transform our worlds.

The story of Camelot is the organizing metaphor for this book because it emerged from a period as perilous as our own. When most of us think of Camelot, we think of a kingdom known for unparalleled peace, prosperity, and justice. But the Camelot story actually begins with massive social disarray, similar to what the world is experiencing today. When Arthur came to the throne, the old order no longer existed and society was threatened with dissolution as rival lords, most motivated only by their own narrow ambitions, fought over the power to rule. As in the world today, community was crumbling into rival factions and interest groups. At first the signs of chaos were much stronger in Camelot than were the hints of a new order. In Camelot, as in our world, magic sustained and nurtured an emerging social vision.

When I began writing *Magic at Work*, I had not planned to use the Camelot legend as its frame. Yet whenever I sat down to write, Camelot stories entered my mind. They simply would not leave me alone. Why is this? I wondered. What captivates me and others about the Camelot legend? Why does a tale of medieval knights, castles, grails, and romantic love remain so popular that we all know it?

For myself, I realized that I am frustrated by the fragmentation of American society, by the ethnic strife erupting throughout the world, and by rising tensions between groups. I know in my bones that it is possible for people to have a sense of community and commonality without losing the value of their differences or retreating to inequitable and anachronistic social roles. Yet all around me I see individuals and groups blaming and scapegoating one another. The Camelot legend attracts me because it offers a mythos that can help restore community to a splintered society.

To begin with, this great legend distills the best wisdom of Western (European) culture—wisdom that has informed the traditionally male domain of enterprise. At the same time, scholars such as Jessie Weston (in *From Ritual to Romance*) tell us that the Grail stories are derived from ancient mystery rituals that were part of indigenous, life-venerating religions— religions that worshipped goddesses as well as gods.[4] Moreover, says scholar H. A. Guerber, although the Grail stories were Christianized in Spain, their origin was Moorish.[5] Grail stories have multicultural roots, which is why they may have become popular at another time of cultural awakening. The mingling of different cultural traditions makes possible a great catalytic eruption of empowering thought.

In just such a way, this book offers unifying frame stories that can serve as guides to living in the pluralistic, complex world of the In-Between. Such roomy and inviting mythic frameworks call on us to give up being right at the expense of other individuals or groups, and to learn from diverse wisdom stories. Moreover, they challenge us to walk away from the battlefield of the war between the sexes, so that we can enjoy mutually honoring gender partnerships—for the good of our society, our workplaces, our children.

Marion Zimmer Bradley, in her best-selling novel *The Mists of Avalon,* sets the Camelot story between the time of the great goddess civilizations and the rise of patriarchy. Camelot was at its height when masculine and feminine forces were in balance. Camelot fell when patriarchy took a firmer hold. At that point women lost power and magic disappeared from our cultural lives; those practicing goddess religions were burned as witches. Magic eventually became associated with Satanism.

It is no accident that the Magician archetype is reemerging today as women reclaim power, theologians celebrate the feminine face of God, and Jungian psychologists (and others) extol the return of the feminine to the culture. Accordingly, a goddess figure—the Lady of the Lake—is the cosmic director of the Camelot story as it unfolds. It is she who rises from the lake and hands Arthur Excalibur (his magic sword), and she who rescues him and others at key moments in the action.

Hovering in the background of the action, the Lady of the Lake embodies a quality of feminine consciousness that can seem as mysterious and ineffable as a mist rising above a lake. Although this goddess magic is difficult to describe, we experience it every time we fall in love, lose ourselves in the pleasure of our work, feel life to be great adventure, or experience the awe and wonder of what we commonly call "magical moments."

The constant sense of another, more transcendent mythic world blending with ordinary reality (embodied in the symbol of the goddess rising from the lake) allowed the knights and ladies of Camelot to find greater pleasure, depth, and meaning in the active world of enterprise than we often do today. The Lady of the Lake is now inviting us to remember how to live magically, so that our spirits as well as our economy will flourish.

The Camelot story describes the process of creating a society so lovely that the word "Camelot" has become a synonym for "utopia," just as Merlin has become synonymous with Magician. Camelot speaks to our yearning for a more perfect world. We all have this longing, whatever our race, religion, or gender. I am not suggesting that you pattern your own utopian vision on the literal story of Camelot. In that time, after all, technology was primitive, peasants had few rights, and women's social roles were circumscribed. Rather, the story can challenge you—by example—to imagine *your own contemporary* utopian workplace and then create it.

Deep down, most of us hunger to lead lives that matter. In contrast to the antiheroes who crowd modern literature, the characters who fill the Camelot story strive to live nobly, love deeply, and sacrifice greatly. We know their names: Arthur, the just, fair, and noble once and future king; Merlin, the Magician who foretells it all and is the power behind the throne; courageous and devoted knights—Lancelot, Percival, and Gawain; the fair Guinevere, loved by Arthur and Lancelot; and the sorceress Morgan le Fay, whose power rivals even Merlin's. We find conflict, even villainy, in these stories—but never a focus on the banal subjects found in modern management literature: how to have the right image, how to achieve security, status, and wealth by exploiting your "human capital."

In many workplaces today, people act as if the bottom line of money were all that mattered. Consider this: If you had all the money in the world but had few friends, no sense of mattering and meaning in your life, and trouble facing yourself in the mirror every morning because you had compromised your own ethics, would you feel successful? Would you be happy? Similarly, if your organization operated "in the black" but your employees lived in fear, worked so hard that their health and personal lives suffered, or produced a product or service in which they did not believe, would you call this a successful company? Would you want to stay there?

You can start learning from Camelot by imagining what Merlin, Guinevere, or King Arthur would advise you to do if you found yourself in such an unsatisfactory situation. They might encourage you to live up to your highest values and contribute to the greater good of the work. They might urge you to find coworkers you respect and a setting for your work that allows you to reach your highest potential. They might tell you about chivalry, the importance of kindness to those in need, and the courage necessary to face the great challenges of your life.

Then you might begin to practice thinking mythically. If you have a problem, think of it as a dragon to be faced. If you feel a sense of nameless yearning, think of it as a call from a grail that urges you to seek greater enlightenment. If you supervise others, imagine yourself as King Arthur creating a Round Table that supports each person's highest attainment. If you fantasize about your future, imagine that you are Merlin having a vision for the world you might someday inhabit.

How do you get from fantasy to reality? To tap into the power of your Magician within, shine the light of consciousness on it through your imagination and immerse yourself in stories of magic.

Merlin and his magic helped Arthur throughout his life— just as magic can help each one of us today. Merlin arranged the secret meeting between Arthur's parents, King Uther and Igraine, that resulted in Arthur's birth. He served as teacher when Arthur was a growing boy and as trusted advisor when he became king. He advised him of auspicious times to go to battle, and about which nobles might form important political alliances through marriage. He warned of potential dangers, was instrumental in building the Round Table, and in one night lured the sacred stones of Stonehenge from Ireland to Britain by singing a magical song. Although Merlin may have preferred escaping to his cave—and however necessary to his magic these retreats might have been—his ultimate responsibility was to stand beside Arthur and lend his wisdom and magic to the creation of a prosperous and noble kingdom.

The figure of Merlin is larger than life. Merlin "had superhuman powers . . . He could speak as soon as he was born and he grew up able to change shape, to create all sorts of illusions and to see into both the past and the future."[6] Few if any of us think we have the kind of power ascribed to Merlin or even to King Arthur. These are archetypal figures and we are mortals. We may aspire to live responsibly, creatively, and with the power to be change agents in our communities, families, and workplaces, but we do not feel as grand as such figures of legend. In some ways, it is just as well that we do not. To do so in this democratic, egalitarian age would be to court grandiosity. No one of us has to be quite as kingly as Arthur or possess the magical powers of Merlin, because no one person needs to carry the archetype of the Ruler or the Magician all by himself or herself. This does not mean that we must settle for lives as antiheroes. We can carry these archetypes together—and together create a real utopia, one as wonderful as the Camelot of legend.

When read carefully, individual stories in the Camelot legend can help ordinary people to thrive in the In-Between. In the following chapters we will examine various characters who engaged in some sort of magic—Merlin, Arthur, Percival, Guinevere, and a host of lesser-known figures with connections to the Grail: Kundrie, Morgan le Fay, Titurel, Dindraine, the Hideous Damsel, and others. We will explore how their adventures metaphorically shed light on the everyday events occurring in the contemporary workplace of the In-Between.

However, at a time of rapid economic change and uncertainty, it would be folly to read these stories as permission to live out pie-in-the-sky, escapist fantasies. Real-life examples throughout this book show how the principles of Camelot magic can work to restore prosperity as well as dignity to our individual and collective lives.

To understand the mystery of Camelot and its significance for our time, we have to read it as a metaphor or parable. Most of us have never had a literal grail appear to us. We have, however, experienced our own calls to various quests. Though we do not sit at King Arthur's Round Table, we can find ways to minimize hierarchy and to create a sense of personal integrity and group camaraderie. We cannot lure Stonehenge to our locations, but we can celebrate our organizational vision and values to create a sense of meaning and sacredness in our work. We may not entertain great visions as Merlin did, but we do have hunches and can learn to follow them. We may not be able to change shape, but we can learn to be flexible.

Read in this metaphoric way, the legend of Camelot teaches us how individuals and organizations can become magical enough to thrive in the In-Between. To cooperate with the magic inherent in our time, it is important that we learn to do what Magicians do. We also can think more widely about the Magicians we know from story and legend.

In conducting interviews for this book, I was aware that managers are expected to be wizards. In the workplace of the recent past, leadership was relatively simple. You knew your industry. You figured out what needed to be done, told employees what to do, and if they didn't do it, you fired them. Today you are expected to be an expert in human relations, to understand and motivate people, even those very different from you. Rather than telling people what to do, you are expected to create consensus around shared goals, and when conflict arises, to find win/win solutions. Moreover, leadership in the modern organization is dispersed. Every employee is expected to share the consciousness of leadership—looking out for the good of the whole—and exhibit leadership skills in dealing with one another as well as with customers or clients. Furthermore, in today's fast-paced economy, you are expected to anticipate future trends and plan for them. You may not use a crystal ball, but you feel the pressure to be a miracle worker.

Today effective managers do long-range and short-range planning for the same reason ancient Magicians gazed into crystal balls: to prepare for the future. Crystal-ball gazing is not like watching television; it is about envisioning a future so compelling that people will want to make it happen. It also is about envisioning potential calamities in order to avoid them. Merlin, the great Magician, was famous for his power as a seer to do just this kind of magic.

Magicians also are known for using herbs, potions, and spells to heal the sick, raise the dead, and help people find love. Today effective managers institute their own spells and charms: employee assistance and training programs can help revitalize lifeless employees, while team building and diversity workshops help people learn to value one another. As Magicians once used rituals to create community, leaders now use meetings, conventions, and celebrations to create a common sense of mission and identity.

Finally, good Magicians are inventors, creating the tools of their trade. Modern managers are reinventing or reengineering just about everything in the workplace, and our lives are being transformed daily by the latest electronic miracles. The Camelot myth is filled with magically crafted objects: the Round Table, Excalibur (the sword of invincibility), and the Grail itself. Magical buildings also have important power roles in the story: the Grail Temple, the Grail Chapel, even the Castle of Camelot. Inventors in the story include the architect Titurel and Merlin, as well as others.

Before turning the page, you might stop a moment to motivate yourself by picturing a contemporary workplace with the virtues of Camelot. You and your coworkers have lives filled with meaning because you know you are contributing to a more peaceful, prosperous, and beautiful world. You sit at a round table, which simply means you work in relative equality with people enjoying a sense of mutual respect. Leadership carries true moral authority—because outer position matches inner ability—and inspires you with a vision worthy of your efforts. Beyond that, everyone shares a sense of dignity and nobility because everyone knows that what is being done is important. Conflict is faced and resolved, allowing all to be of one mind on outcomes. Work roles are congruent with employees' true talents and inner sense of purpose. No one is just putting in his or her forty hours.

Imagine yourself doing the work you most love, surrounded by people you respect and like, and contributing to the betterment not only of your workplace but of the larger world as well. Hold this image, for it can be the catapult that helps launch you toward your own personal Camelot.

The Education of the Magician

We live today in a work world that is wildly out of balance. Ambition, achievement, and persistent "doing" take more than their fair share of our time and attention. A CEO of a large corporation complained to me that he felt like the "Energizer bunny": he "kept going and going." We can protect the environment, improve productivity, and save ourselves from burnout if we understand the magic of the circle. It tells us not just to keep doing more of what we are doing but to stop and analyze what part of the wheel is being ignored and devalued. When we reestablish balance, magic is restored.

Magic happens not just because of what we *do* but because of what we are willing to become. Magic is an art, not a science. Like great painting, writing, or music, it emerges from the soul of its creator. Although it does require technical competence, skill alone is not enough. People tend to believe that Magicians, like great artists, are better than the rest of us. We believe this only because we have not yet learned that we all possess the potential to connect with our depths. We can learn how to do so just as we can learn technical skills. The Camelot legend and the symbol of the Wheel of Creation teach the possibility of having magic in our lives and of creating lives that express our essence.

The belief in simple magical answers demeans magic. In the world of magic, changes occur because consciousness changes. To achieve magical results, we first must learn to *be* magical. Many of us have had the experience of taking a course or a workshop that sounded great; most likely we were guaranteed success if we used a few easy tools. Yet friends of mine with self-esteem problems have gone to countless workshops and still grapple with an undermining lack of confidence. Like many academics, I am totally capable of reading a book on good nutrition and thinking that somehow this will make me healthier (and even thinner). Then I put down the book and eat just the way I'm used to!

We have to use and integrate skills in a way that changes consciousness and behavior. People often mistake understanding a few concepts for being able to employ them. My favorite example comes from a friend. A man she knew claimed to be a very powerful shaman. He was totally broke—but offered to teach her to have infinite power if she would just provide him with a free place to live! Undoubtedly, he had studied shamanism, but he did not know how to use it in any practical way.

How do we learn to be magical? Ancient Magicians such as Merlin and Morgan le Fay apprenticed with master Magicians from whom they learned the rudiments of their craft. However, the best students surpass their teachers, furthering knowledge and furthering life. Today most of us don't learn about magic from any mystery school but from the school of hard knocks. You may be lucky enough to find a magical mentor, but if not, remember that you have a Magician within you. Because magic is awakening in today's world, the Magician archetype probably is stirring within you as well.

People today are going through a modern version of the stages of development experienced by ancient shamans. Anthropologist Robert Ellwood notes that great shamans from indigenous cultures typically went through five stages before accepting their destinies. In stage one they received, but resisted, a call. In stage two they went through a kind of initiation, which often involved facing and healing some serious pathology. In stage three they underwent an ordeal, leading to stage four, in which they experienced illumination. In the final stage they accepted shamanistic missions.[7]

As I researched the Camelot legend and interviewed modern-day magical leaders, I modified Ellwood's model some-

THE LAST TEMPTATION OF CHRIST AS A SHAMAN'S JOURNEY

The pattern Robert Ellwood describes is exemplified tellingly by the movie version of Nikos Kazantzakis's *The Last Temptation of Christ*, which portrays Jesus' life as a classic shaman's journey, a very human story in which he, like most of us, sometimes is confused about his identity. However one feels about the historical Jesus, and whatever one's religious beliefs, the movie is interesting for what it suggests about how people today, living without a cultural context for shamanism, respond to the call to magic.

For most of the movie, Jesus is presented as not knowing his destiny. He continues to have self-doubts until the end. He experiences a call to be a Magician but resists, continuing to make crosses for the Romans in the hope that God will hate him and leave him alone. Rather than coming as a blessing, his great love and compassion for humankind weigh on him like a curse, one from which he yearns to be free. He is healed of his resistance and despair when he joins a group of monks in the desert and has an initiatory vision. His ordeal includes being misunderstood by others, being tempted by Satan in the desert, even being crucified. Illumination occurs when he imagines the impact on humankind were he to fail in his mission to defeat death: hope would be gone. He then fully opens his heart and willingly accepts his destiny—to overcome death so that others might live.

what: the Camelot narrative presents the stages in a different order, and a slight modification of the names of two of the stages made more sense in a contemporary urban context. Accordingly, the stages that form the basis for this book are: initiation, trial by fire, call, illumination, and mastery.

Modern-day magicians go through these stages, but not

necessarily in a tidy, linear order. In fact, we can spiral through them many times and in different orders. Moreover, this means that going through the stages is not like climbing a ladder, where we step to successively higher rungs. Rather, we go through each stage to get (and keep) its gift. We do not graduate from it when we go on to the next stage; instead, we expand our reality to include more. If we overstay our time in any one stage, we can regain balance by revisiting whichever stage has been undervalued or underlived.

For example, we may receive a call on numerous occasions —every time we notice a new opportunity and every time we face a seemingly impossible challenge. Similarly, we undergo many initiations and trials and have many moments of illumination. We spiral through these stages at different levels of sophistication and depth, and become wiser and more effective in the process. Anytime we feel stuck, it is a challenge to advance or to return to a stage that has a lesson for us.

In studying Camelot lore, I also came across Merlin's theories about the creative process, and found that they correspond to the stages of the journey described above. Like most magicians before and after him, Merlin employed the language of the elements to describe the process of doing magic. The elements are used throughout the world in the process of creation, for healing, and for reestablishing balance (within the body, within communities, or between society and the natural world). Such traditions include European alchemy, Tantric polarity, Ayurvedic medicine, Chinese acupuncture, and American Indian and other indigenous shamanistic practices. Although many labels are used to describe the elements, the most frequent, especially in the West, are ether, air, fire, water, and earth. Although some traditions have four (not five) elements, the distinction generally is a semantic one, since ether sometimes is defined as the space in which the elements move or their primal cause rather than as an element per se.

Although elements are used in virtually all magical traditions, the meaning ascribed to each varies somewhat from one tradition to another. For this reason I treat the elements as archetypes, corresponding to ways our psyches order the physical world. Briefly, earth relates to solids, water to fluids, fire to energy, air to gases, and ether to space (as in outer space). Elemental thinking is implicit in expressions such as "spacy" (ether), "fiery," or "going with the flow" (water). In the *Vita Merlini*, Merlin describes the creation process (God's creation of the world or our creation of our lives) as beginning in the heavens with ether. It then moves down into the sky and the winds, the element of air; into the stars and the element of fire; into the oceans and the element of water; and onto dry land and the element of earth.[8]

This five-element step-down process is similar to that used in the ancient system of Tantric polarity to describe the continuous re-creation essential to all life. It moves from inspiration (ether) to an idea (air), to a desire or intent (fire), to a feeling (water), and, finally, to an action or achievement (earth)—and then back to inspiration (ether).[9] It was fascinating to me to realize that the stages of the indigenous shamans' journeys described by Ellwood correspond to the step-down process of creativity in the Camelot stories and Tantric theory. Patterns such as these, which recur across cultures and in different historical periods, likely are archetypal, meaning that they are natural to the human psyche in all times and places. This is why I would ask sophisticated contemporary readers to take them seriously.

The stages of the journey help us gain the gifts of the elements. The call helps us align with spirit so that we can discern a true inspiration from temptation (the gift of ether). Initiation frees the mind and expands the consciousness so that our ideas are empowering ones (the gift of air). Trial by fire clarifies our intent so that we both know what we want and have aspirations worthy of our best selves (the gift of fire). Illumination opens our hearts so that our actions are compassionate and we feel one with ourselves and others (the gift of water). Finally, mastery helps us create the practical structures that ground our dreams in the real world (the gift of earth).

Each of the following chapters focuses on a stage in the Magician's journey, exemplified by an important character, theme, and/or symbol of the Camelot legend, to show how we can attain the qualities of mind and heart that allow positive magic into our lives. We begin with initiation and the story of Merlin—for it was Merlin's transformed consciousness that created the vision for Camelot. Next we turn to trial by fire and the example of King Arthur. Without his competence, determination, and fiery spirit, the vision never could have been realized. Then we explore the call of the Grail to the assembled knights, following the adventures of the great knight Percival. From there we consider illumination, illustrated by the story of Queen Guinevere and her gift to the court of the Round Table. In the concluding chapter, we explore mastery, with a focus on the people, buildings, and practices that served and housed the Grail: Titurel (architect of the Grail Temple), Dindraine (the Grail Maiden), Morgan le Fay (priestess of Avalon), the Grail Hermit (guardian of the Grail), and Taliesin (Merlin's mentor).

Each chapter has five circles, or parts. Circle One provides an overview—including the gift brought by the stage and its element, as well as a case study of a magical leader who illustrates the virtues of this state. Each of the next four circles provides more specifics about the journey within the stage. The movement from the first circle of each chapter to the fifth is like that of expanding concentric circles. Circle One presents the heart of the matter; the next four circles expand our understanding of the particular stage and its gifts.

The number five is important to this book because if four is the number of psychological wholeness, five represents such wholeness manifested in the world. The principle of the macrocosm and the microcosm is illustrated by having five concentric circles within each of five chapters. Each chapter in this book constitutes an elemental circle that could be placed in one of the four directions or in the center of a medicine wheel or magic circle. Further, the repetition of the number five is meant to invoke the principle of the holograph, since each part of a holographic image carries the entire image within it. The pattern is a little like the picture on the cover of this book, where a Magician's hands keep pulling hats out of hats out of hats.

The diagram that follows might appropriately remind you of a medicine wheel. (You will see this diagram again in Appendix A, where you can use it to chart your individual and organizational Magician's journeys.) In many indigenous magical traditions (American Indian, for example), the shaman or medicine person literally draws a circle in the earth to create sacred space, placing magical objects in the four directions and the center to honor and invoke the elements. Erecting such a physical structure invites a balance of the elements into our lives, asking the power of the invisible realm (inspiration, thoughts, feelings, passionate intent) to help us create beauty on a physical, visible plane. Such external magic circles are paralleled by internal ones. Jung found that his patients often dreamed of or drew mandalas (whose shape is similar to those of magic circles or medicine wheels) when they were approaching wholeness and integration. The spirals emanating from the magic circle image are meant to remind you that the five elements are part of a spiral journey that helps us release the highest and best potential in our individual and cultural lives.

We experience a call on numerous occasions—every time we notice a new opportunity and every time we face a seemingly impossible challenge. Similarly, we undergo many initiations and ordeals and have many moments of illumination leading to a deepening sense of vocational mission. We spiral

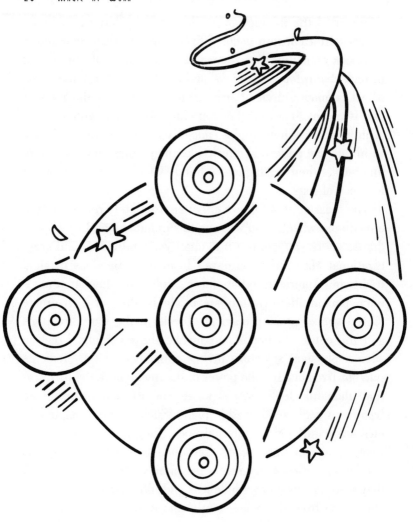

through these stages at different levels of sophistication and depth, and become wiser and more effective in the process. Anytime we feel stuck, it is a challenge to advance or return to a stage that has a lesson for us.

Although we may consider ourselves ordinary and be unaware of our uniqueness, the choices we make have ripple effects that emanate out into the world like magic. They can help transform the world. If we examine our work lives and workplaces right now, it might be difficult to believe that magic is afoot. In fact, when we are most conscious of the ordeal or the initiation stages of our journeys, we may feel anything but magical. The journey is much more painful when we do not know what is going on; thus, having an awareness of life as a journey can be helpful. When Arthur was being readied for kingship, most people did not know that he was preparing to create Camelot. *Not even he knew that!* So things looked pretty hopeless then, as they might sometimes to us today.

The journey, as described here, is primarily an evolution of consciousness. We travel from ordinary consciousness into a deepening awareness of the magic already present in life and work. This shift, in and of itself, increases our openness to magic. It takes time to develop a magical consciousness, but you probably are on the journey. The chapters that follow are designed to help you recognize the magic already present in your life today and to suggest practical strategies for greater success and well-being.

THE EXERCISES

Before beginning the lessons included in this book, you may wish to take the self-tests included in Appendixes A and B to find where you are in the Magician's journey:

Appendix A: Includes "The Magician's Journey Index for Individuals" and "The Magician's Journey Index for Organizations."

Appendix B: Included as a service to readers of *Awakening the Heroes Within* who would like to integrate theories discussed there with those of *Magic at Work*. It includes "The Heroic Myth Index" (HMI), which helps you discover which of twelve archetypes currently is active in your life, and "Heroic Allies of Magic," which helps you identify how these archetypes relate to the stages of your magical journey.

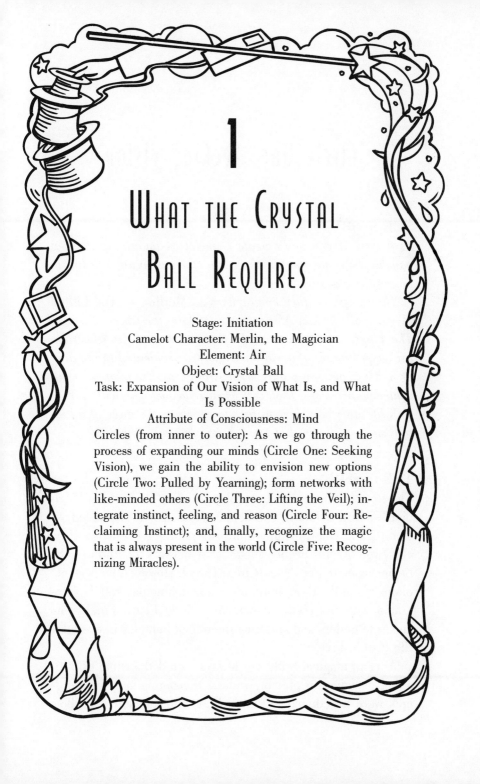

1

WHAT THE CRYSTAL BALL REQUIRES

Stage: Initiation
Camelot Character: Merlin, the Magician
Element: Air
Object: Crystal Ball
Task: Expansion of Our Vision of What Is, and What Is Possible
Attribute of Consciousness: Mind

Circles (from inner to outer): As we go through the process of expanding our minds (Circle One: Seeking Vision), we gain the ability to envision new options (Circle Two: Pulled by Yearning); form networks with like-minded others (Circle Three: Lifting the Veil); integrate instinct, feeling, and reason (Circle Four: Reclaiming Instinct); and, finally, recognize the magic that is always present in the world (Circle Five: Recognizing Miracles).

Circle One: Seeking Vision

THE STORY

As a seer, Merlin helps create Camelot by imagining the best possible outcome for his time, and then devoting his life to making it a reality.

The twelfth-century biography Vita Merlini *(or* The Life of Merlin*) tells us how Merlin came to claim the power of a seer. The biography is particularly powerful because it illustrates archetypal stages of initiation as they are evidenced in the story of a life. The events may seem strange and unrelated to our contemporary time. However, when read metaphorically, Merlin's life story can show us how to negotiate the stage of initiation successfully so that we, too, can become seers.[1]*

THE LESSON

The story of Merlin illustrates the initiation stage of the Magician's journey. Merlin's unhappiness motivates expanded vision (Circle One), leading him to reframe his worldview (Circle Two). As he becomes part of a network of initiates, he begins to share his vision (Circle Three). However, he does not claim his full power until his wild, instinctual self is integrated with his civilized persona (Circle Four). Finally, he comes to understand and trust the role of miracles in everyday life (Circle Five).

Ancient magical traditions always included a ritual of initiation, designed to promote radical transformation. When adepts were introduced to the tradition—to its sacred symbols and rites—their eyes were opened to new visions, new possibilities.

The stage of initiation challenges us to take the time we need to find our bliss. The process is one of constant expansion as we grow and change to become ready to inhabit our perfect world. We are more likely to trust this process as a guide to the future if we see how it has acted in the past. The more we are able to trust the way life has unfolded to this point, the greater our faith in the future. The strength of our optimism protects us from clinging to present realities, allowing for an openness to change.

In the In-Between, we can be mindless and either allow ourselves to be swept along by the winds of fate or chain ourselves to a rock and refuse to budge. Merlin's story teaches us an alternative: we can become conscious. If we take the magical path, we can imagine the future we desire and then grow to be worthy of it.

If we were being formally initiated into a magical tradition, we would have had a teacher to guide our thinking and our practice. In the modern world, our teacher is likely to be an eclectic set of books, experiences, mentors, friends, colleagues, teachers, or workshop leaders. Many of us today are exposing ourselves systematically to new ideas that fundamentally change the way we view the world—this is our self-initiation, our preparation for the moment we gaze into the crystal ball and recognize for ourselves the future that is perfect for us.

What does the crystal ball require? It demands that we embrace change—in the world and in our selves. When we do so, life becomes an adventure.

Magicians often are portrayed as shape-shifters, even appearing at times as animals or spirits. Magicians today may not literally change shape, but they do adapt quickly to changing circumstances. In *Leadership and the New Science,* management consultant Margaret Wheatley describes how protons, in response to other subatomic particles, change form for a time. This leads her to the conclusion that protons are possibilities in search of relationships. Like protons, Magicians live in the world of possibilities where different potentials are expressed in changing relationships. The difference between the Magician who shape-shifts and someone who is all things to all people is integrity.

Initiation requires constant reevaluation of one's principles and values in the light of new information. As we are exposed to new ideas and different cultural assumptions, we may come to see our old values as provincial, defined by the socialization of our particular group. We may sense that our values are limited—or even that they hold within them elements of prejudice. If so, we may want to rethink our values, asking ourselves as individuals, "Now that I know more, is it appropriate for my values to change?" As we grow, we may find that our values or principles need to grow with us, so we ask, "Are my values still current? Are they adequate to the situation I face in the complex world of the In-Between?"

Philosopher Brian P. Hall, author of *The Genesis Effect*, argues that as values evolve, so society evolves, and vice versa. He identifies four major states of consciousness that produce different values. At level one, people value the satisfaction of physical needs: food, shelter, pleasure. At level two, they value social acceptance and strive to fit in. At level three, they value self-actualization; they begin to find themselves. At level four, they value the well-being of a global community and want to be responsible for the good of the whole, not just themselves.[2] Merlin had to have been at level four or he could not have created the vision of a Camelot—a social order that made the world a better place.

A CASE STUDY

Magical consultant Charlie Smith, of Charles Smith and Associates, helps managers invoke a modern-day initiation rite that he calls "the Merlin factor": "The Merlin factor is the process whereby leaders transform themselves and the culture of their organizations through a creative commitment to a radically different future." Smith's two-step process invites individuals and organizations to create their own Camelot—first by articulating their highest aspirations and then by living as if those aspirations could be accomplished. In doing so, they make them come true.

Smith is fond of talking about Merlin's ability to "live backward," and he enjoins others to do likewise, quoting T. H. White in *The Once and Future King:*

> "Ah yes," Merlin said, "how did I know to set breakfast for two? . . . Now ordinary people are born forwards in Time, if you understand what I mean, and nearly everything in the world goes forward too. This makes it quite easy for ordinary people to live . . . But unfortunately I was born at the wrong end of time, and I have to live backwards from in front, while surrounded by a lot of people living forward from behind . . ."[3]

Magic, Smith says, is action motivated "by compelling vision." We can have memories of what can be and then live into them, he maintains.

Smith becomes energized as he cites organizations that made a commitment to a future which, like Camelot, would have seemed virtually impossible to others—but which had such power to inspire people that the organizations' goals were achieved:

- NASA's commitment to putting a man on the moon by the end of the decade
- Caterpillar's commitment to forty-eight-hour parts service anywhere in the world
- Holiday Inn's commitment to "no surprises"
- Maytag's commitment to ten years of trouble-free operation

Magical leaders, Smith continues, must first make a "radical commitment to an impossible future" and then act as "ambassadors" from the future to the present—to speak for the interests of "a conjectural future state of affairs, negotiating with others to bring it into being." He argues that a memory of the future has more grip than a memory of the past."

Smith emphasizes the necessity of affirming an inspiring future vision, even if you have no idea how you are going to get there. This works for individuals as well as organizations. In fact, it is impossible for organizations to live backward from their highest aspirations if the individuals within them do not do so.

THE SAVAGE FOREST

John Matthews and Marian Green (in *The Grail Seeker's Companion*) note that knights in the initiation stage typically spent time in the Savage Forest, a space that seemed like a maze going nowhere. There they experienced adventure after adventure that expanded the questors' horizons and caused them to question all their values and beliefs. "It is an area which must be traversed before the true lands of the Grail are reached . . . [m]any kinds of delusions await those who come without purpose or direction . . . yet, at its heart, in some almost forgotten glade . . . lies the first rumour of the Grail."

Wandering in the Savage Forest can feel as aimless as "a dog chasing its own tail,"[4] but eventually it leads to a change of vision achieved, not in a directed, linear way, but as a gradual expansion of consciousness as the circles traversed become wider and wider. Like Merlin or Charlie Smith, you may have had times when you felt that all your wide-ranging studies, interests, or adventures were getting you nowhere. You were stuck in a maze, going round in circles, until at last you discovered the meaning and purpose of your apparent aimless wanderings.

Smith's life is a case in point. Early on, he had a yearning to be a catalytic agent for change, and took what to others might seem a meandering, even labyrinthine path, one of "following his nose"—which eventually led to the founding of a consulting company that gave form to his vision. His education included an M.B.A. from Harvard Business School, a Ph.D. in organizational behavior from Case Western Reserve University, and certification from the Gestalt Institute in Cleveland. He also studied T-groups, sensitivity training, bioenergetics, conflict resolution, and many other techniques of transformation. Though he had only the vaguest idea where all this was leading, he followed his interests until he settled on a mission: being a Merlin to King Arthurs. Today he searches for CEOs with character and ability and teaches them to find a vision compelling enough to pull themselves and their businesses into the future. In doing so, he finds that he, too, must grow and change continually, and continually refine his personal aspirations.

When initiatory leaders find they are living the life they once only dreamed of, they raise their aspirations still higher —a process that recurs throughout life. The strength of this approach, in fact, lies in the way it promotes continual growth and improvement. Its drawback—if it is not balanced by the other stages of the journey—can be a tendency toward eternal dissatisfaction as images of success recede ever farther into the horizon.

THE GIFT

Initiation utilizes the archetypal element of air. Air is, by nature, expansive. Initiatory leaders live expansive lives—always growing and changing. Air provides the quality of movement (as exemplified in wind) and is associated with the wide-ranging vision of birds in flight. Initiatory leaders are like birds in the sky, visionaries who help us see the big picture and scan the environment for new opportunities. As we inhale and exhale, we learn about the enlivening quality of change—experiencing and letting go.

As air comes in and out through our nostrils, we gain information about the world around us by using our physical sense of smell. Initiation can awaken a sixth sense, which works in a similar way. Initiatory leaders rarely know where they are going. Instead, they "follow their noses," trusting an intuitive sense of where to go next—even when they do not know for sure where they actually are heading. The gift of releasing the highest and best potential in any situation begins with sniffing out possibilities, with gaining discernment about what "stinks" and what "smells like a rose."

THE EXERCISES

FOR INDIVIDUALS

- Identify aspects of yourself and your life right now that you like and value. Tell or write a brief biography showing how the choices you made (consciously and unconsciously) created your life even when you had no idea where you were going.

- Allow yourself to imagine something you would like to do, be, or achieve in your future. Then tell or write a story (or ideally several stories) about how you would get there from where you are now. (The stories can be fanciful and fun if you like. You are not making a plan at this point. You are opening up a mental pathway for imaging the dynamic process of success.)

- Look at the results of your HMI (Appendix B) as a story in progress. These HMI results tell you which heroic archetypes are active in your life right now. As you read the archetypal allies descriptions, you might speculate about which archetypes have been more active in the past. Which archetypes are active in the present but have not been in the past? These are important now to help you learn something you need for this stage of your life. Which archetypes seem attractive to you, beckoning you to change? These are like signposts, urging you on to a new stage of your journey.

- Brainstorm as many wonderful futures as you can imagine. Let yourself go. Some can be zany, others serious. Some you actually might want to live out. Others might simply make you smile.

FOR ORGANIZATIONS

- Identify what is best about your organization and write or tell a history showing how events in the organization's life created such a positive outcome. Be aware of when the organization made the right choices as well as when it was blessed with serendipity.

- Imagine some goal you would like to achieve for your organization. Create as many stories as you can, describing how you would get from where you are now to where you would like to be. (Feel free to be fanciful and even outrageous. The goal is to open your mind to imagining that greater success might be possible.)

- Consider some problem facing your organization and brainstorm as many solutions as you can. Allow yourself to have fun. No idea is too zany to consider. Set a rule that no one is allowed to criticize an idea—he or she should just generate as many ideas as possible. After you have finished brainstorming, imagine possible futures for your organization—again, as many as you can. Do not judge the futures, just put them out there. However, the goal is to generate the maximum number of positive futures.

Circle Two: Pulled by Yearning

THE STORY
Merlin has been a successful king, but after a particularly bloody war he is so devastated by grief that he retreats to a forest cave, where he suffers from madness and philosophizes about the nature of weather (a concern motivated by his discomfort as winter approaches and his inability to get warm). Merlin begins to envision Camelot because he is overcome by the brutality, injustice, and superficiality of the world around him. There in the forest cave, he imagines a unified kingdom in which peace and prosperity are restored. His dream of Camelot arises out of his own dissatisfaction and alienation. He wants to be part of a community, but not one that drags him down. He yearns for a community that is ennobling and high-principled, one that will bring out the best in him and others.

THE LESSON
The dissatisfaction we feel when faced with some unfulfilled need or wish can help us clarify what we want. Creation out of dissatisfaction is essential to the magic of enterprise.

In a minor way this works if you are thinking of starting a business but do not know what kind. You go to the shopping mall and experience the desire for an espresso. You imagine going to a coffee bar, but you find none there yet. So, you open one. Others reap the advantage of your entrepreneurial imagination.

In a more major way, this operates when you are miserably unhappy with your job and begin to daydream of alternatives.

At first you may simply have rescue fantasies—like winning the lottery—but eventually, if you allow yourself to dream, you will begin to get ideas about a new job, going back to school, or starting your own business.

Or perhaps you like your work but feel somewhat alienated and lonely in your workplace. You wish you worked in a friendlier environment. You have a sense of how work could be if people cared about one another. Most people might just complain that someone should do something. The Merlin factor occurs when you take the initiative to fill the gap—beginning to network, bringing people together, modeling a more cooperative and supportive atmosphere. In this way one person sometimes can change the environment of an entire office.

Unhappiness makes us think as well as dream. Merlin's fundamental approach to life shifts in the forest cave. Grieving about the war and wondering about the causes of winter (i.e., suffering in human life), he is forced to think deeply. He begins to ask fundamental questions about the nature of reality and how life was created, because he needs to re-create his own life. Using the medieval theory of the elements (emphasizing the four archetypes of air, fire, water, and earth), he draws a circle with four quadrants. In each quadrant he positions an element, a season of the year, and a stage of life. Through this process, he comes to see that suffering is merely a natural part of life, just as winter is. Moreover, neither defines reality. They simply are part of a reality that is always in flux.

This also can work in reverse: thinking can make us temporarily unhappy. For example, it is not uncommon for students who attend college to get depressed once they learn critical thinking. All of a sudden they have a tool to see what is wrong with ideas, institutions, and philosophies, undermining their faith in the status quo—even perhaps their religious faith and their patriotism. The result can be a creeping depression that causes a reformulation of values. Similarly, in times of difficulty or in midlife, anyone might begin to feel down—and the desire to cheer up motivates us to grow and change.

The more we open up to new information, the greater the likelihood that our worldview will change. In *The Structure of Scientific Revolutions*, Thomas Kuhn popularized the concept of the "paradigm shift"—the transformation that results from an accumulation of data that do not fit the old scientific model. Suddenly a change in perception makes possible a whole new organizing principle.[5] Have you ever had a time in your life when all the attitudes that used to work for you no longer served? If so, you have company. Many people in workplaces today are living and working in an outdated paradigm. Increasingly, what used to work no longer does. Our first response usually is just to work harder—doing more of what is not working, until finally, like Dorothy in *The Wizard of Oz*, we realize we are "not in Kansas anymore."

Disillusioned with war, Merlin stops being defined by the Warrior archetype and allows the Magician archetype to awaken in him. In so doing, he stops thinking that he should be able to stop oppression and suffering by the force of his will. He begins to understand the need to cooperate with the natural cycles of life.

The Warrior archetype provides us with a way of thinking that explains reality in terms of separation and of forces in opposition. Problems are solved when right triumphs over wrong. The Magician archetype provides quite a different mode of thought, one in which problems are more likely to be solved when we expand our vision. In the Magician's worldview, we are all cocreating the universe together, and each of us has a critical and important contribution to make to this evolutionary unfolding. Everything is interconnected on an energy level and through what Jung calls the "collective unconscious." Consciousness creates the world. If we want to transform reality, we begin by changing (without blaming) ourselves.

As we move through the initiation stage, we may begin to notice and question patterns of behavior that we formerly took for granted. Contemporary business analyst Peter Senge, author of *The Fifth Discipline,* uses systems thinking to identify what here I will call the Warrior template, noting that the dynamic pattern of the arms race "is a generic or archetypal pattern of escalation, at its heart no different from turf warfare between two street gangs, the demise of a marriage, or the advertising battles of two consumer goods companies fighting for a market share." When we recognize archetypes, we can see how such seemingly diverse realities are similar and related, and how the same mode of thinking pervades them all. We then can notice, as does Senge, that these plots always follow the same path. We can choose whether we want to go down that path again—and if so, whether we are creative enough to find a way to change a pattern so entrenched and seemingly inevitable.[6]

In many instances, however, problem solving requires changing our basic assumptions. When we expand our experiences, we need new categories. Stephen Covey, author of *The Seven Habits of Highly Effective People,* observes that it does not matter how good your map-reading skills are if you are trying to find your way around Chicago using a map of Detroit —even if, or especially if, Detroit is your hometown and you know it well.[7]

Pattern recognition, which takes account of the archetypal roots of behavior, also can help us see the similarities between an ancient legendary Magician like Merlin and the modern manager who is vision-driven, trusts his or her intuition, and seeks win/win solutions.

Many women and minority males recognize that their outsider status, which has made success so difficult, has its gifts as well. They do not take for granted that "reality" is defined by how things have always been done. Sally Hare, dean of graduate and continuing education at Coastal Carolina Com-

INITIATION AND EXPANSION

Initiation does not replace one set of beliefs with another. Rather, it expands what we already know. For example, scientists do not stop using or teaching Newtonian physics because they learn Einsteinian physics. They just know more. Similarly, as we open our minds to magical ways of working, we do not necessarily give up the old ways that have worked for us. We build on them with new options that expand what we are capable of doing.

Warrior thinking finds what is right by eliminating what is wrong. Therefore, if we think like a Warrior about archetypes, it might seem necessary to determine whether the Warrior or the Magician is better, more right, or more effective. But this is not how magical thought processes work. Magic—especially the initiatory magic of the air element—is expansive. It seeks to increase options rather than substitute one choice for another. Therefore, Magicians prefer not to denigrate Warriors. They view issues contextually. They determine whether the Warrior or the Magician or any other archetype is "right" by the needs of the situation. The Magician as seer helps us imagine a world without war. In the process of getting there, we may well still need the Warrior. King Arthur could not build a peaceful kingdom without being willing to stand up to aggressive, even ruthless challengers.

munity College, explains her magical perspective and her ability to solve problems this way: "I had the advantage of being a female—often the only, or one of a few—in a so-called man's world. So, I could form my so-called minority perception, recognize alternatives or different ways of being." Newcomers and the young also excel at divergent thinking—simply because they do not just assume that things should be done the way they always have been.

Merlin, however, is an insider. He has been a king. He becomes an outsider when, in his forest cave, he begins to challenge the dominant ideas of his time. The story of Plato's Cave describes this phenomenon well. Plato says that most of us are like people shackled in a cave, with a fire behind them that casts shadows of the reality outside the cave onto the cave's inside wall. These people think these shadows are all there is. If they leave the cave and return, others will see them initially as crazy, deluded, or dangerous. Nevertheless, their responsibility is to share what they know to liberate humanity.

Of course, Plato assumed that it was the great educated men who would do this and that they would possess the Truth. In the modern world, truth is more complicated. Different individuals among us leave the cave by different doors, so we each come back with different pieces of truth. Therefore, as in the Sufi story about five blind men describing an elephant (each holding a part and thinking it the whole), we can argue about the details (who's right) or we can contribute our own piece to complete the puzzle.

Suffering can be a source of potential initiation for us, as it was for Merlin in his grief. The great pianist Arthur Rubinstein spoke movingly of the vision that immediately followed his failed suicide attempt when facing bankruptcy and mourning the death of his four-year-old daughter:

> Out on the street, however, a sudden impulse made me stop. Something strange came over me, call it a revelation or a vision.
>
> I looked at everything around me with new eyes, as if I had never seen any of it before. The street, the trees, the houses, dogs chasing each other, and the men and women, all looked different, and the noise of the great city—I was fascinated by it all. Life seems beautiful and worth living, even in a prison or a hospital, as long as you look at it that way . . . My "rebirth" brought yet

another surprise: it created a revolution in my whole psychic system. I suddenly started to think . . . Let me say only that in this chaos of thoughts I discovered the secret of happiness and I still cherish it: Love life for better or for worse, without conditions.[8]

However, initiatory insights do not *require* suffering. Suffering simply motivates us to become self-aware and know ourselves. The clarity that results from self-reflection increases the frequency of intuitive insights or visitations from the muse.

You can meditate, record your dreams, write in a journal, pay attention to your hunches, and talk honestly with a friend or counselor. All such activities free your intuition. Creative artists, writers, and inventors come to expect, and even rely upon, "aha!" experiences, as do managers known for trusting their hunches. Initiation can be as small as today's "aha!" experience or as large as a major invention; as ordinary as any moment of inspiration or as radical as a religious or political "conversion"; as mystical as a visionary moment or as rational as a scientific paradigm shift.

Great insights often come in a moment. Einstein dreamed of riding a white beam of light and awoke with the famous formula $E = mc^2$. Molecular biologist Phil Lipetz was meditating when he saw himself within the DNA molecule; he later verified the helix shape of DNA and used his findings to conduct further research on cancer and aging.[9] Nobel Prize–winning biologist Barbara McClintock came up with the "jumping gene theory" when she imaginatively empathized with the corn she grew for her genetics experiments.[10] True, each one of these people had worked hard and long on a specific problem, but the breakthrough came in a moment.

Most people think such insights just happen. That's how it feels. But it does not mean that we cannot increase our creative receptivity. The journey to the underworld taken by most ancient Magicians can be interpreted as a journey within. The more we know about our own inner world, the more likely it is that we can receive clear intuitive guidance. Too many people today fear their own inner world and stubbornly refuse Socrates' dictum to "know thyself." They are like many of us who know how to use our computers but have no earthly idea how they work. Using preprogrammed software works up to a point —we can do simple word processing or data analysis—but we cannot break new ground. To do that, we need to understand programming. Opening ourselves to magic is in part consciousness expansion and in part psychological housecleaning, knowing how we are programmed mentally.

Merlin was forced to develop self-knowledge so that he could sort out visions from hallucinations. You may develop an interest in your inner life because you want to overcome emotional or learning difficulties, because you yearn for a more fulfilling life, or simply because you want to become conscious enough to live a life that matters.

Ancient Magicians, as part of their apprenticeship, learned to travel in "different worlds," to change consciousness at will. Nevill Drury (in *The Shaman and the Magician*) explains that mediums, epileptics, and schizophrenics share with the shaman the ability to move into a "trance condition." The shaman, however, "is able to control the trance dimension and . . . to explore the realms of the cosmos which his altered state of consciousness opens for him."[11] Merlin's visions come while he is in trance, and once his madness is healed, his journeying to other worlds is in his control. Shaman Don Juan, in Carlos Castaneda's anthropological novels about apprenticeship, uses drugs to create the altered consciousness necessary for such journeys. But the same effect can be gained through drumming, deep breathing, trance, or biofeedback machines. The object is to learn to shift from beta to alpha and even theta brain-wave states in order to go in and out of trance. Shamans have to be, in this way, masters of their own minds. If they are unconscious or afraid of their own feelings, desires, or memories, they cannot do magic.

In a performance-oriented culture, people short-circuit this

PARADIGMS AND POWER

Agnes, the title character of Lynn Andrews's novel *Medicine Woman,* explains that "the purpose of medicine is power. You go to a psychiatrist and he tells you your head is fouled up. What he is doing is helping you to introspect and learn about your own character. But since native people have observed the four-legged and winged ones and all the forces of nature for thousands of years, we know your closest kinship. When I tell you you're the black wolf, you look within yourself and you know that you truly are. When you understand the powers of the black wolf, you too will have those powers. All the Medicines are good and have power."[12]

inner journey—to their own detriment. Once upon a time, there was a man who experienced enlightenment while eating coconuts on a boat. He returned to his village and told his story. The next morning the village was empty. He looked around and found all of the villagers in boats on the river eating coconuts! Becoming magical is not about following the right rituals; it requires learning to, in neopagan Magician Starhawk's words, "change consciousness at will."[13]

In an interview, psychologist Patricia Sun shared with me how, after years of meditating, she began to have psychic flashes where she "just knew" what her clients' issues were. As she meditated regularly, this ability grew and her capacity to help clients heal quickly was greatly enhanced. While meditating, she also explored her own inner world, eliminating beliefs, defense mechanisms, and other unconscious patterns that held her back. According to Sun, the challenge of our time lies in the development of mature minds. The immature right brain creates monsters and is scared of the dark; the immature left brain is dogmatic, rigid, and hierarchical. The mature right brain, however, gets direct information about reality; the mature left brain scientifically sorts information to support the right brain's perceptions. The integrated and mature expression of both sides of the brain can allow us to solve the great problems we face today. However, we cannot do this until we clear away the psychological blocks that stultify our thinking—most of which are the result of emotional trauma and repression.

The more Sun worked on her own consciousness, the clearer she became. She expanded her concept from individual client issues to larger issues of social transformation. Now she travels throughout the globe teaching people how their own expansion of consciousness can contribute to the evolution of culture.

SCRIPTURAL PROPHECY AND MAGIC

Patricia Sun referred to a scriptural prophecy that God would make a new covenant with humankind, based not on our following outward forms, practices, or laws but on our following our own inner truths. I include it here because it anticipates the emergence of the Magician archetype in large numbers of people: "But this is the covenant which I will make with the house of Israel after those days, says the Lord: I will put my law within them, and I will write it upon their hearts; and I will be their God, and they shall be my people. And no longer shall each man teach his neighbor and teach his brother, saying 'Know the Lord,' for they shall all know me, from the least of them to the greatest, says the Lord; for I will forgive their iniquity, and I will remember their sin no more."[14]

THE GIFT

People become more creative, and find it easier to see themselves as the creators of their own lives, when they give themselves the time and space to reflect on existence and to imagine a better future. This is a necessary step to creation and healing. Some may enter therapy to free themselves from limiting family and societal scripts; others may practice some form of meditation, active imagination, or other means of listening to their inner wisdom; still others may imagine a better future and then live their lives as if it really was possible. Any or all of these practices—when done following an inner sense of goodness, using wholesomeness as a guide—will break up old patterns of accumulated negativity or dysfunctional thought. This is the process that makes "miracles" possible.

THE EXERCISES

FOR INDIVIDUALS

- What dissatisfies you about your workplace? What outcome do you desire? How can you change or grow to provide your workplace with what you find missing?
- What dissatisfies you in the world? Envision the outcome you desire. What might you do through your job or in a volunteer capacity to further it?
- What dissatisfies you about yourself? Begin a process of self-reflection to see how you got to be that way. (Perhaps you are unconsciously carrying on attitudes of one of your parents or of the culture in which you were raised.) What might you do to change yourself?
- Look at your HMI results (Appendix B). What dissatisfies you about them? What would you prefer them to be?

FOR ORGANIZATIONS

- What do you dislike about your organization's present performance? (Perhaps productivity is low, customer service is inadequate, or employees do not seem to care.) How would you prefer it to be? How might the organization, and the people in it, change in order to achieve the results you desire?

- What do you dislike in the world around you? (Perhaps you are concerned about environmental abuse, crime in the streets, etc.) How can your organization change in order to contribute to the social outcome you desire?
- What are people dissatisfied about in your organization? How would they prefer things to be? What would have to change to make things better?

Circle Three: Lifting the Veil

THE STORY

Merlin's sister, Queen Ganieda, begins to worry about whether Merlin can withstand the hard winter in the forest. She sends musicians to play for him, to soothe him, and to awaken his desire for culture, so he will return to the royal court. Merlin's alienation from court life is so great that he must be forcibly restrained. When Ganieda's husband, King Rhydderch, affectionately brushes a leaf from her hair, Merlin's inappropriate laughter prompts the king to inquire further. Merlin agrees to explain his outburst in exchange for his freedom. He tells the truth—that the leaf results from an outdoor tryst between Ganieda and a lover. To show Merlin for a fool and thereby prevent her husband from believing him, Ganieda dresses up a young boy from the court in different costumes, asking Merlin how the boy will die. Merlin gives three different answers: by falling, hanging, and drowning. His seemingly ludicrous responses arouse laughter from the court, but the king honors their agreement and grants Merlin his freedom. Years later, the boy has a tragic accident: he falls off a horse, catching his foot on a tree branch, as he hangs from it, his head falls into the water and he drowns.

As Merlin leaves the court, he laughs two more times: first at a beggar who sits on a pile of gold and does not know it, and next at a young man who buys patches for his shoes, unaware that he will die tomorrow.

THE LESSON

Initiation often begins with disorientation. In some ancient societies, initiates were sent into a labyrinth or maze—an experience that can induce mild trance. I often have been puzzled by the fact that when I am driving to what will be very important, life-changing events, I frequently get lost. People who attend my workshops also report having such experiences. We may be replicating maze experiences unconsciously!

Merlin is disoriented by the trauma of war. The music that Queen Ganieda has her musicians play for him helps him find his way back to himself. In medieval times, music was believed to connect people with the underlying order of the universe. Thus it could alleviate ordinary disorientation—or even soothe madness. The highest form of music could connect people with the music of the spheres.

Many years ago I worked with counselor Anne Wilson Schaef, who uses deep process techniques to help remove blocks to self-knowledge and self-expression. She would encourage participants in her workshops to engage in deep breathing as a means to access their genuine feelings. Often they would cry, or get angry, or even revert to childlike sounds and motions. One woman I vividly remember relived a number of emotionally very difficult events, but then began to sing a hauntingly beautiful song. Later, when she shared her experience with the group, she said she was "singing the music of the stars." Such spontaneous spiritual experiences replicate ancient initiatory moments of oneness with the cosmos.

Ancient initiates also were shown symbolic visual images designed to shift their worldviews, so that suddenly they would see beyond the surface of things to understand them at a deeper level. In Merlin's story the leaf in his sister's hair may have held such significance. Until he sees the leaf, he is locked into his own self-absorbed feelings of alienation from court life. The leaf introduces a discordant element, reminding him of the cycles of natural life. Most likely Merlin's psychic ability has kicked in and he realizes his sister knows more than is apparent to the eye. The leaf is not evidence of a sordid affair.

Readers familiar with the Camelot period, or who have read Marion Zimmer Bradley's novel *The Mists of Avalon,* know that Arthur and others of his time felt perfectly comfortable combining Christian and nature religious practices. Ancient fertility rites still were practiced. The monarch's marriage to the land was symbolized by intercourse with an anonymous person who ritually represented the land. This rite not only ensured the fertility of the land but also celebrated a covenantal relationship between the monarch and the kingdom—rather like marriage.

However, during this time more and more people—clearly including Ganieda's husband—disapproved of such practices. Therefore, pagan initiations began to be held in secret. It is particularly significant that the queen would keep them quiet, since they were holdovers from goddess-worshipping rites. In these traditions the queen would have been at least as important as the king; moreover, in the goddess tradition queens would not have been expected to be monogamous.

In contemporary times it is unlikely that ordinary people are practicing sexual religious rites in the forest. However, some of us may have had experiences we feel we must hide from our coworkers. Men who have followed poet Robert Bly and other men's movement leaders into the woods to drum and dance and get in touch with their feelings may not tell the guys by the watercooler what they've been up to. Similarly, women who have been exploring an interest in goddess-oriented spiritual traditions may participate in full-moon rituals, read tarot cards, and burn candles for mystic purposes; but they may not tell their coworkers or even their mothers. The mayor of a small town confided to a friend of mine that she regrettably stopped participating in Native American sweatlodge ceremonies because she feared what her constituents would make of it.

The more visible your role in the world, the more likely you are to avoid doing anything that might seem unusual or indicate that you have problems. Going for psychological counseling can ruin a political candidate, even though many people enter therapy in order to grow. Even if your paradigm-changing focus is simply cerebral—such as an interest in the implications of chaos theory or other aspects of the new science—you may work with people who would regard you as weird if you talked much about it. The same is true with medicine. You may be seeing an acupuncturist or other alternative healer, and you find you do not discuss it in certain circles. The same is true even in mainstream religions. People who have life-changing conversions often are viewed with suspicion. Therefore, they may be quiet about their experiences for fear of being seen as "religious nuts."

This reminds me of the time of Galileo, when people were fearful of his idea that the world was round and revolved around the sun. Threatened with execution, Galileo pretended to agree that the world was flat! Today we are unlikely to be executed for heretical ideas, but we can be exiled—if we have grown beyond the consensual reality where we work. Exile may take the form of being laid off. Or it might take the form of social ostracism.

The result is that millions of people who have experienced paradigm shifts act at work as if they had not (or reveal it only to their close friends there). When I go into organizations as a consultant, people often whisper to me that they are catalysts for change in their workplace, but cannot talk too openly. In workshops, people complain that they feel as if "their hands are tied" (like Merlin's, we might add) because they cannot use their best thinking. To them, the way people around them are thinking seems superficial and anachronistic.

The good news is that a critical mass of people who have

experienced paradigm shifts is developing, so that they can begin to stop self-censoring. And when we bring our deeper wisdom to the problems we face in the workplace, they have a greater chance of being solved.

When Merlin sees the leaf in Ganieda's hair, he laughs— partly at the king's obliviousness but also in relief. Like many people I talk with, Merlin feels lonely. Recognizing a kindred spirit in his sister, he lightens up, knowing he has company. Like him, his sister knows more than what appears on the surface. He has someone he can talk with. For people today, something similar happens. When we discover we are not alone, we cheer up, stop feeling so hamstrung, and start sharing what we know.

We have to be careful, however, of people who have a vested interest in appearing to share in the perspective the boss holds. In laughing, Merlin also breaks a cardinal rule of initiation. He blows his sister's cover and puts her in a vulnerable position with the king. For this reason, he allows his sister to trick him and lets the court think that he is a fool. Today many budding Magicians hide what they know from old-paradigm people. For example, try convincing a boss whose Warrior archetype is dominant that we are all interdependent!

If your horizons have expanded beyond those of many of your coworkers as a result of therapy, a recovery group, the women's or men's movement, the human potential movement, serious participation in a spiritual path or religious group, or trying an alternative medical approach, you may feel like a member of a secret society. It's not that you know a secret handshake or anything as tangible as that. When you realize you may have found another possible initiate, try out some cutting-edge ideas to see if the person is on your wavelength. As you find more people, a network forms, and soon an alternative, informal power structure develops. Marilyn Ferguson (in *The Aquarian Conspiracy*) described this phenomenon in the 1970s. Since she wrote her bestseller, the phenomenon has increased a thousandfold.

Such networks provide support as well as information, and that support breeds confidence. Merlin is not just covering his tracks to save his sister when he says that the same boy will die by falling, hanging, and drowning. He actually is teaching in parables, as Jesus did, so that those who are ready to learn will understand. Others, who would misuse or trivialize the information, find it merely laughable or irrelevant. The laughter of the uninitiated who hear his prophecy is derisive. For others, his words can be like a Zen koan (such as "What is the sound of one hand clapping?"), a riddle that helps the listener reach enlightenment.

What do his words mean if taken metaphorically? In some tales Merlin himself experiences the deaths he predicts for the boy—by falling, hanging, and drowning. In *The Mystic Life of Merlin*, Camelot scholar R. J. Stewart likens the meaning of this threefold death to the tarot card of the hanged man, which shows a man hanging upside down from a tree, looking serene.[15] If you were to receive this card during a fortune teller's reading, it would indicate that you were ready to go beyond ordinary ways of thinking about the world: it is a card of everyday, in-the-world initiation.

In his cave Merlin drew an elemental circle in order to understand that the seasons of the year paralleled the seasons of a life: air is the element of birth and the season of spring; fire is the element of youth and the season of summer; water is the element of adulthood and the season of fall; and earth is the element of old age and the season of winter.

In the ancient mysteries, the secrets of spiritual life paralleled the patterns of physical life. Physically, we are born, grow, and die. In the natural world, flowers die in the winter but are reborn in the spring. Fertility religions taught, therefore, that either reincarnation or an afterlife followed this one. Peter Senge writes, as do other systems theorists, about the "S

ELEMENTS AND THE THREEFOLD DEATH

Stewart connects the threefold death with four-element theory: "falling from a great height = Air; hanging upside down in a tree = Fire to Earth, crossing the Abyss from light to darkness by the most direct path; drowning = Water. If we locate this triple death or triple movement upon the Wheel of Life, it travels East, South, North, West. This *serpentine* motion cuts across the Wheel and acts as a path of liberation from the cycles of life, death, and rebirth."[16]

---

curve" in businesses. In any new endeavor, a high-energy period of growth often is followed by one of gradual decline. To keep our workplaces alive, we need to infuse them with new ideas and new projects while phasing out or redefining old ones. Otherwise, the life goes out of the enterprise. Change is more often cyclical than linear in its processes. We are relearning what the ancients knew—that the patterns of our lives mirror those of nature: birth, growth, death, rebirth.[17]

Initiation facilitates spiritual metamorphosis. You die to your small self and are reborn to your great self. In modern psychological language, we might say that we move beyond ego to a deeper, truer sense of self. What this means is that we move away from trying to have the right image—or from rebelling against having the right image—to becoming authentic. Students going to college, or managers involved in transformative training, grapple with how hard it is to go home again once they have experienced a radical transformation of their ideas while others have stayed the same. Many today fear this isolation; they want educational experiences simply to give them tools and information without changing them in any way.

In contemporary business, people who resist growth are liabilities. The workplace is profoundly interesting today because the rate of change requires everyone to keep learning and developing all the time. We have to learn new technologies, information, methodologies, and behaviors. We do not expect to be initiated at work, but in today's world we almost have to be. Whether the initiatory process is spiritual, psychological, or educational, it either changes us or does us no good at all.

Organizations are most likely to change when they experience the equivalent of the threefold death—when their very survival feels threatened. Ron Stupak, consultant, University of Southern California professor, and experienced executive, says that organizations typically bring him in when they are in trouble. Otherwise, his capacity for divergent thinking, as well as the "sixth sense" that helps him know what he has no rational way of knowing, scares them. When things are going well, many organizations shy away from letting in too much new information, but, Stupak says, the same strategies that save endangered organizations can prevent such straits.

Stupak insists that "to mix a magic potion" in organizations, one must add the unknown. Someone who does not think like an insider—a consultant, a new hire, or someone just passing through—has to see outside the envelope. Stupak uses a simple exercise to dramatize this with clients. He puts up a chart with sixteen boxes and asks them how many boxes they see. At first they see sixteen, but then they see more, noticing that groupings of boxes and the frame also form squares. In really creative groups, however, someone always makes the leap to go outside the frame altogether, noticing all the squares in the room, including the outline of the walls, windows, ceiling, etc.

Effective consultants, Stupak says, come into organizations unencumbered by the mental boxes that are limiting the organization. He also helps clients lighten up and play, so they begin to relax and expand beyond their former mindsets. It is this differentiation, he says, that makes his interventions so effective and thus allows him to pick and choose his clients.

Stupak is not afraid to exercise leadership or to demand that his clients do the same. Everyone, he says, is client-driven today, but that is not enough. "The guy who invented the minivan never received a single call from a parent or scout leader asking for one." Instead, the inventor scanned for trends and anticipated customer demand. Good leaders *lead,* they do not simply respond.

According to Stupak, most people instinctively hoard leadership, but to be a powerful leader, you need to give it away. Sharing power expands the amount of power available and makes everyone more successful. Matrix and modular management—mixing and matching teams for various tasks—provides ways of sharing power as people are moved out of role-bound thinking and relationships. The rigor of the 1990s, he says, is "flexibility leading to greater creativity."

Stupak's interventions as a consultant are whole-organization initiations that ask leaders to move from closed systems to open ones. As they let in the air of new ideas, their organizations become more prosperous as a result.

The image of the beggar sitting atop a buried pile of gold is used in a variety of spiritual traditions to represent the unenlightened state. We are cautioned to see ourselves not merely as physical bodies defined by the need for shelter, food, and pleasure; we are invited to wake up and realize that we are spiritual beings as well. In a psychological sense, as we dig up the buried gold, we explore the riches of the unconscious, discovering the power of archetypes and other unseen forces in our lives.

As an educator, I also see in this symbol the potential richness that education bestows. It often is said that even the most educated of us use only a fraction of our brains. Even so, education makes us wealthier—literally as well as metaphorically. It is an initiation process. We are changed by learning more. In the In-Between, we all need to be lifelong learners. Moreover, the more we learn, the greater our chances of prosperity. In most advanced countries, the single greatest predictor of individual affluence is educational attainment. Collectively, the more educated a people, the more prosperous their society.

Buckminster Fuller defined the world's wealth as consisting of two basic components: physical (energy) and meta-physical (know-how). From this he reached two major conclusions: (1) humankind is always in the process of becoming more affluent; and (2) our combined activity produces synergistic action that results in a pattern of economic progress. To back this up, Fuller explained that as know-how increases, wealth increases. For example, "in this century alone we have gone from less than 1 percent of humanity being able to survive in any important kind of health and comfort to 44 percent of humanity surviving at a standard of living unexperienced or undreamed of before. This utterly unpredicted synergistic success occurred within only two-thirds of a century despite continually decreasing metallic resources per each world person. It happened without being consciously and specifically attempted by any government or business. It also happened only as a consequence of man's inadvertently becoming equipped synergistically to do progressively more with less."[18]

In other words, the more we learn, the more prosperous we become—individually and collectively. As a larger and larger percentage of the population gains access to quality education, and as the per capita percentage of time devoted to education increases over a life span, we cannot help growing more wealthy. Initiation, then, creates prosperity.

Seeing beyond a narrow definition of "reality," Merlin knows that the beggar does not need to be poor. The solution is right there. When we find and develop our talents, we have the potential for rich lives, not only in the money we make but in the intrinsic joy we can take in every day. When we learn how to help all citizens find their gifts, the nation will be wealthy beyond compare. This is why all workers need to develop their full potential—and bring that potential to their work. That's what creates prosperity.

Merlin also laughs at the young man repairing his shoes, ignorant of his own impending death. In the cases of both the beggar and young man, Merlin sees us trapped in ignorance of where we are in time. While it may seem callous to laugh at a man planning for a future he will not have, the parable shows the folly of linear projections that confine our sense of possibilities and life's complexities. The young man assumes his life will systematically proceed forward—that therefore we can predict the future and thus prepare for it. In fact, argues Barbara Mossberg, a philosopher concerned with thinking in more productive, rational, and optimistic ways, discoveries by the scientific community confirm what the arts and humanities knew all along: that linear projections are illogical. Currently Senior Fellow at the American Council on Education, and the Mount Vernon Institute's Distinguished Scholar, she develops models for planning based on "reality principles of how the world works," illustrated by the arts, humanities, and sciences. According to these theories, such linear thinking is unrealistic. Planning based on linear projections will leave us stranded over time.

For example, chaos theory reveals a world of constant change in which one change leads inexorably to another because of the interdependence of everything in the system. The changes that occur over time cannot be wholly predicted, but we can count on the fact that things will change. This theory inserts mystery into our strategic deliberations. Planning mandates that we insert the element of mystery into our projections. Chaos theory also shows, according to Mossberg, how "we are cocreators of the mystery. We are part of it all."

As Mossberg explains, chaos theory describes how things work in terms of the whole time/space continuum. Any seemingly little intervention in the system—a butterfly, our own dreams—can make enormous differences to the system. In this long-range perspective, what looks momentous now (either great or terrible) may seem a trifle later on, and vice versa —"especially vice versa: what initially seems trivial or inconsequential causes mayhem—over time. Thus a diplomatic incident in a community in a small country is seen to cause a world war and political, economic, and cultural realignment of the globe; a handkerchief is discovered and Othello murders his wife; a dam project prevents a tiny fish from spawning and an entire food chain and world ecosystem are threatened. Chaos is where Shakespeare, nature, and the stock market converge."

In the stock market, for example, "a rumor late in the day, about an impending ruling on regulatory liability for one product for one company, or one company executive's husband's purchase of a retirement condo, may give rise to increased trading, which will shoot the market up or down. Money is made or lost that no one could have predicted even at noon that day. If we make long-term investment decisions that do not factor in the susceptibility of the system to such short-term variations, based on the interdependence within the system, we risk losses. If we look at the behavior of such market ups and downs over history, we see patterns in fluctuations, even as they are caused by external variables no one can predict or control. Any change will destabilize the system. But over time, these patterns become manifest. Based on these patterns, we can predict that the market is going to fluctuate on an hourly and daily basis in ways that cannot be predicted. Nonlinear planning takes into account the behavior of interdependent systems over time, knowing that even trends and cycles will be affected by continually new changes in the environment— changes you can count on."

In lectures and consulting, Mossberg integrates the wisdom of the sciences and the arts to help leaders of organizations think of "the whole" and of the reality of how change happens. She relates connections between truths expressed by writers

and by the discoveries of science to a comic and hence optimistic worldview. When I once told Mossberg that her theories
reminded me of the Merlin story, she said, "Merlin is a brilliant example of a nonlinear thinker. Merlin's wisdom is a
function of a holistic vision—seeing the continuum. He has a
long-range point of view—what has happened, what will happen. We need this to be wise. What if we saw the bare
branches of a winter tree and concluded that the tree was a
failed project—not knowing that leaves, blossoms, and fruit
will appear in time, and that this stage of the tree is in fact
crucial to the development of those leaves? What if we saw the
blossoms as the end result, not knowing that the seeds from
the fruits still need to fall so that the tree can be nourished
and new life occur? If we cut down the tree without leaves, or
if we planned on a tree with blossoms year-round, we would be
acting foolishly. The Merlin parable is about wisdom: what
makes us wise is the ability to see things in perspective and in
context of the long run. Merlin is a *realist.*"

When he laughs at the discouraged beggar or the man
patching his shoes, Mossberg continued, he shows the disparity between how we perceive a situation at any moment and its
real import over time. We might conceive a traumatic incident
later as a funny story—because we survived to tell it. "Comedy's happy ending is that the world goes on, even if things
appear disrupted, disorganized, topsy-turvy," Mossberg said.
"Strindberg argued that the fall of a great tree should not be
viewed as tragic, since it was great news for the ferns and
other life below, which now had a chance at the sun. Comedy
and tragedy are all about perspective—from where and when
you're looking. The happy ending that chaos theory shows is
that the world continues, reshuffled, realigned, in some config-
uration or other. True, we may be demoralized or humbled by
our inability to control or to predict—or even to know what
things mean as they happen. But this keeps us from being
complacent or even discouraged. There is no logic to despair.

We cannot say that what now appears tragic will appear so next month or year. We can be wise by planning for change, knowing that in an interdependent world our own plans and actions, however small they appear, will influence what happens. The slightest effort can go a long way and make a difference. We have a solid basis for hope! The point, then, is not to not plan; it is to plan for change, to seed the soil for serendipity."

If we work with this long-range and flexible perspective, and do not fight the reality of Merlin, we can be optimistic, even—or especially—when our lives or organizations throw us curves. "As, of course, they will," promises Mossberg.

THE GIFT

If Merlin and Arthur had believed in a linear model, moreover, they would have concluded that there was no hope for Britain. The future looked bleak. Instead, they held fast to their vision of creating Camelot—an irrational belief in a chaotic time. The Newtonian worldview tells us that present trends are causes, and the future is the effect. Ancient magical thinking tells us that cause exists in another realm—the realm of mind.

When we realize this, we, like Merlin, can lighten up. Initiations in ancient times were designed to help people look beyond the veil of ordinary thinking to see the truth of the gods. As we experience initiatory ideas, and in the process find a supportive network to help in their development, we find that we gradually shift from alienation to optimism. We realize that the future is not determined by forces outside our control. Rather, it is determined by the expansiveness of our minds, for imagination is the key to freedom from the restraints of conventional thinking.

THE EXERCISES

FOR INDIVIDUALS

- Describe experiences you have had that felt disorienting, or that threatened to undermine the way you saw the world, or where your habitual approaches would not work. How did you respond to these experiences? How have you been initiated into a way of thinking or acting that is somewhat different from what many around you experience?

- How do you recognize people who have been changed in ways similar to your own? Do you have a sense of community with such people? If so, how has this group affected your life or that of others?

- What changes have made your life seem richer? What unexpected or serendipitous events have affected the course of your life? What dreams have you had that came true?

- Looking at your HMI results (Appendix B) and thinking about initiatory experiences you have had, identify the archetype or archetypes that best characterize your new thinking. Are these archetypes honored in your workplace? Who speaks for them? What happens to you when you speak for them? Who supports your new thinking (at work or outside work)? Which archetypes seem to embody what others expect from you?

FOR ORGANIZATIONS

- Describe events in your organization that are baffling or disorienting. How have they changed you? Are you operating very differently than you did several years ago?

- Do you have a group of people who have opened to new ideas and new approaches? Do they seem to be free to speak honestly, or do they translate most of the time?

- What changes have increased the productivity or quality of life in your organization? To what degree were these changes planned? What unexpected challenges and opportunities helped shape your world? What visions did you have of the future? Which of them have come true?

Circle Four: Reclaiming Instinct

THE STORY

As Merlin's power grows, he feels called once again to go to the forest to strengthen his powers. He disdains the bitter tears his wife Guendoloena, sheds over his departure. Feeling above the need for marital intimacy, Merlin grants her permission to remarry. However, when she actually does so, he interrupts the wedding, rips the horns from the stag on which he is riding, and kills her new husband.

THE LESSON

Initiation is not an escape into the head but a unifying experience connecting intellect and instinctual bodily knowing. Merlin's hard-won ability to look at reality dispassionately is not complete until he experiences primal passion fully. When Merlin kills his wife's new husband, he is in the grip of the negative power of an archetype. The stag and his horns are associated archetypally with male sexual power. (In medieval drama, men often used stag horns to kill a rival lover.) Merlin's initiation inevitably requires him to integrate that power so that it is under his control—rather than taking him over.

Merlin was initiated by the tenets of a fertility religion. Such nature or life cults focus on the power of love, sexuality, birth, and death, with the body as a source of wisdom and of power. However, Merlin also was influenced by other, more ascetic traditions, which develop spirit by sublimating or repressing the flesh. Medieval Christianity distrusted the body as leading to sin. This approach encouraged a kind of dissociation from carnal concerns, with the purpose of developing higher, more spiritual ones. This made sense for the time. This is one example of the way Warrior archetype thinking always moves us into duality. To get something that is good, we assume we must kill or suppress something else. However, once we know we are not just bodies—and once our archetypal perspective shifts from Warrior to Magician—our task is to link body knowing with intellect and spirit. When we deny the wisdom of the body too long, our lives become fleshless and enfeebled—passionless. Today many of us have become so desensitized that we can walk past the homeless, witness the despoiling of the wilderness, and discuss the carnage of the latest war with little or no sense of horror. Like Merlin and his wife, we forget that we need one another.

Men and women today, encouraged by books like Clarissa Pinola Estes's *Women Who Run With the Wolves* or Robert Bly's *Iron John*, seek to find the "wild man" or "wild woman" within in order to reclaim primal instinctual power. Merlin's magical power eventually increases as he integrates the wild man of the forest with the wise seer who instigates the founding of Camelot. The dissatisfaction Merlin experiences in both his forest retreat and the royal court mirrors the split between these two parts of himself—a split that causes emotional numbing, a phenomenon we are very familiar with in today's world. His wild man feels at home in the forest. His civilized self prefers the court.

Initiation is first about expanding the mind. When we become more educated and cerebral, we are likely to cut ourselves off from more primal feelings. Like Merlin, if no one helps us understand this phenomenon, we may reconnect only with the wild, instinctual power within as it takes possession of us.

Imagine how embarrassing it is for Merlin to act so irrationally. First he tells his wife she is free to remarry. When she does so, he is overcome with jealousy and kills her new lover.

Merlin here is possessed by the archetype of the wild man rather than integrating it into his consciousness.

We may feel removed from this story if we take it literally. Even in these violent times, most of us do not kill other people. However, read metaphorically, the story is similar to scenes we all have experienced. Many of us have seen two human stags fighting as if to the death—for a contract, for the boss's good opinion, or just for the thrill of the contest. This behavior often is totally at odds with business success, since it usually undermines teamwork. However, it often is unstoppable unless the "stags" become conscious enough to moderate their behavior.

If you get locked into an irrational power struggle with a coworker, stop and think, but do not try to repress the strength of your feelings. The passion of your response cannot be denied. Often we feel as if we were fighting for our very survival —when really the only thing at issue is a slight advantage in status or pay.

Suppose that two men who have started a business together split it up because they cannot get along. Of course, the same unresolved issues that have kept them from working together surface as their lawyers try to sort out who gets what. Actually, only a rather small sum of money is at stake. Each partner feels exploited by the other—and that he has to fight for his life not to get cheated.

In reality, what's at stake is self-concept. Neither partner feels respected or appreciated by the other. In the past each has given in to the other to keep the peace when he should have held firm. The fight gets nastier and nastier until the more conscious partner calls a halt and suggests that they talk with a counselor about the emotional issues before settling the legal ones. The counselor helps the men express their anger directly, and to see, as they do so, that survival is not really at stake in the legal issues. It just feels that way.

In a different situation, two real estate agents get locked

into constant, ferocious competition, which gets so out of hand that they start playing dirty tricks on each other. You would think it was the Cold War. Each is afraid to give in, for fear of losing face. Eventually, the more conscious of the two recognizes that they both are getting a bad reputation in the business. Other real estate agents, who often help each other out, steer clear of them both. Customers pick up their desperation for a sale and go elsewhere.

As the more self-aware real estate agent begins to recognize this negative trend, he decides to channel his drive into achieving his own goals and helping people find the homes they need (rather than defeating his competitor). His sales go up precipitously.

A contemporary manager who has groomed a younger protégée may be completely done in when that protégée pulls away and seemingly bites the hand that has fed her. There has been a strong bond between them—similar in intensity to the relationship between father and daughter. If the mentor looks deeper, he may see the underlying pattern: coming of age. Just as adolescents often act out when they are beginning to separate from their parents, so do workplace protégés when they are ready to separate from their mentors. This is such a deep pattern that it often happens unconsciously.

The protégée is ready to go out on her own, but she stays out of fear of the unknown. Unconsciously, she begins to do things to alienate her mentor so that he will mistreat her, her underlying purpose being to convince herself that he cannot be trusted and she must get out. If he understands that her actions represent the workplace equivalent of adolescence, the mentor can keep his equilibrium, even pushing the protégée out of the nest if need be. But if he understands only the surface behavior, he will feel terrible. Being aware of the deeper, archetypal pattern will allow him to lighten up, to see the unpleasantness as a sign of successfully completed mentoring. He may need to grieve for his own loss, but he also can celebrate his protégée's readiness to try life on her own and be comforted knowing that if she were not terribly attached to him, she would not need to cause so much pain in order to leave.

For some people, the issue is not too much primal passion but too much censoring of that passion. Take the case of Linda, a mild-mannered woman with little sense of competitiveness or personal power. She had thought everything was fine, but then her hands started trembling. She went to her doctor, who said there was nothing wrong with her physically —but that the stress feeding the tremor eventually could damage her health. As they talked, she confided that she was furious and did not know what to do. A very popular coworker with a sweet, childlike persona took credit for her work, and then acted innocent when Linda tried to talk with her about it. Not being very assertive, Linda was afraid others would not believe her. Eventually, she realized that she was trembling with the effort it took to repress her natural instinct for self-preservation. She stopped repressing it. But rather than going to extremes, she just set up better boundaries between her work and her coworker's, and her trembling ceased. Even though her coworker pouted, sulked, and complained, Linda's body relaxed because she no longer was allowing herself to be exploited.

Primal mythic patterns often take over whole organizations. In the contemporary workplace, the minute something goes wrong, people immediately want to get rid of the leader or some other scapegoat. We may better understand this tendency by examining historical precedents. Ancient societies literally killed the king every few years to ensure the vitality of the kingdom. In some places in the world today, coups routinely act out the same script. Democratic countries provide a benign way to oust the old leader by holding regular elections.

Too often this primal urge for sacrifice takes over and precludes any rational thought. To take one recent example, a financially strapped mental health center was ready to ask its leader to resign. The cause of the problem was not really the leader's fault; an economic downturn in the local community and changes in insurance policies had greatly curtailed reimbursements for therapists. Fortunately, the management and professional staff understood that the sacrificial archetype had been activated. They looked for ways to reinterpret their primal urge. After analyzing the situation, they realized that instead of having to fire their boss, they could save money by having everyone share in the sacrifice. I am aware of other organizations that have been taken over by the need for a public hanging in situations like these. People feel better for a while, but of course the problems continue.

THE GIFT

Consciously experiencing such instinctual and mythic patterns restores vitality to individuals and organizations without leading to irrational and self-destructive behaviors. It also connects the conscious with the unconscious mind and the mind with the body. When this is accomplished, we can begin to trust the wisdom of our bodies. People who have connected consciousness with instinctive patterns often can evaluate a possible course of action by the way their body either comes alive or feels dead. You may have had the experience of rationally analyzing a situation and then deciding on a course of action. However, when you start to implement your decision, you lose all energy and feel like lying down (or having a cup of coffee or a stiff drink to get you going). Or, you have ideas of things you would like to do that make no rational sense at all, but when you think of them, your body tingles with aliveness. The initiated consciousness does not filter out these body cues, for the wisdom of the body is a window on the soul.

THE EXERCISES

FOR INDIVIDUALS

- Have you ever had a bodily symptom—from listlessness to illness—that seemed to be related to a person, an activity, or a job? What did you learn from that symptom? What could you learn if you thought about symptoms as clues to your needs?
- Notice if there has ever been a time when primal feelings took you over. Examples: having inappropriate erotic feelings about a coworker; being involved in a fierce power struggle or competition; making someone a scapegoat. What did you do, or could you have done, to regain appropriate conscious control? What did you learn?

FOR ORGANIZATIONS

- What kinds of symptoms are current in your organization? Can you see any patterns that may give insight into what feelings are going underground and being somatized?
- Notice if there has been a time when primal instinctual patterns have taken over whole groups of people in your organization. Examples: acting like a lynch mob; over-idealizing a charismatic leader ("you can rescue us"); engaging in lemming behavior (following the leader off the cliff). What did you do, or could you have done, to make this pattern conscious enough so as to defuse it?

Circle Five: Recognizing Miracles

THE STORY

Queen Ganieda finally gives up trying to make Merlin live at court. She worries, however, that his health will suffer if he stays in a forest cave in winter, and she builds him an observatory, according to his specifications. He lives there in winter and observes the stars. This structure has seventy doors and seventy windows—corresponding by a factor of ten to the seven planets. Seventy scribes record the prophecies that result from his observations of the stars. After this, we see a new Merlin, one who writes about the wonders in the world rather than about what is wrong with it.

THE LESSON

When initiation is complete, we feel at home in the world. When Merlin finally has a home—one just perfect for him— we know that he has arrived. In his observatory Merlin practices astrology, the science of his time, tracing the correspondences between the movements of the stars and human events. The recurrence of the number seven suggests that he is in perfect alignment with the heavens. He has created "heaven on earth" for himself, just as he earlier helped create Camelot —"heaven on earth" for others. If you ever have felt that you were completely in the right place for you—even if only for a time—you know this phase of initiation. It leads to a sense of acceptance and appreciation of the world, making you less needful of changing it.

The purpose of initiation is to help us live in accordance

with natural and spiritual law. When this is achieved, happiness is the inevitable result. A number of signs let us know about Merlin's contentment. He visits a healing fountain, and is cured once and for all of his madness. He is no longer lonely, for people he loves come to live with him: Ganieda, his sister; Taliesin, his mentor; and Maeldinus, a longtime friend and comrade. When Maeldinus eats a poisoned apple and goes mad, Merlin knows what to do: he takes him to the healing fountain, where Maeldinus is restored to his right mind.

Rather than wondering about the origins of human suffering, as Merlin used to do in the cave, he now celebrates natural processes. He recognizes that the way the Creator used the five elements to create the universe is the way Merlin creates Camelot and his own life. Merlin no longer feels estranged from the world, because he recognizes his capacity for cocreation. He explains in his writing that beyond the physical world is another world, an "island of apples" ruled by nine sisters. This otherworld is the home of the platonic ideal (or, we might say, of archetypes). All kinds of possibilities are contained in this otherworld—some good and some that feel bad but teach us valuable lessons. The creation process allows these possibilities to enter the physical world. Each of us, as a cocreator of the world in which we live, allows in some possibilities and blocks others.

A medieval audience would have immediately connected the references to apples (the isle of apples and the poisoned apple that deranges Maeldinus's mind) with the Garden of Eden. Eve and Adam fall from grace because they eat an apple from the Tree of the Knowledge of Good and Evil. In other words, Adam and Eve are suddenly initiated into dualistic thinking—in a form that separates spirit from flesh. Thus, the sign of their fall is an alienation from their bodies and the natural world. They are suddenly ashamed of their nakedness. Moreover, Eve is cursed with the pain of childbirth and Adam with difficult and painful work.

The healing fountain, which Merlin sees as connecting us

FINDING YOUR PLACE OF POWER

Carlos Castaneda writes about leaving the shaman Don Juan in a room with the task of finding his power spot, the place in the room where he feels the best. Much of any Magician's power lies in being able to sense the right place to be—the right job, for example, or the right city. Doing so requires paying attention to the moment, getting calm inside, and discovering what feels right.[19]

with this otherworld, can heal Maeldinus or you or me from a dualistic alienation from our bodies and from nature. What this fountain represents is the power of the imagination to express the truth of the human soul and to continually free our minds. In his journey, R. J. Stewart explains, Merlin uses imagination to expand his perspective as he moves through and beyond duality. Merlin alternates between madness and sanity, and he is sometimes the wild man of the forest and at other times the urbane advisor of kings at court. Similarly, in the modern world, we often assume the need to pick between dualistic choices—like being true to ourselves or being successful, or being kind or getting ahead. When we think dualistically, we suffer. Expanded consciousness asks more benign and imaginative questions: How can I be true to myself and get ahead? How can I be compassionate and rise to the top? The Grail myths exemplify paradoxical thinking, which heals the split between being and doing by teaching that effective lives come from being true to our own true natures and to the order of the cosmos.

By the end of Merlin's life, his consciousness is expanded to the point where he has healed the split between spirit and matter, so that he can understand paradox. Moreover, he understands that his earlier suffering was necessary to the attainment of greater wisdom. He then begins to realize that there is no need for estrangement: humans are part of the natural order, and we can trust instinct, the wisdom of our bodies, and the processes of our lives. He writes a catalogue of birds, which expresses wonder at the ability of cranes to fly in formation. "It is therefore the nature of the cranes, as they go through the air, if many are present, that we often see them in their flight form a figure in one way or another. One, by calling, warns them to keep the formation as they fly, lest it break up and depart from the usual figure; when he becomes hoarse, another takes his place." There is a natural order, Merlin realizes.[20] In learning from it, we not only have good science, we also have effective magic.

Writing from the perspective of modern science, Margaret Wheatley discovers wonders similar to Merlin's cranes. She celebrates the tendency of natural systems to structure and restructure themselves. As managers, most of us assume that when a problem arises, we should intervene and do something about it. However, many problems simply take care of themselves. Organizational systems, like ecosystems, have a tendency to reorganize or reconfigure themselves. Wheatley quotes K. C. Cole as saying:

> It is natural for any system, whether it be human or chemical, to attempt to quell a disturbance when it first appears. But if the disturbance survives those first attempts at suppression and remains lodged within the system, an iterative process begins. The disturbance increases as different parts of the system get hold of it. Finally, it becomes so amplified that it cannot be ignored. This dynamic supports some current ideas that organizational change, even in large systems, can be created by a small group of committed individuals or champions.[21]

Wheatley concludes with the image of clouds as self-organizing systems, "changing into thunderstorms, hurricanes, or rain fronts with the influx of atmospheric energy or foreign particles." Limited management thinking tells us we have to be firmly in control, managing change all the time. According to Wheatley, when we understand that we neither can nor need to do so, we can observe the emerging order and trust the magic at work in the system: "After all, how do you hold a hundred tons of water in the air with no visible means of support? You build a cloud."[22]

Both Merlin and Wheatley are noticing the great miracle of what Wheatley calls "order for free." Modern science tells us that order exists in the universe—it is just very complicated. This means it is not always readily apparent. So, we have to trust the process of our lives. We always have reason to fret, and plenty of reason to hope. Which would we prefer? Often we see only in retrospect how some apparent difficulty was just what we needed in order to grow. For example, in hopes of solidifying a big order, you rush to send a fax. The fax is lost in transmission, and as a result no order is forthcoming. You are angry—until you learn later that the client was on the verge of bankruptcy. Chances are, had you gotten the contract, you never would have been paid. Thus, you can learn to have faith in synchronicity, the meaningful coincidences that help things work out rather magically in our lives.

At this level of initiation, the universe begins to feel friendly. As Hugh Prather has said, "It is safe to be happy. It is practical to trust. It is intelligent to love. It is not only dignified and honorable—it is glorious to be kind."[23] This does not mean that we should be naïve. Rather, we should have faith not only in our own creativity but in that of others. We also can trust the deeper wisdom of the collective unconscious, the universe, God—or whatever name we use for transcendent consciousness responsible for synchronous occurrences. Therefore, we exercise our imaginations, we trust our synergy with others, and we notice the gifts offered to us by the universe.

RECOGNIZING MIRACLES

The film *Grand Canyon* is set against the backdrop of Los Angeles—a city with so much violence and potential for violence that the audience sits on the edge of their seats. Life seems so dangerous that it begins to feel like a miracle every time characters make it through a day without mishap. The movie focuses on a middle-class couple, Mack and Claire, who are going through a midlife crisis. In the midst of it Mack's life is saved by Simon, a kind and wise black tow-truck driver. Claire finds an abandoned baby. "Something happened," she argues; "you can't go back and have it not happen. Some kind of connection has been made and it has to be played out." When Mack does not immediately understand, she continues, "Maybe we don't have any experience with miracles, so we are slow to recognize them."

Scholar Gareth Knight, writing on the Grail legend, sees magic—as Claire does in *Grand Canyon*—as a natural part of life. "There is no gulf or barrier," he notes, "between magic and the ordinary world. We all use magic in order to live our lives; just as we use prose to express ourselves—without necessarily being consciously aware of the fact." What we call magic is the process through which imagination creates reality —or, poetry influences history. We are using magic every time we have a new idea and then act on it.

Therefore, Knight says, all attempts to outlaw or ban magic are ill-conceived. "One might as well try to outlaw perception or metabolism. The only point at issue is how consciously it is used, for an increase in faith and intention renders its operation more effective, just as a forced draught will enhance the powers of a natural fire . . ." Magic, in fact, is nothing more than "basic life principles" or "various 'processes' of consciousness."[24] We do not need to make them happen; we just must take note of them. This awareness provides the air that fuels the fire. Magic, therefore, actually increases when it is noticed.

Noticing order and other positive events is a magical act— that is, if it does not move us into denial. Similarly, focusing too much on the negative tends to reinforce it. For example, a problem employee should not be allowed to act badly. That would be denial. However, constantly harping on the negative can dispirit people without changing them for the better.

Management consultant David L. Cooperrider promotes the idea of "appreciative inquiry," where the impulse to change emerges from exploring what the organization or the individual currently is doing right. Such an approach is based on faith in organizational systems. They are not wrong and in need of fixing. Rather, they have their own logic and order that need to be recognized and celebrated. Cooperrider cites studies showing that "the rise and fall of images of the future precedes or accompanies the rise and fall of cultures. As long as a society's image of itself is positive and flourishing, the flower of culture is in full bloom. Once the image begins to decay and lose its vitality, however, the culture does not long survive."

Magicians do not deny problems, but they call attention to the best of the present in order to enlighten faith in a positive future. Winston Churchill was able to do this in England's darkest hour. As Dutch sociologist Fred Polak puts it, "Churchill's impact and the guiding images he helped create were the result of his towering ability to cognitively dissociate all seeming impossibilities, deficiencies, and imperfections from a given situation and to see in his people and country that which had fundamental value and strength. His optimism actually did not come from denial: it came from seeing in the 'crystal ball' of a highly developed consciousness a deeper truth about his people and their situation. Because he saw it— and proclaimed it—the Britons believed it so much that they were able to live up to his image of them. Any time people collectively are able to express their highest and best selves, failure is impossible." If you want to be more successful, notice what is right about you, your coworkers, and your organization and celebrate it. Do not hide your light under a bushel. Flaunt it![25]

We can see that Merlin successfully inspired the British people not only because he saw the potential for Camelot but, even more, because he saw in them the capacity to create a utopian society. His role in Camelot was to be a namer of possibilities, individually and collectively, sharing with people what he saw as the highest and best outcome for their lives. He convinced Arthur that he could be the greatest king who ever lived. He inspired the knights to embody the chivalric ideal. His legacy can inspire you and me to dream big dreams and then become big enough ourselves to express those dreams in the real world of our lives and work.

THE GIFT

We lend our energy to what we notice. Better and worse alternatives always coexist in every person, organization, or society. Initiation teaches us to reinforce the best of these alternatives by our attention, words, and deeds.

When we begin to have visions of what we can be, it is easy to be dispirited by the discrepancy between where we are now and where we want to go. We gain confidence by noticing and celebrating any signs that we already are realizing our potential. Similarly with others. Sometimes we do need to give people negative feedback, especially when they are way out of line. However, we can make the choice never to end a conversation without sharing a positive vision of what the other person could be—and what it is about his or her present abilities and skills that makes us think that individual is capable of growing into this vision. The same is true for organizations. Once we have identified a particular vision for an organization, we can celebrate those aspects of it that already demonstrate signs of the desired reality.

Reinforcing the good also can be very tangible. Morale always flags when incompetent or destructive behavior is re-

warded. The most obvious ways to reinforce the good in organizations include not only verbal praise but money, increased
power and responsibility, and perks—such as greater autonomy, more attractive surroundings, and time off. Whatever we
reward in our organizations will flourish. Whatever we ignore
will fade out. For example, if we talk about integrity and social
responsibility but reward ruthlessness and self-centeredness,
ruthlessness and self-centeredness will increase exponentially. The gift of initiation teaches us to notice and reward
whatever it is we would like to encourage in the world and to
ignore and neglect whatever it is we would like to see disappear. The initiated consciousness in the media, therefore,
would focus much less attention on what is wrong with the
world and more on what is right with it.

Margaret Wheatley has a personal trust in the miracles that
inform her work. In my interview with her, she immediately
brightened when I asked her about magic, identifying three
areas where she regularly trusts magic in her work: intuition,
purpose, and ease. As I listened, I realized she practiced "appreciative inquiry" with herself, others, and the world.

Before speaking or consulting, she pauses to get centered
so that she can speak from an attitude of service, not ego.
Often she finds herself going off on what appears to be a
tangent, saying things she did not plan to say (or even things
she did not know she knew), but she has learned to trust her
intuitive process. Afterward, someone almost always will indicate that Wheatley's unplanned example or anecdote was
transformative or that it touched the person deeply. When she
and I met, she had just come from consulting with the Chief of
Staff of the U.S. Army, and she described how she had felt
prompted to talk with him about his role in history, about how
as a pioneer in these turbulent times he would not be able to
accomplish all that he wanted. He immediately grabbed some
paper and began writing notes, indicating that this was the
issue he wanted and needed to address.

When she feels called upon to write something, Wheatley

has a sense of ease about it because she knows she is supported by "unseen help." Knowing there is purpose in the world also means that she does not obsess about methodology or have to do a complete literature search on her topic. She trusts her eclectic and random studies, reading only what she is attracted to at a deep level: "If I do what I am attracted to, it will all work very well." Laughing, she said she hated to quote a popular source like *The Celestine Prophecy*—but "there are no coincidences." Everyone she meets, she assumes, is in her path for a reason.

Years ago, Wheatley said, she had been touched when the theologian Parker Palmer told her that most of us ignore our true gifts because we live in a culture that believes accomplishments are not valuable unless we struggle to achieve them. When we are operating out of our true gifts, Palmer explained, we experience ease. Right work, Wheatley told me, is effortless. Every one of us has a purpose. We find the gifts that support that purpose by developing those skills, abilities, and interests that come naturally to us.

In her consulting work these three priorities—intuition, purpose, ease—translate into three principles that help managers ask the questions that can open up their organizations to operating effectively in the In-Between. First, an organization can collect and make widely available "open, abundant, and even superfluous information" so that people can follow their interests, learn what they need to know, and use their intuition to know what to do and say. Second, people in the organization can have access to everyone in it without being hemmed in by structures, status, or rules. Third, people can have a clear sense of the organization's mission to thrive in chaos. Purpose helps us greet and trust change with ease, without fear of any loss of identity. Institutional barriers to magic—hoarding information, locking people into an inflexible chain of command, expecting people to follow orders from above, whether or not they agree or understand—block the expression of everyday miracles. As with the Berlin Wall, it is time these institutional barriers came tumbling down.

Wheatley is describing ways to create preconditions for learning and growing—for continuous initiation—without stress. Her deep faith in an underlying and benevolent order to the universe means that she can trust her own inner guidance. We can do the same. We can rightly expect all the events we experience and the people we meet to provide just the right avenues for the next step in our learning. Above all, we can trust that we are not wrong. Each of us is just right for the work we are here to do. Even when things appear to be the most chaotic or painful, we can rest in our assurance that there is a deeper order that will not let us down. We can stop fighting the messiness of life, stop thinking we have to create order. We can let go. We live in a universe that gives us "order for free."

THE EXERCISES

FOR INDIVIDUALS

- Imagine as many solutions as possible to a current problem. If at first you think you have only two choices, be sure to come up with at least one more.
- Notice and list examples of good in the world. Describe any problems that seem to have solved themselves. Describe any synchronous events in your life—apparent coincidences that either benefit you or seem to set you back. With regard to the former, be grateful. As for the latter, consider that they may be stopping you from a course of action on which you are set but which ultimately may not be in your best interest.
- Describe what is right about you, your family, your job, your friends, and anything else important to your life. Redo your résumé to truly highlight everything good

about yourself. Think about other ways to make your positive qualities more noticed and noticeable in the world.

- With reference to your HMI results (Appendix B), notice what archetypes are reflected in what you really like about yourself. How might these archetypes help you create the future you desire and deserve?

FOR ORGANIZATIONS

- Describe what is right about your organization, its employees, its management—anything at all that is positive. Find ways to tell the story externally (in your ads, a video, or a marketing campaign) and internally (in speeches, an employee newsletter, etc.). Keep feeding back to the organization its own strengths.
- Describe the best potential found in your organization as if it already existed.
- List ways to reinforce good behavior—actual and potential.

2

THE CHALLENGE OF THE MAGIC SWORD

Stage: Trial by Fire
Camelot Character: King Arthur
Element: Fire
Object: Magic Sword
Task: Clarify Intention and Act on Commitments
Attribute of Consciousness: Will

Circles (from inner to outer): As we act to make our dreams come true (Circle One: Trial by Fire), we learn to persevere through life's ordeals (Circle Two: Pulling the Sword from the Stone); recognize our purpose or mission (Circle Three: Claiming the Sword of Invincibility); set and achieve goals (Circle Four: Achieving Your Goals); and, finally, let go of illusions about ourselves and the world so we can do our part in the cosmic plan (Circle Five: Learning What the Sword Demands).

Circle One: Trial by Fire

THE STORY

King Uther of Britain asks the advice of Merlin about the untempered fire of his passion for Igraine, the wife of the Duke of Tintagel. He desperately wants her love, but he does not want to inspire the enmity of her husband or the judgment of the court. Merlin offers to bring him to Igraine that night transformed into the likeness of her husband—on the condition that, should a child be born of their union, that child will be Merlin's.

Although the duke is killed in battle and Igraine and Uther soon marry, Uther keeps his word and their son, Arthur (who is as passionate and spirited as his parents), is given to Merlin. Arthur, who has no idea of his parentage, is raised in an outlying court, where he is tutored by Merlin.

When Arthur is a young man, King Uther dies and the kingdom seems in danger of splintering. Many different dukes are claiming the right of succession. In the churchyard of the greatest church in London a sword appears, stuck into a stone and an anvil, with letters declaring "Whoso pulleth out this sword of this stone and anvil is rightwise king born of all England."[1]

As you might imagine, only Arthur can pass this trial, pulling the sword from the stone when all others fail. When Arthur does so, Merlin tells him of his royal descent. Although Arthur soon becomes king, his job is not an easy one. Uther has been a weak king and England is fragmented. Arthur's first task is to recruit an army. Eventually, he unifies the country, selling his vision of Camelot, vanquishing rivals in battle, and arranging marriages to solidify the state. He is besieged on every side throughout his reign, but he has a zest for life that helps him rise to meet each challenge. The results of his efforts are truly miraculous. He unifies Britain and then expands its territory as far north as Norway and as far south as the Roman Empire. Arthur liberates the people wherever he goes, establishing justice, rule by law, prosperity, and a sense of honor and nobility in life. As a result, he is as loved as he is respected.

THE LESSON

The trial by fire stage of the Magician's journey is illustrated by the story of King Arthur. Arthur's life demonstrates the virtue of action in the service of a higher cause (Circle One). As he pulls the sword from the stone, Arthur accepts his destiny as king (Circle Two). Later, Arthur receives Excalibur, which symbolizes the clarity of purpose and mission that make him invincible (Circle Three). Next, Arthur sets and achieves his goals by enlisting others in his noble effort (Circle Four). Finally, after anticipating potential defeat, Arthur realizes that he must not succumb to ego: he remembers that the source of his power is the Divine (Circle Five).

The magical principle demonstrated by this stage is that each of us has a purpose for being here—and the talents to realize that purpose. When we have the courage to come through the fire to express our best potential, we also help to release the highest and best possibilities in the world around us. This is how we release the inner fire of our will and enthusiasm and claim our own form of greatness.

While the air element is expansive, the fire element allows us to find our own part in the cosmic dance. One's internal fire (as in the expression "fire in the belly") can be expressed as ambition, anger, vision, or passion. The fire element is energetic, focused, and achievement-oriented. It also can transform. We heat materials to purify them, or to change them from solid to liquid or from liquid to gas. However, fire can burn down the house if it does not have proper boundaries. Properly bounded, it can heat a home or drive an engine.

We contain our fire with the structure of a formed identity.

We do this automatically as we discover our own talents and commitments, channeling our fire in a positive direction. Without such a structure, fire can burn out of control and wreak havoc—as with unbridled anger or ambition. Too much fire and we burn out from overactivity or become willful and stubborn. Too little fire and we are easily distracted or discouraged—so nothing much gets done.

The sense associated with trial by fire is vision, as in keeping our eyes on the prize. The issue for this stage of the journey is persistence and clarity of intent. Fiery leaders often pull rabbits out of hats simply by the power of their will. They will not give up. If the element of air helps us expand, fire helps us focus. Too much fire and we burn out. Too little fire and we wimp out.

A CASE STUDY
Mabel Phifer, president of the Black College Satellite Network, exemplifies the confidence and energy typical of fiery leaders. When Phifer was just a little girl, her parents told her she could do anything, and she believed them.

Throughout school Phifer gravitated to leadership positions. She is such a natural leader that, even today, she has to limit her involvement with organizations because inevitably she is drafted to leadership. In talking with her, I could see why. She exudes confidence, competence, and self-esteem. Working sixteen-hour days does not seem to faze her. Indeed, not only is she undaunted by challenges, they seem to energize her.

When Phifer was just twenty and a recent college graduate, she was hired to teach home economics in a high school and manage the cafeteria. The school had one year to get the cafeteria out of the red. Phifer, who was supervising people two or three times her age, determined that they would stop buying prepared food and utilize free government commodities, which had been piling up in the storeroom. She began daily workshops, teaching a reluctant staff to bake bread and yummy deserts and to use the ingredients available to make main courses that adolescents like. Not only was the cafeteria in the black in six months, it also was acclaimed for the quality of its food.

Phifer's confidence did not result from privilege. For an ambitious African-American woman growing up in the segregated South, the very conditions of social life required a comfort in trial-by-fire situations. When Phifer was hired as one of the first African-American teachers in a predominantly white school, she refused to allow herself to be defined by others, even though the principal had gone on record with his strong opposition to ever having a black teacher. She quickly rose to be the chair of her department and took on responsibility for home visits. Although she was visiting primarily white families in a racially volatile time, she did so without incident (because *she* was comfortable in a mixed-race situation—in part because she came from a racially mixed family—and her ease made others comfortable). After she left for another job, the formerly resistant principal called her every year for several years trying to entice her back to his school.

Phifer's life mission is to empower people to achieve excellence, and her career exemplifies the qualities she strives to develop in others. Matching her talents with her commitments, she decided to become a higher-education administrator. She rose through the ranks of college administration, first in career development and then in fund-raising. She earned a Ph.D. in educational administration with a concentration in business management because she believed that too few higher-education administrators truly understood the science of management.

After graduate school Phifer had an informational interview in which she freely shared her views and aspirations with Dr. Frederick Patterson, president of the Robert R. Moton Institute. He was so impressed that he created a position for her. She did not disappoint him. In fact, she was so successful in developing programs that provide technical assistance to the 126 colleges served by the institute and in raising money that when Patterson stepped down from the presidency, she was selected unanimously by the board as his successor.

In the early 1980s Phifer began to be convinced that satellite technology was the wave of the future. She proposed that the Moton Institute raise funds to create an information highway connecting black colleges, community centers, schools, and churches in order to expand the quality and availability of information and developmental opportunities for students, faculty, and people in the community. She was undaunted by initial cost estimates (close to a billion dollars) and by the active discouragement of Fortune 500 leaders, who told her it could not be done. When the board of the institute expressed fear that this project might divert the organization from its other work, she realized she was too committed to this dream to back off, even though her commitment meant spinning her dream off from the institute.

The early days of the network were so difficult that she cashed in her retirement fund to keep it going. When asked what enabled her to persevere, Phifer explained, "People said it could not be done," and behind these discouraging words were racist, sexist, and defeatist assumptions. "I had to do it," she explained, "to prove a point."

She threw herself into learning the science and technology required so that she could "hold her own" with the engineers. Over time, she raised in excess of $50 million and built the Black College Satellite Network from the ground up. Not only has she realized her vision, she has surpassed it. Now this international network serves the U.S. military, schools and colleges throughout the globe, churches of all denominations and of all races, and diverse community groups. In these ways, the BCSN speeds the spread of empowering information so that people can learn from what is working in "pockets of excellence," which, Phifer reassures us, are found "everywhere."

Asked how she sees herself, Phifer emphasized her commitment to being a visionary activist, someone who believes that "if I don't dream big, I don't dream at all." She loves to pass on her enthusiasm and zeal to the next generation, describing the gratification she feels when she gives young interns projects that require them to deliver at a level beyond anything they thought they could do. As they explain to her that what she has asked cannot be done, she just smiles. When they eventually succeed, she tells them she knew they could do it.

She loves live telecommunications because (like life) you cannot tape it, edit it, and make it perfect. You have just one chance, and you have to do it right. Moreover, she loves the gratification the network gives her, like being able to sit right in her own studio and provide assistance, for example, to educators in South Africa. Of operating a system that empowers people throughout the globe, Phifer says, "That's power!"

THE GIFT

The crystal ball helps us find a vision worth our commitment and then begin to *be* the kind of person who can manifest that vision. Trial by fire is about determination, persistence, and a can-do spirit without which nothing really is achieved. People who have the gift of the fire element have great energy. They know how to keep their eyes firmly on the goal. They are not easily discouraged or defeated. Their motto is often "Where there's a will, there's a way."

THE EXERCISES

FOR INDIVIDUALS

- Think of some time in your life when you have persisted to meet a goal. What helped you keep your focus? What was it like to achieve what you wanted?
- Make a list of things you care enough about to sacrifice other goals and activities in order to achieve.
- What are some goals you will commit to right now?

- In Appendix B, look at your HMI scores for Warrior, Magician, and Destroyer. These are allies of the trial by fire. How much support do you have for this stage of the journey?
- In Appendix A, notice what your "Magician's Journey Index" score is for "A" (the stage of trial by fire). If it is high, you are well into this stage of the journey. If it is relatively low, you may be called upon to experience this journey—especially if your problem takes the form of indecision, low energy, or lack of persistence.

FOR ORGANIZATIONS

- What are some important goals your organization has achieved? What strategies have helped the organization stay focused?
- What are the organization's goals today? How firm is the institutional commitment? Which goals are most important to it?
- In Appendix A, check the "Magician's Journey Index." Notice the organization's scores for trial by fire. If they are high, the organization may be called to experience the stage of trial by fire.

Circle Two: Pulling the Sword from the Stone

THE STORY

Arthur demonstrates his destiny to rule England (1) by his unique ability to pull the sword from the stone, and (2) by his determination to persevere until his countrymen recognize the meaning of his feat. All the barons and lords in England try to remove the sword and fail—all, that is, except Arthur. Because he is an obscure personage, people won't accept him as a potential king even when he holds the magic sword in his hand! On Pentecost everyone tries again, and when Arthur again prevails, he is crowned King of England. Arthur is not successful pulling the sword from the stone because of superior physical strength; many lords probably are stronger than he is. He pulls the sword out because it is his destiny to be king.

THE LESSON

In the Camelot story, swords are symbols of truth, destiny, authenticity, and power. Arthur claims his own mission to be king by pulling the sword from the stone. By attempting the task, he is responding to the invitation at hand—and he perseveres even though at first others fail to see the potential within him. When he succeeds, he accepts a particular destiny that he lives out, even though at times it is not much fun.

As we commit to a major in school, to our first and subsequent jobs, to career goals, and to taking various leadership roles, we have to step out with energy and faith—even if we are not completely sure we will succeed. If others do not see our potential, we may feel lonely in making the choices we do. Part of success lies in not letting that sense of being isolated and out on a limb stop us.

Circle Two is what Robert Ellwood describes as an ordeal. At this point, we face a challenge that helps us confront what we most fear, so that we can be free. In Ellwood's example of the ordeal, the shaman experiences a loneliness so extreme that he feels "cut off from all life . . . the most ghastly experience that is possible for any human being to have."[2] While we in the modern world may or may not experience loneliness of this magnitude, some tolerance for loneliness is required if we are to go our own way.

Anyone who wants, as a friend of mine put it, "a life that is handcrafted, not mass-produced," faces the loneliness that comes when we are willing to risk individuality. As long as we are conforming to what is expected in a relationship or group, we can find it comforting to merge into something larger than ourselves. This feeling is pleasant because it replicates the oneness of early infancy, where little distinction exists between mother and child. The recognition of separateness that occurs incrementally over a life span can be very isolating. Yet being willing to suffer this loneliness is essential to finding out one's own true talents and perspectives.

Some years ago I was in a support group that was very important to me. We were so close that we called the group the Cozi, and we fantasized that we still would be meeting when we were elderly women rocking on the porch of a retirement home. Then the group decided to go in a direction that did not fit for me. Even though *I* was choosing not to continue, I felt alienated and rejected—sad that they all would choose to go on a new path without me. Yet, thinking about it, I had to realize that they were not doing anything *to* me. *I* was the one differentiating from the group.

Virtually all of us are aware that groups can and do ostracize people who go their own way. In one office I consulted with, everyone talked about how close they were. They agreed about almost everything, played cards at lunch, and knew the ins and outs of each other's lives. That is, everyone but the boss. She did not do everything with them or tell them much about her personal life. They took her separateness as a rejection, and consequently they wanted her fired. Her difference felt threatening to their unity.

The boss felt caught between a rock and a hard place. She alienated the group when she stood apart from them, but when she tried to fit in, she felt like the odd woman out. Her values and her lifestyle were just too different. Eventually, she decided to switch positions and move to an office with more tolerance for individuality. Claiming oneself requires courage, and part of that courage is to face the possibility of being alone, unloved, and unappreciated. Being willing to be lonely and unappreciated—at least temporarily—is essential to having clear enough boundaries to claim one's own power. This is especially true for those who aspire to be leaders or innovators.

When any of us take on a leadership role, we may experience a predictable sort of loneliness as we recognize that, as President Harry S Truman put it, "the buck stops here." Others can advise, blame, or complain, but they do not share the same responsibility. Such authority requires an ability to make independent decisions—which can feel isolating, particularly when others sit back critiquing our performance as though work were a spectator sport.

Furthermore, people who experience leadership at virtually any level know how cut off they can feel when others project onto them personal issues involving parents or other authority figures. It is as if the leader were an invisible screen onto which they throw their own fears and traumas. Once when I was the vice president of a college and was having a routine meeting with a middle-aged faculty member, I realized to my horror that she was not really talking to me at all. Although her actual words concerned business at the college, in truth she was feeling about thirteen and replaying tapes from her relationship with her mother. I felt the powerlessness of not being able to connect with her. I was just a stand-in in her ongoing drama with her parent.

You may remember that during President Bill Clinton's first hundred days in office, journalists and pollsters kept asking "How is he doing?"—as if one man's actions would determine the fate of the country. I kept wishing they would ask "How are *we* doing?" Most organizations I consult with have a similar problem. They set up their leaders as heroes and expect them to leap tall buildings at a single bound. When managers show signs of being normal, flawed human beings, they may be condemned as villains or great failures. As a result, leaders often feel misunderstood and abused.

The more innovative we are, the more likely our trial by fire —like Merlin's and Arthur's—will involve being misunderstood, put down, and underestimated. People thought scientist Barbara McClintock's ideas about genetics were crazy. Even though she could not get a research or academic job, she knew she was right and persisted. Eventually, she won a Nobel Prize for her work. James Lovelock's theories about ecology were denigrated until he published *The Gaia Principle* and they gained widespread public acceptance. Similarly, creative people I interviewed told me how little they are understood and how patient they have to be day to day. Yet, creativity demands the ego strength to go our own way whether others understand or not.

Being lonely or misunderstood is only one aspect of the ordeal we experience in Circle Two. Others are failure and the hard knocks that inevitably are part of paying our dues. There may be times when we try our hardest and still fail—until our actual skill level catches up to our ambition. Often the hardest part is the self-mistrust that can undermine confidence. Most of us think that career advancement is great, but we can be so fast-tracked that the Peter Principle takes effect and we find ourselves having reached our level of incompetence. In such cases, wisdom calls for humility, for stepping down until we are ready for the next challenge.

Success takes time. It took time for Merlin to learn to discriminate true vision from hallucinations, just as it took time for Arthur to curb the impulsiveness that frequently put his life unnecessarily at risk. Merlin and Arthur—like you and me—went through trials that were no fun at all but that helped develop character and strength.

Dwight Judy, director of the Institute for Transpersonal Psychology, is not surprised that people find this alternative graduate program so magical. But what they miss, he says, is an understanding of how much sheer hard work goes into creating such a school. While the end product of creation is transformative and magical, the process of getting there involves not only hard work but drudgery and dogged persistence against all odds.

Most of all, the ordeal challenges us to act even when we are frightened, when we feel invisible and unappreciated, and when the outcome of our efforts is uncertain. Such uncertainty is fostered by the In-Between, with its wide economic and market fluctuations. Fortunes are made and lost very quickly. People feel anxious and unsettled. This very uncertainty throws us back on ourselves, because we find no pat answers to get us through. Many people who have come to my workshops made fortunes and concluded that they had "created" their lives. Then they lost all their money. Their challenge, then, was to avoid the temptation of bitterness and cynicism and to use the experience for learning and growth.

Robert Levit, former director of human resource development at MCI and now a professor and management consultant, talked with me about the difficulties many human resource development people are facing in organizations going through

THE GODDESS DEMETER AND TRIAL BY FIRE

The importance of trial by fire was recognized by the Greeks long before the Camelot stories were written. The Greek goddess Demeter disguised herself as a nurse so she could care for a baby. Every night she held the infant in the fire. The horrified mother eventually caught Demeter doing this and sent her away. As she left, Demeter sighed in frustration that the baby was only one night away from becoming immortal. So it is with us. We may want to say "enough" just before the breakthrough. Often the difference between greatness and mediocrity is simply having enough grit to persevere when things get tough.

the ordeal stage. Often training budgets are limited or are being phased out, or the director's hands are tied. Worse, in many organizations "King Arthur has forgotten to listen to Merlin, and the organization begins to lose its magic." Levit also stressed the isolation that can result when you are ahead of your time, "which must be accepted and dealt with," as well as the need for tough-mindedness that others may not be willing to share: "For every creation, there is destruction. To realize a new potential, one other potential must fail to be realized. To create one thing is to deny the creation of another. That which we create is often denied to us." Many leaders, consultants, and trainers leave situations where they have created magic for others and find themselves alone and unsupported—precisely because others see them as so powerful that they do not need support.

All of us experience an ordeal to some extent just by living in the modern world. The demise of the Soviet Union into warring factions, world hunger and economic uncertainty, international conflicts, terrorism, the undercutting of traditional values, and violence in our city streets—all are part of the disorder characteristic of Circle Two. The surround of our lives is alienating and anxiety-producing. We, like King Arthur when he pulls the sword from the stone, must act even though the future seems so uncertain and unpredictable.

The ordeal stage also requires us to deal with constant change. Our challenge is to sacrifice the old ways and give birth to better ones. Some would have us try to turn back the clock, but "the genie is out of the bottle." We cannot go back —as individuals, as organizations, or as a society. The only way out is through. The task of each of us is to live consciously, learning by our triumphs and our failures, so that our lives can be positive forces in the collective transformation we all are experiencing together. This challenges us to find our own purpose, so we can claim the sword of our invincibility.

THE GIFT

Many of us think that others succeed where we fail because they are just more talented than we are. All of us are potential geniuses at something, but we have to pay the price for that genius to bloom—and that price is hard work. When people get really good at what they do, moreover, it looks easy. It is easy to forget that their ease usually is hard-won. As the late Pablo Casals (who practiced six to eight hours a day) put it: "I have been told I play the cello with the ease of a bird flying. I do not know with how much effort a bird learns to fly, but I do know what effort has gone into my cello . . . Almost always, facility results only from maximum effort."[3]

THE EXERCISES

FOR INDIVIDUALS

- Have you had experiences in your life that have felt like ordeals or times of testing? If so, describe them. How did you sustain yourself through such periods? What did you learn from them?
- When have you felt lonely or misunderstood? How were

you different from those around you? What did you learn
from the experience?

- Consider where you are in your apprenticeship. What are
  you learning? What do you need to learn next? (These
  can be task, people, or attitudinal skills.) Chart out a
  learning plan.

FOR ORGANIZATIONS

- What has been your organization's most difficult time of
  testing? What was it like? Did the organization persist
  and prevail?
- Consider where you are as a learning organization. What
  does it know how to do? What is it learning? Chart out a
  plan for future learning.

Circle Three: Claiming the Sword of Invincibility

THE STORY

When Arthur first pulls the sword from the stone, he is as surprised by his success as others are. He needs, over time, to grow into a sense of himself as King of England. Perhaps because the circumstances of his early life (not knowing his parents, living as an orphan in an outlying court) did not inspire overconfidence, he has a natural humility that enables him to learn from Merlin, from his other companions, and from experience.

As he grows into a more secure sense of mission in his role as king, he is given a second sword. In chivalric tradition, highborn ladies rewarded knights who demonstrated great courage and ability by giving them some object as a token of their esteem. When Arthur has demonstrated his courage and ability, the Lady of the Lake rises out of the mists and gives him another sword, Excalibur, and a scabbard that make him invincible.

THE LESSON

By the time Arthur receives Excalibur, he has developed such confidence and enthusiasm that the challenge of building an empire feels more like an adventure than an ordeal. In fact, Arthur is so fiery, enthusiastic, and filled with joy at this phase of his journey that he can serve as a model for how to enjoy the ongoing challenges of leadership. In his youthful exuberance, he begins a tradition in the great court of Camelot of not starting dinner until those assembled have experienced some great adventure or wonder. And they always seem to have one.

Commitment to action releases our internal fires, energizing us to accomplishment. When lightning strikes, it does not just come down. Energy simultaneously emerges from the ground to meet it. Similarly, we release inner fire when a genuine need in the world—especially one we feel passionately about—matches our own ability to meet that need. The initiation stage helps us clarify such a need and define our own vision for the future.

Trial by fire helps us recognize what *we* can do to fill that need. Probably we all have had the experience of recognizing that some particular thing needed to be accomplished—and then seeing that we (or our organization) had the capability to make it happen. The result was a quick release of energy—"I want to" matched with "I can." This is what it means to grasp the sword of invincibility.

For many of us, grasping that sword is complicated by an uncertain sense of self. Even if we have completed the stage of initiation successfully and recognize what it is that we care about accomplishing, we may have difficulty recognizing how much we are capable of doing. In my many years working with women, I have been made painfully aware of how many of them are unable to fulfill their potential because they are weighed down by "too much/too little" dilemmas—namely, they fear that they are so accomplished, powerful, and smart that they will be threatening to others and, simultaneously, that they are too inadequate, unprepared, and dumb to amount to anything. *What I came to understand was that we are always too much or too little for everything but our own life.* To find our own mission or purpose, we need to identify the middle way between inflation and inferiority.

When Arthur realized he could be King of England, he might have been paralyzed by fear that he was not up to the task, or that others would punish him for presumption. That might have been the case had not Merlin been there to push him toward his destiny. In my own life I have gone through two or three times of great stress when someone has sat me down to tell me that I was on the right course. Or occasionally, when I strayed into an area that did not fit for me, someone kindly (or not so kindly) redirected my efforts to something that did. I have been very fortunate in this regard, and try to pass on this favor to students and colleagues.

A basic premise of magic, which informs the Magician's journey, is the belief that each of us has a purpose for being here. This means that if we are completely true to our own best potential, the results will be magical—although not always immediately. In *The Nibble Theory and the Kernel of Power*, Kaleel Jamison urges each of us to actually write out a statement about our life purpose, saying it is the key to our personal power. Because careers come and go, she counsels us to go deeper than saying "I am a doctor/writer/etc." to something more fundamental.[4] For example, one person I interviewed expressed this "kernel of power" as a "commitment to social justice," evidenced through a talent for community organization. Another said her purpose was to use her ability as an educator to help people see their beauty and value. Still another saw his purpose as creating machinery that improved the efficiency and hence the quality of people's lives. Success coach Cheryll Neil told me she helps people find their purpose by discovering what activities give them energy and release their passion for life. Clearly articulated statements of purpose allow us to change careers without losing our identity, because we do not link our purpose to a single career or job.

Although all of us benefit from the feedback and advice of others, we can get stuck in our "too much/too little" dilemmas when we focus on what others will think of us rather than trusting our own inner truth. When we constantly monitor others' opinions, we give away our power. We live to please them and to live out their sense of purpose, not our own.

We also lose power when we live in the future rather than

the present. Often when I envision a future goal, for instance, I want it immediately. Yet I have not always had the skills or resources to realize my visions right away. Some take years. If we get ahead of ourselves, we become frustrated and unhappy. Similarly, we dissipate our energy with idyllic dreams that we never even begin to make real.

Magic requires us to be where we are in time—where we are in our development—rather than pretending to be more (or less) than we are, which takes us off-course and decreases magical results.

Virtually all of Greek tragedy warns of the danger of hubris —of getting above ourselves. The Greek myth of Daedalus and Icarus teaches us about the danger of flying either too high or too low. The great Magician Daedalus was in the employ of King Minos of Crete. Daedalus was forced to create the Labyrinth, which housed the monstrous Minotaur. When Daedalus helped Theseus, who killed the Minotaur, a furious King Minos threw him and his son Icarus into the Labyrinth. Daedalus then invented the wings that would help Icarus and himself fly out of it. He warned his son to fly neither too low, where he might get pulled down into the waves, nor too high, where the sun would melt the wax holding his wings together. Icarus ignored him, flew too high, fell into the sea, and perished. But Daedalus chose the middle way and survived—because he knew the magical path of staying on course.

Many people suffer the consequences of the Peter Principle —being promoted to the level of their own incompetence. If they are too proud to find their way back to a job they can do well, they will suffer greatly and so will everyone around them. Conversely, people can get tracked too low, or just sideways— in fact, anywhere they do not have the necessary aptitude— and the same effect occurs. Although Cindy was creative and innovative, she was counseled into the secretarial track in school because she was a girl. But she had no aptitude for clerical work, and her self-esteem plummeted until one of her

---

THRIVING WITH INTEGRITY: TRIAL BY FIRE

The integrity check of trial by fire can be made in answer to the question "Is this mine to do?" Although this is not an easy question to answer, people who have learned to be honest with themselves often trust their visceral physical reaction. Somewhere deep inside, you do know the answer. You can tell if it is a yes or a no by whether your body comes alive or goes limp.[5] As a check against complacency, you might also ask yourself, "If not now, when? If not me, who?" Marsha Sinetar (in *Do What You Love, the Money Will Follow*) reminds us of a Spanish proverb: "Choose what you will and pay for it." A life of integrity requires choice and commitment.[6]

---

bosses pulled her aside and suggested she go to college. She did—and later became very successful in the field of design. American University professor Morley Segal stressed in his interview the importance today of having the good sense to recognize not only what you are good at but also what you are *not* good at, and essentially cutting your losses by tailoring what you do to your genuine talents and abilities. His own success—as a scholar and the cofounder with Edith Seashore of the prestigious American University/NTL Institute Master's Program in Organizational Development—resulted from careful self-reflection. Achieving such self-awareness can be complicated if one is part of a group experiencing discrimination. Doing so then requires a complex ability to sort useful feedback from prejudice. Members of very privileged groups may have a similarly tough time achieving a realistic self-concept because the world may mirror back an inflated reflection.

We may experience pain anytime we are temporarily out of place. "Sin" literally means being "off the mark." Rev. Amalie Frank, minister of the Unity on the Hill Church in Washington, D.C., said that "we are not punished *for* our sins, we are

THE GOLDEN MEAN AS A MIDDLE WAY

When Aristotle talked about the golden mean, he was espousing the essence of magic. Magicians know that when we are faced with a dualism, the answer is almost never to choose one pole. Generally, it makes more sense to find the golden mean, or the point of balance between two extremes. In today's workplace, many people believe they have to choose between such dualisms as:

- Being honest or making money
- Being human or being efficient
- Being fair or being kind
- The good of the individual or the good of group (rights vs. responsibilities)
- Quality or equality.

In such cases, choosing any one side without the other is a horror. The magical answer is to find the golden mean, where neither value is sacrificed to the other.

punished *by* our sins." This may sound strange, but it really is quite simple. When we do things we believe are wrong, our self-esteem plummets. When we engage in unhealthy habits (gluttony, drunkenness, debauchery), our health suffers. When we substitute image for substance, we feel progressively more and more empty inside.

A popular joke teaches us about the magic of finding our true place—by contributing our best talents and perspectives —and the concomitant evil sorcery that occurs from the ripple effect of leading with our worst traits: Heaven is where the police are British, the cooks French, the mechanics German, the lovers Italian, and it all is organized by the Swiss. Hell is where the cooks are British, the mechanics French, the lovers

Swiss, the police German, and it all is organized by the Italians.

Why, you might wonder, would you want to lead with your less developed traits? It is easy. Perhaps you have been taught to believe that your particular gifts are not very valuable, or perhaps the culture you are in does not reward them very well. Of course, you might then try to be like someone else—someone you believe has traits that are superior to your own. We all want to be valuable. If we lack respect for our gifts, we can end up being much less than we should be—by being a lesser copy of someone else. What we were meant to give is then missing from the world, causing a void that hurts us all.

If you as an individual try and try and still do not succeed in your current job, it is likely that you are in the wrong place. Get career counseling to help find your genuine vocational skills, and get feedback from others. You do not want to give up just before your breakthrough, but it also makes no sense to keep hitting your head against the wall if this is not the work for you. Each of us has the seed of some real gift inside us. When that seed is unfolding organically as it should, your life eventually blossoms.

Organizations as well as people can stray from the mark. The sustained economic growth of the 1960s and '70s, followed by the wave of mergers and takeovers in the 1980s, encouraged businesses to diversify until they had no real mission or core. When I was working with the United Food and Commercial Workers Local 400 in the late 1980s, the leadership shared with me their concern that grocery stores were being taken over by financial holding companies with no commitment to the grocery business. The union depended on management's knowing its business. The healthiest companies have a strong sense of organizational mission that corresponds to a genuine need—generally called a market niche.

FINDING YOUR OWN GENIUS, FINDING YOUR PARTIALNESS

Educators and educational psychologists have been unconsciously dualistic and hierarchical in their thinking, focusing for example on IQ tests and on the design of tracking systems that separate students by ability. The assumption is that some people are smart and others are dumb. However, cutting-edge work in education and brain research is going another way. Theories on learning styles such as those of Howard Gardner (*Frames of Mind: The Theory of Multiple Intelligence*), David Kolb (*Experiential Learning*), and others, as well as theories of psychological types (Isabel and Peter Myers's *Gifts Differing* and the Myers-Briggs Type Indicator), all look at human ability very differently. Every type of person, such experts argue, has gifts. Not everyone has the same gifts, but we all have abilities that need to be developed and used. The point is not to identify the gifted students but *to identify the gifts within each student.*

An example often used to illustrate different gifts is the supposed "dumb jock" who plays football but has difficulty with math or English. Yet football is a very complicated sport. This young man can memorize complicated plays and keep track of a constantly moving field of bodies in a way that might completely befuddle a classmate who was better at writing a paper on the modern novel. This athlete is not "dumb"—he is smart in a different way from the scholar.

Magical educators also are trying to understand the way the mind works so that they can unleash the potential of every student. Their efforts are strongly supported by research that suggests virtually all of us are using only a fraction of our brains' capacities.

This new way of looking at things has one catch. *We all may be geniuses, but that genius is inherently partial.* The old view posited a way to be on top, above everyone else, seemingly complete in one's own excellence. The view of different gifts says each of us is a genius at something, but none of us is good at everything. Thus, we all are imperfect—and that imperfection requires that we rely on one another.

To discover your own talents, it is important to know your preferred learning and work styles (so you can find work that fits your talents and preferences). The Myers-Briggs Type Indicator, which measures psychological types, can give you some basic information on both. Gardner's *Frames of Mind* or the Kolb Learning Style Index (LSI) can help you identify your preferred learning style.

Difficult financial times force individuals and organizations to find out what businesses they really are in. If they do not, they are likely to go under eventually. By recognizing that it is not just in the business of cutting and fixing hair, a beauty salon can diversify to supplying a variety of services designed to help people look and feel more attractive. By recognizing that its true mission is to get knowledge and information to the public (not just to sell books), a bookstore can meet the needs of changing times by selling tapes and computer programs and by offering lectures and workshops.

THE GIFT

A sure sign that you have claimed the sword of your invincibility is that suddenly your life makes sense as preparation for what you are doing now. David Merkowitz, director of public affairs at the American Council on Education, is a kind of Renaissance man (and also my husband). He's held positions in higher education, journalism, and politics. As he followed his interests, he wondered whether he would pay a price for avoiding the linear career path that seemed increasingly the norm. Yet his present position—in which he develops communications strategies designed to help shape public policy, and which requires a knowledge of higher education, the media, and the political process—draws on this eclectic background. What he calls his "checkered career" helps him spot emerging trends and issues to which his organization must respond. Moreover, his job gives him the chance to contribute to making his social vision a reality: a vision of a truly participatory society where equal opportunity for all is accompanied by a strong commitment to quality performance.

Visitors frequently ask David why he keeps a rabbit doll in a magician's hat displayed prominently in his office. "That's what we do here every day," he replies. "We pull rabbits out of hats." He credits his ability to perform "everyday magic" to his diverse experience and the similarly rich backgrounds of his associates. David stresses how much he enjoys the synergy of working with highly professional and committed people—people who have achieved excellence in their chosen fields. He tries to serve as a "bridge" between the different parts of his organization, identifying connections between their activities and concerns. He finds it highly rewarding to put in place processes that accomplish more than the sum of their component parts, both because he enjoys it personally and because it allows him to live his social vision—right now in his own corner of the globe. This experience constantly renews his energy and excitement about living, even when his workload is almost out of control!

Everyone has a purpose for being here. When you find yours and focus your energy to hone your skills, synchronicity starts working for you and you feel lucky. As I was concluding the writing of this chapter, Betsy Polk, the coordinator of the Mount Vernon Institute, got the news that she had been admitted to graduate school. She had held off applying for several years because she was not sure what advanced degree was right for her. She shared with me her understanding that she might never have heard of the American University/NTL Institute Master's Program in Organizational Development if she had not followed her own intuition in accepting the job at Mount Vernon. She described the sense of joy she felt inside, knowing that this program is the perfect place for her to prepare for the work she is to do in the world. "How do you know?" I asked. She smiled and said, "I just know."

When we pull our own swords from the stone, like David and Betsy, we accept our place in the human family of things. The gift is a sense of radical rightness, of being at the right place at the right time for who we were meant to be. It is a great feeling and worth the experience of all the hard knocks that redirect us until we recognize the sword of our own destiny.

The Exercises

FOR INDIVIDUALS

- First, make a list of things you are really good at. Next, make a list of things that give you energy when you do them. Finally, list issues you care passionately about— that is, where you want to make a difference to the world.
- Complete the following in order to find a provisional purpose statement: I will use my abilities to (fill in the top three things you are good at) in order to (fill in what you care passionately about accomplishing), using a process that (fill in what gives you energy).
- Examine your current work role to determine the degree to which it reflects your mission.
- Based on your HMI scores (Appendix B), which archetype or archetypes seem most important to your own sense of purpose?

FOR ORGANIZATIONS

- Make lists both of things your organization does very well and of things that give its employees energy when they do them. Then describe the issues that the employees care about.

- Complete the following in order to find a provisional mission statement: We will use our abilities to (fill in things the organization does best) in order to (fill in what its employees care about), using a process that (fill in what gives them energy).
- Examine your organization's current policies and structures to determine the degree to which they reflect its mission.

Circle Four: Achieving Your Goals

THE STORY
King Arthur begins reunifying and then expanding his country, bringing together the best and the brightest men and women of his time. Highly charismatic, he convinces many by the force of personality that his dream of Camelot is possible. Others he wins over by carefully arranged marriages. When tyrants stand in the way of his dream of compassionate rule by law, he fearlessly goes to battle. Throughout the years he hones his powers until he exemplifies empowering leadership. Under his direction, Camelot becomes known as the most uplifting and noble court of all time. Eventually, his power and influence grow until he governs much of Western Europe.

THE LESSON
We can see in Arthur's life a case study in magical career and strategic planning. Trained by Merlin, Arthur has been through initiation. This means that he has focused on his "I want" and developed a vision. He then clarifies his own role in achieving this vision, which gives him a sense of purpose or mission. Next, Arthur enlists the support of others, showing them how they can help make the dream come true and how they can combine a personal sense of purpose with a collective sense of mission. Finally, he translates all this into a workable plan—with goals, timetables, and strategies for implementation.

Arthur is essentially an entrepreneur, growing his country until it occupies much of Western Europe. He knows how to release the fire of a group, matching the group's vision ("we want") with their mission ("we can"), and he knows how to sell his own compelling vision. His attention to individuals is phenomenal. Many strategic planning initiatives today fail because, although management is committed, employees do not know how they fit in. Arthur understands that individuals have to know their part in the overall plan. When people understand what they personally can do to realize a compelling vision, their energy level and commitment increase exponentially.

Magical strategic planning initiatives include the following (here associated with different stages of the Magician's journey):

- Scanning the environment for opportunities (initiation, air)
- Articulating a vision (initiation, air)
- Determining an organizational mission (trial by fire, fire)
- Developing goals, objectives, strategies, and timetables (trial by fire, fire)
- Achieving consensus around the plan (illumination, water)
- Evaluation (mastery, earth)[7]

Today, unfortunately, the fiery elements of strategic planning too often are implemented solely in a Warrior mode. Merlin and Arthur make the process magical as well as martial.

First, Arthur's approach to success is vision- rather than competition-driven. He is less concerned with defeating opponents than with manifesting the vision of Camelot in the world. Moreover, since he does not try to convince others to do his will as a way of winning, his fiery enthusiasm for a beautiful and attainable future ignites their own hopes and dreams. In the process he liberates the best and most magical part of his citizenry.

We can liken this to an enlightened sales approach that prides itself on connecting people with products that will help them. Frequently, I have been turned off by the aggressive stance of car and condo salespeople who get hyped up to sell at any cost. This is a self-defeating sales approach: to get the customer to do what you want, irrespective of what he or she wants or needs. Such salespeople often make sales the first time, but more magical approaches yield repeat business.

Second, if people are blocking the expression of Camelot in the world, Arthur does something about it. Using magic does not mean being a wimp. Arthur prefers to get people on his side by persuasion or compromise, but he is willing to get tough when necessary. A modern analogy is a corporate executive who is tough enough (1) to fire people if efforts to make them productive members of the team fail, and (2) to use the sword of truth (the media, the courts, etc.) to expose and stop negative forces in the environment that block the realization of a worthy vision.

Fire is an aspect of will. To express your fire in accomplishment, you must commit to an intense "yes" and enforce your commitment by the willingness to say an equally firm "no." Otherwise, you will end up living out other people's dreams and goals.

Third, Arthur's own goals are always contingent. His ultimate aim is to express the highest and best potential in the world at any given time. Therefore, he alters his course according to Merlin's visions, his own prophetic dreams, and his own experience.

I have seen people stick to their goals inappropriately, so they end up beating their heads against the wall. Many of us have participated in strategic planning initiatives in which we were to set goals and later be judged by whether we attained them—as if the outcome were truly in our control. When we set goals it is best to add the magical invocation, "This or something better."

THE STATUES OF THE TWELVE DEFEATED KINGS

In one version of the Camelot legend, Arthur defeats twelve
kings, buries them beneath Camelot, and erects statues in their
honor. Doing so suggests his desire to integrate the virtues of
all kingdoms and perspectives in Camelot. Arthur clearly sees
himself as releasing impediments to a natural unity rather than
defeating and enslaving enemies.

These twelve statues, each holding a torch, ring the inner
castle walls. Remembering the twelve apostles, the twelve
signs of the zodiac, and the twelve heroic archetypes in *Awakening the Heroes Within*, we can see that Arthur is invoking
symbolic images of unity and completeness.

People who teach visualization, such as Shakti Gawain in
Creative Visualization, emphasize the magic of imaging:

> Imagination is the ability to create an idea or mental
> picture in your mind. In creative visualization you use
> your imagination to create a clear image of something
> you wish to manifest. Then you continue to focus on the
> idea or picture regularly, giving it positive energy until it
> becomes objective reality . . . in other words, until you
> actually achieve what you have been visualizing.

Creative visualization, she continues, is more than mere
"positive thinking," for it requires not simply superficial
change but "exploring, discovering, and changing our deepest,
most basic attitudes toward life."[8] We learn that we can have
what will fulfill us—if we are being true to our purpose.

Creative visualization is quite simple. Just see, in your
mind's eye, the outcome you desire as if it were happening
already. To reinforce the visualization, practice kinesthetic
and auditory techniques. To add body knowing, imagine how it

would feel in your body to get what you wanted. To add an auditory component, verbally affirm, in the present tense, that you have what you desire. (You can justify this, even when your goal is not realized in the ordinary sense of the word, by seeing the goal as reached in your consciousness, knowing that a time lag always exists between aligning your mind to achieve a goal and achieving it in the world.)

It is not necessary to know *how* we are going to achieve our goals. Sometimes the goals will be achieved by serendipity. The phone rings. We run into someone. We see just the right ad in the paper. This is how magic works. As we focus our will and attention on an outcome that we desire and that is appropriate for us, we attract positive results.

The reason for making plans, strategies, and timetables is that they convince the mind that the goal is possible. Moreover, they build in some accountability, so we do not simply use visualization to deceive ourselves. Actually, the more roads to success we can imagine, the better. They make us more confident and more flexible. Moreover, making plans keeps us realistic and makes us set priorities. Arthur could not have taken over much of Western Europe all at once—he had to do it a little at a time.

Fourth, Arthur listens readily to others—especially to his knights—and as much as possible moves forward by consensus, trying to create a climate in Camelot where his knights and ladies are "of one mind" about the outcome desired. In many organizations today, leaders settle for surface compliance, or manipulate or coerce employees, and then wonder why these workers lack commitment or behave in a passive-aggressive fashion. When employees are involved in the strategic planning process, they feel a sense of ownership that releases the fire, the energy, and the commitment of the team.

Fifth, Arthur emphasizes innate ability over imposed hierarchy, seeking to match a natural hierarchy of talents with the needs at hand. For example, Merlin does not try to be king and

BECOMING OF ONE MIND—WITHIN

Becoming "of one mind" works within us as well as without. It means we have internal unified intent. Often, when we fail to accomplish our goals, some aspect of ourselves is secretly at war with our stated intentions. For instance, we may say we want to advance in our job, but some part of us may sabotage our efforts because of fear or a simple wish for more leisure. When we are internally "of one mind" about a goal, our chances of success improve immensely.

For example, Robert Johnson, a psychoanalyst and author of *Inner Work*, writes about a rebellious part of himself that wanted to be a beach bum. In fact, he realized, this part of him was responsible for his forgetting appointments with clients or acting in ways that drove them away. Johnson then held an imaginary conversation with his internal beach bum, who said he just wanted to have fun; Johnson warned how little fun they would have if they had no income. The inner dialogue continued along this line until Johnson agreed to have more fun—go to more movies, actually spend time on the beach—and his beach bum self agreed not to ruin his practice.[9]

Arthur does not aspire to be the court seer. Indeed, Arthur cultivates such tolerance and honesty that his knights are open about their limitations as well as their achievements.

Well into the Camelot story a second sword appears in yet another stone, its engraved message warning that only the greatest of the knights can remove the sword. An attempt by anyone else may prove fatal. Arthur encourages Lancelot to try —because everyone believes Lancelot to be the greatest knight in the world—but he declines, saying the greatest of the knights is yet to come. Shortly thereafter Galahad appears and successfully pulls out the sword.

Arthur's contribution here is to create a kind of modified

hierarchy in which all the knights matter and none get their way simply because of their position. I would guess that Arthur knew how to recognize someone's true ability, even if the person did not see it himself. Great leaders can release the fire in coworkers or employees (or even bosses) by seeing what they are good at and encouraging them to take on tasks and move into roles that best utilize their gifts. Anyone who understands that everyone has a contribution to make to the world has an innate respect for others that is contagious. People come to respect themselves, and when they do, their work improves.

This affects what hierarchy means. Even Arthur does not expect blind obedience. He knows he has to earn the loyalty of his knights, ladies, and subjects by the quality of his rule.

Finally, Arthur does not sit around agonizing about whether he is doing the right thing. Once his purpose becomes clear, he acts with certainty. Otherwise, he could never have achieved so much in one lifetime. A current example of a similarly aggressive leader is Henry Gradillas, former principal of Garfield High School in East Los Angeles. Gradillas believes in the adage "It is easier to ask for forgiveness than permission." When he sees a problem, he acts.

Gradillas was the principal when math teacher Jaime Escalante (made famous in the movie *Stand and Deliver*) demonstrated that it was possible to take Hispanic teenagers from a poor neighborhood who had been written off by almost everyone and teach them all to pass the advanced placement test in calculus. How was this accomplished? Gradillas and Escalante saw what many other people knew: these Hispanic teenagers were going nowhere without an adequate education. They knew these kids were just as smart as kids anywhere. To make up for inadequate preparation, the pair provided time for longer study hours—after school, before school, summers, holidays. Although the parents and students complained, the youngsters also appreciated being taken seriously. With

---

THE SEAT OF DANGER

Until Galahad appears, there is an empty seat at the Round Table, called the Seat of Danger. Anyone but the greatest of knights who dares sit there will die. Eventually, Galahad safely claims it as his own. This seat, like the second sword in the stone, reinforces the importance of an accurate self-appraisal. It is not so important to be the best knight. What is important is knowing who you are and what you can do. All the knights are valuable—except any who suffer from delusions about who they are. They pose a danger to the magical order.

Gradillas's support, Escalante turned indifferent, unprepared math students into excellent ones, year after year. In fact, even today Ivy League colleges make special trips to Garfield High to recruit students. Unfortunately, even after the movie *Stand and Deliver* chronicled their accomplishment, other educators claimed their success could not be replicated in a more ethnically mixed environment.

Both Escalante and Gradillas took on that challenge. When Gradillas took his next position, he noted that the students in the honors class of the ethnically mixed high school were Caucasian—mainly Jewish and middle to upper class. The kids in the industrial sewing classes were predominantly Latino and poor. Gradillas closed the industrial sewing classes and declared that everyone was going to take serious academic subjects. If students had trouble passing, teachers would work with them after school, weekends, summers, holidays—whatever it took. The result: once again he proved that with enough perseverance and hard work, virtually every student can succeed.[10]

THE GIFT

Leaders like King Arthur and Henry Gradillas demonstrate the virtue of fire. If magic is the art of releasing the highest and best potential in any situation, fire is the aspect of magic that gets us to act. The ideal outcome can occur only when we commit to our vision and take the risk of acting on it. Others may criticize us; that is not the point. The point is to do what is right.

Fiery leaders keep their eyes on their goals and act with a kind of fierce commitment. If others do not understand, these leaders leap in to win them over with their charisma and passion. They rarely mind if someone has a different idea or commitment. If someone seems apathetic or lost, they will do everything they can to get that person going—either to find his or her own way or to follow theirs. Their motto is "There is nothing to it but to do it." We know we have completed this level of trial by fire successfully when we become adept at setting and achieving our own goals.

THE EXERCISES

FOR INDIVIDUALS

- Set long-term and short-term goals. Be certain that they fit with your own sense of purpose. Be attentive to internal and external feedback, and alter the goals as necessary.
- Break down your goals into attainable objectives. You may have goals for the year, but to achieve them, you will need objectives for each week or month. Notice if any important actions are postponed continually. What action needs to occur right now? How can you remove the blocks to action and get going?
- Think about the people you work with or want to work with. What would be the ideal relationship with each

person? What do you want from him or her? So many people complain about others without telling them clearly what they want. Get clear in your mind what you want from significant people in your life, and then share your wishes with them (being certain to listen to their feedback about whether your vision fits for them, and also about what they want from you).

- With reference to your HMI scores (Appendix B), consider which archetype you may need more of to fulfill your goals. You can awaken an archetype by (1) ritual invocation, (2) acting the way the archetype acts (go through its rites and rituals and it will come to you), (3) dressing to honor the archetype, and/or (4) finding people who express the archetype at a high level and learning from them. (For example, if you want more of the Warrior archetype, you might take up a martial art or hang around people in the military.)

FOR ORGANIZATIONS
- Work with each unit of the organization to help its leadership set goals and objectives. Be certain they are attainable and congruent with the unit's and organization's mission, and then be alert to the necessity of altering the goals as required by internal and external feedback. What actions need to be taken right now? Identify and remove blocks impeding such action, and get going.
- Take time to be certain that each person in the organization knows how he or she fits in. (Often organizational leaders feel important, but the ordinary employee feels dispensable.) If people do not know what they do well, try to help them find their gifts and then, if possible, move them to roles that fit those gifts.
- Create an accountability system so that people who contribute to the organization are rewarded systematically and people who do not (and certainly those who are negative and sabotage success) either change or go.

Circle Five: Learning What the Sword Demands

THE STORY

Arthur sees a Ship Draped in Silk and is intrigued. When invited to sup with twelve beautiful women, he leaps aboard, where he is wined and dined and put to bed in the most beautiful bedroom he has ever seen. However, he awakens in a dungeon with his men, where he is told he can escape only if he fights the knight Accolon. Arthur agrees. Unbeknownst to him, Morgan le Fay has replaced the authentic and magical Excalibur with a copy, and put the real Excalibur in the hands of Accolon. But Arthur fights so nobly that onlookers are inspired and moved. As Accolon is about to deliver a mortal wound, the Lady of the Lake intercedes—sending Excalibur flying through the air back to Arthur—and saves the day.

THE LESSON

This episode warns us about what can happen if we forget who we are. This is not a prudish story—King Arthur has as much right as anyone else to have a good time. Rather, it is a story about forgetfulness. Arthur is impulsive and leaps aboard out of curiosity, a love of adventure, and the enticement of lovely women. He forgets that as king he is responsible for the safety of all his men. Furthermore, in this forgetfulness we can infer that he has moved into an ego stance. He is doing what *he* wants, without regard for his responsibilities and commitments.

Earlier, when he pulled the sword from the stone, he realized he was successful because of a kind of destiny or purpose. When any of us claims our own mission, things can begin to go rather amazingly right. We may begin to think they are doing so because we are so special. We may then think we can do whatever we want and have the same good luck. Arthur learns differently.

Peter Smith, founding president of California State University, Monterey Bay, talked to me about a similar pattern in his own life. His career began with an astounding story of accomplishment. At twenty-four he had the opportunity to start the Community College of Vermont—and to design it according to progressive educational principles. He spent twelve years of his life making the college the success it is today.

However, such early success made him underestimate the role of serendipity in life. Yes, his idea for the college had been a good one. Yes, he had worked diligently. But he also had been very lucky. As he moved into political life, he expected equivalent smooth sailing. He was elected to the U.S. Congress—but was defeated for a second term! This happened, he told me, because he underestimated how many powerful lobbying groups he was taking on at once. This trial helped him see that it is not enough to be bright, work hard, and be on the side of right. "Several people have to die crossing the bridge before someone does so successfully!"

Asked how he has been changed by his trial by fire, he said he still is willing to sacrifice his own career advancement to improve the quality of the educational system, but that his strategies now are different. He no longer cares about having the last word; he's more interested in achieving positive goals. And he is more attentive to differences in people's styles, so he can develop consensus in a more effective way. Beyond his increasing sophistication is a sharpened sense of purpose and a heightened sense of altruism. He has learned he is by nature "a builder" of educational programs and institutions, and he realizes that his motivation has not been simply to advance his own career but to promote a larger vision of what education is and could be.

What makes the difference between people who are defeated when the magic suddenly does not work and those—like King Arthur and Peter Smith—who bounce back? Consider the moment when Accolon is about to deliver the mortal blow. What goes on within Arthur? In that moment, I would imagine he is remembering that the power he has wielded has never been his own. He has always had supernatural help—simply because he has given over his life to something greater than himself. When he remembers this, Excalibur—that is, his invincibility—returns.

In the popular movie *Field of Dreams,* Ray Kinsella, a young farmer, gets angry when author Terrance Mann (who is a "come-lately" to Ray's enchanted baseball field) is invited to go with the ballplayers (long-dead heroes of his childhood who have returned magically to earth for one final game in Ray's Iowa cornfield) into the otherworld. He reminds the ghost ballplayers that he has risked everything—his farm, his sole means of support—to build their playing field. If anyone gets to go with them, it should be me, thinks Ray. He demands, "What's in it for me?" Shoeless Joe Jackson, one of the ghosts, challenges him abruptly, asking, "Did you do this for *you?*"

Magic is done not because it helps us get our own way but because it represents an act of faith and a concomitant willingness to do our part—whatever that happens to be.

There is a wonderful Japanese story about a simple farmer who quite accidentally insults a great samurai. Challenging the farmer to a duel, the warrior declares he will return the next morning. The farmer is totally distraught. He has no combat skills. How can he fight a samurai? He consults a sword master, who draws a circle on the ground and tells him to stay in this circle for protection. Although the master also teaches the farmer one stroke, which he is to practice all night, he tells

---

TURNING IT OVER AND THE FEMININE

The feminine often is associated with a receptive willingness to live for something beyond oneself. Feminine agency—the twelve beautiful women, Morgan le Fay, and the Lady of the Lake—brings Arthur back to his purpose and his magic when he has become wayward and full of himself. The twelve women who defeat his ego complement the twelve kings Arthur kills. Their presence in the story underscores the theme of androgyny in the Arthurian legends.

---

him, "You cannot escape from this fight. The chances are that you will die. So the first thing you must accept is that you are as good as dead." The farmer practices all night, and in the morning stands with his foot in the circle. When the samurai begins to fight him, the farmer lunges suddenly, wounding his opponent. The spectators are dumbfounded, asking him how he has been able to defeat such a great swordsman. The farmer replies that he has done nothing. He says he was not even there during the combat; he had died the night before. Yet, "as I stood there, a surge of power shot through me and sent my body into that lunge."[11]

A similar story that virtually everyone knows occurs in the movie *Star Wars*. When Luke Skywalker is careening through a space cavern chased by Darth Vader's death squad, he fears he will lose control and crash. Suddenly he hears the voice of his teacher, Obi Knobi, reminding him to "trust the force, Luke." When he turns the steering over to "the force," he is successful at the seemingly impossible task of navigating safely at high speed.

What does this mean in everyday life? Creative people often talk of being visited by the muse. Counselor and interior designer Deborah Marsteller of Making Home, Unlimited, bartered to take my yearlong training course, promising me twelve archetypal banners in return. Two weeks before the end of the course, they still were not made. She went into an almost trancelike creative state, meditating on each archetype in turn. As she began each banner, she would see an image in the silk. She did not even draw the image first; she just started cutting, using a rather complicated mixed-media appliqué process. She trusted she would know what to do and where to find the materials she needed. Some she found in her attic, others in nearby stores. She did almost nothing else for two weeks. The results are astonishingly beautiful. The process itself taught her a different way to live—because she realized being in such a deep creative state allowed her to know what to do and where to get the resources she needed.

For many people, as for the farmer in the Japanese story, the ability to move into this highly intuitive and trusting place comes from facing death. Peggy Williams, president of Lyndon State College in Vermont, when asked about trial by fire in her life, told me about camping in the Arctic with her husband and being surprised by a storm. The tent collapsed from the weight of the accumulating snow. They sized up the situation and realized that most likely they would die. Calmly accepting this fact, she and her husband propped up the tent with a piece of equipment to keep enough air inside so they would not be asphyxiated. They decided it was best that they act as routinely as possible and took turns steadying the tent against the wind and sleeping. The next day the storm abated somewhat, so they abandoned their camping gear and skied to safety!

It is no wonder that when her college faced budget cuts of several million dollars, President Williams refused to see it as a crisis. Because she remained calm, so did everyone else. For years she found ways to cut the budget without truly harming the college. She just seemed to know how to prune judiciously while taking steps to improve college finances. At this writing, Lyndon State College is booming.

An ease with death and loss means that we can meet our goals noncompulsively. A thin line separates being committed to goals and becoming addicted to them. Here's how we can tell. If we feel that our well-being depends on achieving a goal, it has become addictive. That is why it is best that we mentally let go of our goals even while we are achieving them.

My respect for Arthur as a character grew greatly when I read that as a young man he was warned by Merlin that his reign someday would be overthrown by his own illegitimate son, Mordred. But Arthur chooses to fulfill his own mission while knowing that Camelot is destined to crumble. In a way, he has to mentally give up his goals before he even begins. He creates Camelot because it is the right thing to do as well as being his destiny—not because it is a way to achieve immortality by creating something that will outlast him.

When Arthur returns from the high point of his success—his victory over the Roman Emperor—he finds that Mordred has led a rebellion and declared himself king. Arthur tries to avoid warring against his own flesh and blood. However, as the two armies face each other at dawn to negotiate a truce, a soldier draws his sword to kill a viper and the nervous armies begin a bloody battle in which Arthur is mortally wounded. He sends a messenger to throw Excalibur back into the lake, where the hand of the Lady of the Lake emerges to grasp it. He then is taken to a barge in which Morgan le Fay and two other women escort him back to Avalon. Legend has it that there his wounds will be healed and someday he will return to rule again. That is why he is known as "the once and future king."

Everything that is born, dies. Our careers and organizations go through periods of growth and then decay. Any worthy initiative releases energy that, if properly guided and nourished, will grow for some time. However, life is cyclical, not linear. That means that if a business is booming, it may still be on a growth curve, or it may be peaking out—with sales about to drop off suddenly.

Arthur's going to Rome is a great triumph—and the beginning of the end for Camelot. In reality, Arthur has accomplished what he set out to do and likely has overextended to the point where his country now is ungovernable. It is time to let go, to turn it over to a new generation. Often we think that if an enterprise does not last, it has not been a success. Yet successful parenting, therapy, and schooling require people to grow up, terminate, graduate. Careers and businesses that last over time do so because of a continual cycle of new initiatives, with a process of birth, growth, and eventually death. Creativity is freed up when we love the process enough to let go of its results.

I once took a workshop in which the leader had us make statues out of clay, allowing the wisdom of our hands to shape the goddess most important to us. I worked hard at not allowing my mind to override the wisdom of my fingers and was impressed with what I and others created. We shared what our creations meant to us, and then the leader suggested we return our pieces of clay to the center of the circle and press them back into one piece. Some people winced visibly, for it was hard to destroy what we had been so proud of creating. The leader explained that destruction was part of creation: we could not create freely unless we were able to let go of the results.

Parker Palmer tells the Taoist story of Khing, a master carver who was commanded by the ruler to fashion a perfect wooden bell stand, under threat of death if he failed. That's certainly a case of trial by fire. The master carver fasted until he "had forgotten gain and success . . . praise or criticism," his own body, and finally the ruler and his power. When he had achieved a state of complete disinterestedness, he walked through the forest until the "right tree appeared" before his eyes. Then he worked to release the "hidden potential in the wood," the result being so perfect that people thought he had received help from the spirits to produce it.

Palmer concludes that the woodcarver "took care to attend

to reality without getting fixated on results, to the point that he was willing to risk no results whatsoever." Like the wood-carver, Palmer explains, people working to improve the world must keep doing so whether they get results or not. "What they are crafting is not bell stands or justice or peace. They are crafting themselves."[12]

Growth, learning, and innovation always require experimentation. People who have gained the gift of trial by fire do not worry overly much about making mistakes, seeing them simply as part of the process of getting it right. When challenged about how many "failures" he had experienced while trying to invent the lightbulb, Thomas Edison is said to have replied with characteristic confidence that he had discovered a thousand eight hundred ways *not* to make a lightbulb![13] Magical creativity requires letting go of attachment to results —even our ideas about what we are or can be.

Wise leaders in the In-Between know how to cut their losses, and they also know how to protect endeavors with intrinsic worth, whether or not they are profitable or popular. The leadership of LucyAnn Geiselman, president of Mount Vernon College, illustrates such fiery persistence coupled with discretion. Earning a Ph.D. at the University of Chicago, she loved research and teaching and had a facility for both. However, she took a hard look at herself and realized that what set her apart from many of her classmates was an innate ability as a leader and manager. She therefore decided she would be a college president—preferably of a small women's college.

Geiselman is a woman of courage, conviction, and perseverance. In fact, her metaphor for the ideal leader is a tennis player who is never off her game. Geiselman paid her dues, moving slowly up the administrative ladder, developing expertise in fund-raising as well as the academic and business side of collegiate management, taking detours as needed for family and other reasons but always keeping her goal in mind.

After some years she was offered a position as president of

Mount Vernon College, a small women's college in Washington, D.C. As with many of us, however, just when she thought her dreams had come true, she discovered herself facing another test—a formidable one. She knew that small women's colleges were experiencing financial difficulties as a result of demographic changes and market trends, complicated by the recession of the 1980s and early '90s. However, she did not anticipate how difficult things would be. She reasoned that she could take out a loan for the college using the valuable real estate of the campus as collateral. What she had not anticipated was the banking crisis that hit along with the decline of the real estate market—just at the time she took her new and much hoped-for position. Banks were not lending large sums with real estate as collateral. She went to twenty-three banks and was turned down by all of them.

Things looked hopeless. At this point almost anyone would have thrown in the towel. However, Geiselman declared that this little school was not going to roll over and play dead. She believed Mount Vernon deserved to succeed. When she had visited the college for her interview, she was impressed by a student she saw running to a class she had missed the day before; her professor had called to see where she was. This was a place that cared about students, and a place that took women seriously.

The faculty, sophisticated about teaching and learning, did not simply want to find the best and the brightest students to teach; they brought out the best and the brightest in the students they had. If magic means releasing the highest and best potential in any situation, then Mount Vernon faculty and staff did magic with their students.

In a short period of time, Geiselman secured a loan from Georgetown University, doubled the size of the entering class, tightened up financial management, implemented an innovative core curriculum, launched a strategic planning initiative, and secured an exemplary donation of a million and a half

FAITH FUELS FAITH ON A COLLEGE CAMPUS

At one point early in the first winter of LucyAnn Geiselman's presidency, the boiler broke down and the college did not have the funds to fix it. Mount Vernon students were scared—because they were hearing rumors of the school's demise—and they were cold. Without the boiler, there was no heat. Geiselman called on the wonderful "feisty" group of women in the student government to stand with her as she persevered in solving this problem (patching the boiler until funds were available to replace it). The next day student government officials went out and used their own funds to buy cherry trees for the campus—a tangible symbol of their belief in the school's long-term future. As the president's confidence fueled their faith, theirs, in turn, fueled hers, giving her renewed energy for the struggle ahead.

dollars from a pleased parent of a Mount Vernon leader. Asked how she was able to continue to work extremely long days in the face of such persistent uncertainty, Geiselman explained that it was not a sure knowledge of victory that helped her negotiate her way through her trial by fire, but a sure knowledge that the college deserved to thrive. Successful leadership, she continued, requires "grit" and what Vaclav Havel defines as "hope":

> Hope is definitely not the same thing as optimism, it is not the conviction that something will turn out well, but the certainty that something makes sense regardless of how it turns out. It is also this hope above all which gives us the strength to live and continually try new things.[14]

The fire of the Warrior is focused on winning—on the outcome—fearing the "shame of defeat." The fire of the Magician is about faithfulness to integrity of purpose and to excellence, whether one wins or not. In the past we have equated success with stability. Whether we've been talking about our marriages, our businesses, or our projects, we've considered them a success if they lasted. The Magician's idea of success is much more demanding—and more transcendent.

Success, for the Magician, is measured by the quality of the endeavor—the quality of our dreams, our efforts, our interactions with one another. When we say Camelot failed, we can remember that England lived on. "Camelot" symbolizes a quality of experience, not an organizational or political structure. It is always a success when "Camelot" exists at all, if even for a moment.

Whenever we do not get the results we want, most of us blame ourselves or others instead of recognizing that we do not control the universe. As a result, fire erupts as rage and hurts us all. In our society today, we focus our attention on conflicts between political and racial groups, thus intensifying their animosity toward each other. However, the more significant distinction in the In-Between (which is largely ignored) is not between people's politics or skin color, but whether or not they are willing to rise to the challenges of the In-Between. Blacks and whites who hate each other, for example, have more in common than they do with those of their own race who take responsibility for their own growth and development, without hate or blame. Similarly for liberals and conservatives, or any other warring groups today.

This is one major reason it is so important that we learn the secrets of everyday magic encoded in the Camelot legend: they can help us use the In-Between to grow rather than to act out our rage on one another. As individuals, we may not be able to change the climate of hatred and violence in society overnight, but we can do our part.

In *Leading from Within: Reflections on Spirituality and Leadership,* Parker Palmer urges us to be aware of our projections. "We share responsibility for creating the external world by projecting either a spirit of light or a spirit of shadow on that which is 'other' than us. Either a spirit of hope or a spirit of despair . . . We have a choice about what we are going to project, and in that choice we help create the world that is. *Consciousness precedes being.*"[15] As we resist the process of projection and the blaming of others, consciousness evolves and the world improves—as we learn from the inevitable trials of the In-Between.

John Sherer, a consultant I interviewed for this book, told me how he literally walked on hot coals (in a "fire walk" offered by Anthony Robbins). In doing so, he realized that success had to do with committing so completely to something that you would "walk through fire for it." In my heart of hearts, I would rather skip the hard stuff and be a fairy godmother, using magic to make everyone happy, including myself. However, I have had to learn that each of us has different trials by fire which heat up the cauldron in ways which can turn whatever is leaden in our consciousness into gold. When I have most wanted to use magic to transform a situation, I have had to recognize that the situation *was* the magic—transforming *me*. I cannot protect others any more than I can protect myself from this important alchemical process.

THE GIFT

Poet David Whyte tells of an excursion into a cave in the Himalayas filled with carvings of ancient Tibetan Masters. The faces, although carved in wood, looked more loving—and more authentic—than any living faces he had ever seen. He noticed that the carver of these wondrous faces had used the flaws in the wood to create such beauty.

King Arthur recognizes that the swords that give him his power come from the Divine. Similarly, Whyte encourages us to think of ourselves not so much as wielding the sword but as being sculpted by a divine carver of great benevolence and wisdom. Whyte's point is similar to Parker Palmer's: we are never just creating; we also are being created. Whether we experience trial by fire as an ordeal or an adventure, its gift is a chipping away at the inauthentic, allowing our true natures to show through. What we typically see as our inadequacies, then, are the keys to our individuality. Whyte's poem, reprinted here in its entirety, encourages each of us to trust the process of being sculpted by "the blows of the carver's hands."

THE FACES AT BRAGA

In a monastery darkness
by the light of one flashlight
the old shrine room waits in silence.

While above the door
we see the terrible figure,
fierce eyes demanding. "Will you step through?"

And the old monk leads us,
bent back nudging blackness
prayer beads in the hand that beckons.

We light the butter lamps
and bow, eyes blinking in the
pungent smoke, look up without a word,

see faces in meditation,
a hundred faces carved above,
eye lines wrinkled in the hand held light.

Such love in solid wood!
Taken from the hillsides and carved in silence
they have the vibrant stillness of those who made them.

Engulfed in the past
they have been neglected, but through
smoke and darkness they are like the flowers

we have seen growing
through the dust of eroded slopes,
their slowly opening faces turned toward the mountain.

Carved in devotion
their eyes have softened through age
and their mouths curve through delight of the carver's
    hand.[16]

If only our own faces
would allow the invisible carver's hand
to bring the deep grain of love to the surface.

If only we knew
as the carver knew, how the flaws
in the wood led his searching chisel to the very core,

we would smile too
and not need faces immobilized
by fear and the weight of things undone.

When we fight with our failing
we ignore the entrance to the shrine itself
and wrestle with the guardian, fierce figure on the side of
    good.

And as we fight
our eyes are hooded with grief
and our mouths are dry with pain.

If only we could give ourselves
to the blows of the carver's hand,
the lines in our faces would be the trace lines of rivers

feeding the sea
where voices meet, praising the features
of the mountain and the cloud and the sky.

Our faces would fall away
until we, growing younger toward death
every day, would gather all our flaws in celebration

to merge with them perfectly,
impossibly, wedded to our essence,
full of silence from the carver's hand.[16]

Anytime we act to create, we are in partnership with the Creator. The comic book image of the Magician commanding cosmic forces to do his or her will actually is one of inflation or of evil sorcery. People often are attracted to the idea of magic simply because they fear the trials by fire that are part of human life. They want control of—and some exemption from feeling the effects of—the carver's hand.

People who express the Magician archetype in its most positive form are humble. The woodcarver Parker Palmer wrote about, the one who carved the exquisite bell stand, insisted that "I am only a workman"—that there was nothing special about him. True Magicians do not command, they ask. They do not seek to cheat death by using magic to gain immortality. They do not *make* magic happen. They align their wills with positive forces in order to create a space for the magic to flow through. They often do *not* even call themselves Magicians. They see themselves as ordinary—and they are. They just have opened themselves up to allow magic into their lives.

Opening up to magic requires a willingness to do our part—
no matter how small or large the work is that we may be asked
to do. When we want to be more (or less) than we are, we can
fall prey to evil sorcery. The Master Summoner, mentor to
Ged, the Magician in Ursula Le Guin's *A Wizard of Earthsea*,
explains that he was attracted to the Magician's path because
he thought wizards could do anything. However, as his magical wisdom grows, he recognizes that his path is narrowing
until "at last he chooses nothing, but does only and wholly
what he must do."[17]

THE EXERCISES

FOR INDIVIDUALS

- Experiment with letting your intuition lead you. Let your
  inner voice tell you what to do. Or, create something out
  of clay and simply let your fingers do what they wish. Or,
  create a collage, picking pictures that beckon to you and
  placing them where they want to go.
- Write your goals on a piece of paper. Declare that you
  want them, or something better. In doing so, turn over
  your will to God, another higher power, or your deeper,
  wiser self. Then burn the paper. Finally, you might write
  a series of alternative, equally good scenarios of what you
  want to achieve as backup plans to relieve your mind.
- Do the same thing as in the previous exercise, only this
  time write down something you are ready to let go of in
  order to achieve your higher goals. Declare why you are
  letting it go and what you wish in its place. Then burn
  the paper.
- With reference to your HMI results (Appendix B), conduct a written dialogue with an archetype that you would
  like to help you in your efforts.

FOR ORGANIZATIONS

- Encourage discussion in the workplace on how to let intuition serve as a guide. Set goals but let people use their own resourcefulness and creativity in determining how to achieve them. Do not tie people's hands.
- What products, endeavors, approaches are not working? Which ones should be phased out? Which might be modified? Which should be protected because of their intrinsic worth? Where does the organization need to turn over concern with results and just do what needs to be done— and hope?
- Put in a suggestion box for better ideas. Encourage people to tell what is going right and what can be improved, including the organization's goals and priorities! Reward good feedback, even if it is critical. (However, encourage people to share in as constructive a way as possible.)

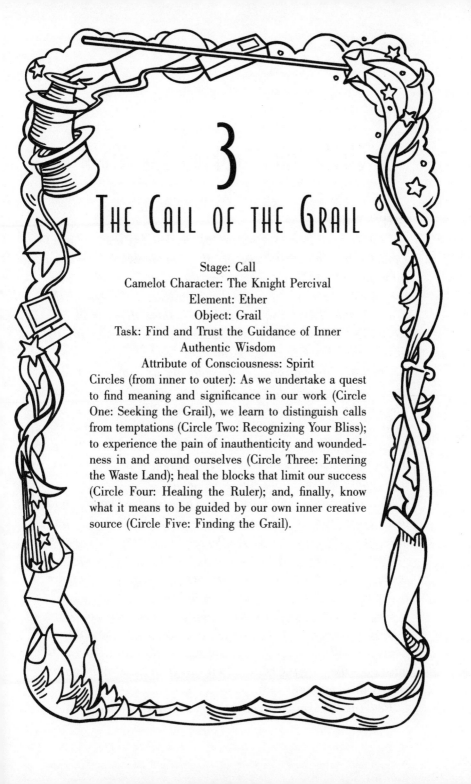

3

THE CALL OF THE GRAIL

Stage: Call
Camelot Character: The Knight Percival
Element: Ether
Object: Grail
Task: Find and Trust the Guidance of Inner
Authentic Wisdom
Attribute of Consciousness: Spirit

Circles (from inner to outer): As we undertake a quest to find meaning and significance in our work (Circle One: Seeking the Grail), we learn to distinguish calls from temptations (Circle Two: Recognizing Your Bliss); to experience the pain of inauthenticity and woundedness in and around ourselves (Circle Three: Entering the Waste Land); heal the blocks that limit our success (Circle Four: Healing the Ruler); and, finally, know what it means to be guided by our own inner creative source (Circle Five: Finding the Grail).

Circle One: Seeking the Grail

THE STORY

On the vigil of Pentecost, when all the knights and ladies of Camelot are gathered together, they suddenly hear a loud thunderclap, and a sunbeam enters the assembly brighter than they have ever seen before, and they all are "alighted of the grace of the Holy Ghost."[1] As they sit there dumbstruck, the Holy Grail appears and every knight and lady is mysteriously furnished with the food he or she most loves.

Then the Grail disappears as suddenly as it appeared, and Sir Gawain proposes that all the knights vow to seek the Grail. The knights accept this "call to adventure." Because "it would be a disgrace to go forth in a group . . . each entered the forest at a point that he, himself, had chosen, where it was darkest and there was no path." Each knight must find his own way, going where no one has gone before.[2]

How amazing it must have been! The assembled knights had long ago responded to King Arthur's call, and they willingly vowed loyalty to him and fidelity to the dream of Camelot. These knights helped Arthur create the most just and prosperous society England had ever known, yet in an instant they are ready to leave it all and search for the Grail.

King Arthur is saddened by the knights' vow. They all have been so successful together. Why leave now, when everything is going so well? he wonders. Yet he recognizes that the knights must go—they are responding to a call from their souls. So he blesses their journey.

Percival, a knight whose story speaks uniquely to a

postmodern consciousness, sets out full of enthusiasm for the quest and confident in his own abilities. After all, he is one of Arthur's most able knights. As he wanders along searching for the Grail, he finds himself in the Waste Land kingdom, a barren, alienating place where the people suffer and the land is ravaged by dryness. He comes across the castle of the monarch of this wretched realm, only to find that the king suffers from a mysterious and seemingly incurable wound. The king invites Percival to a huge feast, during which Percival sees many strange sights—including a ritual procession in which the Grail is carried through the hall. He yearns to ask the king about this but remains silent.

The next day Percival leaves. He wanders for years, feeling a kind of mysterious ennui, until finally a bizarre and ugly woman accosts him and tells him the ancient prophecy about his destiny. It turns out that Percival is destined to heal the King of the Waste Land by asking two magical questions. The hitch is that Percival was to have asked these questions spontaneously and in innocence of the legend; now that he knows it, it is too late.

However, Percival refuses to give up. He returns to the Grail Castle and asks the questions. The king is healed, and the Waste Land blooms once again.[3]

THE LESSON

The story of Percival's search for the Holy Grail illustrates the call stage of the Magician's journey. The Grail appears to the assembled knights and ladies of Camelot, calling them to find their unique creative source: their individuality (Circle One). As Percival begins his quest, he learns to discern a true call from a temptation (Circle Two). In seeking the Grail, he enters the Waste Land and feels the pain of the Wounded King, thus moving through superficiality and denial to acknowledge how much suffering exists in the world (Circle Three). As he faces his own failures, he is able to heal the king, so that the Waste

THE ORIGIN AND MEANING OF THE GRAIL

Moorish tales link the Grail to the goddess of love, and Celtic tales connect it to fertility goddesses. In the Christian tradition the Grail is the Holy Grail, the cup out of which Christ drank at the Last Supper. In all these accounts, however, the Grail calls us to our souls and to a realization of cosmic love. One version of the story says that the Grail was formed from a star that fell from Lucifer's crown when he was banished from Heaven, and that the Grail is a means for transmuting evil into good.

In *The Power of Myth*, Joseph Campbell likens the Grail of the Camelot story to a Roman god holding a cornucopia from which an endless supply of food is pouring: "This is the Grail, the vessel of inexhaustible vitality. The Grail is that fountain in the center of the Universe from which the energies of eternity pour into the world of time. It's in each of our hearts, that same energy."[4] You have the opportunity to find the "grail" inside— the source of your own uniqueness, vitality, and strength, the divine within you—by "following your bliss" instead of following the herd.

Land can bloom (Circle Four). Finally, Percival finds the Grail and "becomes" it by integrating into his daily life all that he has learned on his quest.

In individual or organizational life, the call of the grail may come as a crisis of values or meaning—generally when we have become reasonably successful. We expect to rest on our laurels, and suddenly the bottom seems to drop out of everything. Perhaps some crisis motivates us to begin wondering about the meaning and value of life. Sometimes, as in the classic midlife transition, an inner urgency for meaning emerges, requiring us to revisit our values to see if they still hold true. Sometimes we are thrown into such experiences because we have violated our own ethical imperatives, and we begin to wonder who we are. Such experiences vary in intensity, but inevitably they include a visit to the waste land, where we feel depressed, alienated, or empty. This is the classic "dark night of the soul" about which poets and mystics talk, and which comes before enlightenment.

This chapter is about the process of reaching enlightenment. In the Camelot stories, this does not require a mystic retreat from the world. For example, when Sir Galahad finds the Grail, he exclaims about the mystery of enterprise: "For now I see revealed what tongue could not relate nor heart conceive. Here is the source of valor undismayed, the springhead of endeavor; here I see the wonder that passes every other!"[5] The Camelot stories are parables about spirituality expressed through the active world of public life.

Camelot scholar Dolores Ashcroft-Nowicki reassures us that everyone has what is needed to find his or her own grail. In fact, a child who sits and gazes out the window on a wet afternoon holds the very same key that we need to seek out our inner grail. We call it the creative imagination. Imagination allows us to become the rulers of our own inner kingdoms. "All things have their beginning on the inner levels of existence and work their way outwards," Ashcroft-Nowicki says. That is why the grail, or the imagination, holds the key to valor, endeavor, and enterprise.[6]

The Percival story teaches us that when we begin to notice ourselves surrounded by a waste land world—that is, a life that does not nourish us—we must go inward and heal the part of us that is wounded. Once we do so, we can become a force to transform and heal the world around us.

The appearance of the Grail to King Arthur's court also illustrates a crucial stage in organizational life. At the founding of any organization or the beginning of new organizational initiatives, some leader or leadership team generally carries the torch. If they have charisma and their vision is compelling enough, others will follow. However, an organization can keep going only so long on the energy of its leadership. For the organization to become truly magical, each employee must find his or her own sense of meaning and value in being part of the enterprise.

This stage in an organization's history often feels anarchistic—and it is. Moreover, it usually is attended by negativity. A sign that people are beginning to seek their own grails is that they become critical of the organization or its leadership as they try out their own independent visions. People go their separate ways to find their own versions of the grail. To the degree that they are successful in their quests, they invest at a deeper level in the mission of the organization—or they leave. At the end of this process, however, a new level of consensus is reached where people have greater unity of intent—which, in turn, increases the potency of the magic they can do together. While the pattern of the trial by fire stage tends to be linear and focused, the pattern of the call stage spirals outward, then inward, then outward again. As Ashcroft-Nowicki observes:

> The circle becomes first our own expansion of consciousness, then the Table Round where we take our place, and finally, it becomes the Grail and centers itself within us. In the final analysis God is the Grail, containing the Cosmos within what has become an Entity far beyond titles of God or Goddess, or attributes of sex. "It" is a creative matrix, a life-holder, a Cosmic Grail.[7]

This is the God of the mysteries, not of dogma. Therefore, the quest described here does not lead to (nor does it deny) religion. Rather, it describes a course of discovery that can lead us to find our own deep integrity—and with it a sense of meaning in our lives.

We learn that we cannot find our grails unless we are willing to go through our waste lands. In our organizations and in our individual lives, this means that things may get worse before they get better. When they do, we are forced to reflect on fundamental questions of meaning—questions like "What is the meaning of my life?" or "What is the meaning of my work."

We simply cannot transcend or transmute negativity—or even evil—in the world or in ourselves unless we are willing to face it head-on. Finding our grails is not about easy, quick-fix answers; it is about the deeper discipline or magic that eventually brings with it real power—but power from within, not power over another.

A CASE STUDY

Leaders of the call often are pioneers and scouts for the society. Typically, they feel confined by narrow societal roles and forge their own paths. Iconoclasts at heart, they usually are acutely aware of the woundedness of the culture in which they live, and they yearn to heal it. Known for their empathy and concern for people, they call us to a higher sense of who we can be.

Such a leader is writer and former psychotherapist Anne Wilson Schaef, author of *Women's Reality* and *When Society Becomes an Addict*. Schaef grew up in a small town in Arkansas, where she determined she would become a doctor. After college, recognizing that she was in the business of healing the psyche, not the body, she redefined her career goal and became a psychotherapist.

Asked if she ever had experienced a call, she replied affirmatively: "Since early childhood I knew what I would be doing and I have just trusted and followed that unfolding." Attributing her success to her trust in herself, she explained that she has learned to "wait with awareness": "I often get clear flashes about books I need to write, some new idea or concept. When I keep present to myself and my life, this happens often."

When working the way she prefers, she has let "the task do me."

Listening to her, I also could see a variety of sequential calls that refined her vocation. She was called first to medicine, then psychology, then feminism, then recovery counseling. In the 1960s and early '70s, Schaef recognized that traditional psychotherapy was inadequate for the treatment of women. She began to articulate the differences between what she called the "white male system" and the "female system," focusing on the way the former taught both men and women to trust control and hierarchy over their own emerging inner process.

Schaef's most important work has been the development of an alternative to psychotherapy she calls "living in process," which is based on the assumption that the psyche knows how to heal itself. She began to teach women and men to "feel what you feel, and know what you know" so that they could find and connect with the deep growth processes within themselves. When we try to control our development (for example, by repressing our true feelings in order to perform, be impressive, or avoid pain), we set up emotional blocks that actually are carried in the body. These can be cleared away by fully expressing the feeling—after the fact.

As she worked with clients, Schaef became aware that addictions blocked their growth process. In exploring this idea she became convinced that we live in an "addictive system," which means that our culture actively encourages addictive thinking.

As Schaef became more and more successful as an author, counselor, and consultant, she kept breaking with established thinking and the groups that supported it. Having established her career as a psychotherapist and a feminist, Schaef now believes both psychotherapy and feminism demonstrate qualities of the addictive system, at least in the way they frequently are practiced (see her best-selling book *Beyond Therapy, Be-*

SCHAEF, THE GRAIL, AND THE WARRIOR ARCHETYPE

The traits that Anne Wilson Schaef identifies as associated with the "white male system" and the addictive system—control, hierarchy, stoicism, psychological repression, and political oppression—are associated in this book with the negative aspect of the Warrior archetype. Similarly, what she terms our process, and what I call our grail, refers to the creative source within, which is connected to the ongoing creation of the cosmos.

yond Science). By this she means that whenever dogma and elitism creep in, people are encouraged to live up to some preset image rather than to trust their own process.

Schaef uses a peer rather than an expert healing model to teach people to become aware of their addictions (not only to chemicals but also to processes, such as worry, romance, and excitement). Treatment includes the traditional twelve steps from Alcoholics Anonymous, with special focus on "turning it over" to a higher power and living "one day at a time."

When she and Diane Faschel (coauthor with Schaef of *The Addictive Organization*) work with troubled organizations, they use that same model to stress that they, too, are in recovery. In this way, they identify compassionately with their clients rather than judge them. Schaef believes we all are affected by an addictive society, and therefore we all are ill or recovering.

Schaef told me she admires the Old Testament prophets who sat at the edge of the city in sackcloth and ashes, calling upon the citizens of Israel to repent. Her work is prophetic in just this way. She consistently points out the sickness in individuals, organizations, and the society at large—and that health is within us.

In our interview Schaef gently critiqued the questions I asked. For example, when asked "What would you most like to contribute to the world," her answer was, "I would like to contribute being myself and living my own process. When I get into wanting to contribute a specific thing, I am into the illusion of control and therefore the addictive disease process." Similarly, to a question about success strategies, she replied, "I am constantly creating something new as I live my life, trust my process, and share it with others. I believe 'strategies' would likely destroy that process."

Leaders like Anne Wilson Schaef who demonstrate the positive qualities of the ether element call us to our higher and better selves. In doing so, they demand that we face pathology and evil head-on so that we can heal or transform ourselves and our world.

THE GIFT

The call gives us the gift of ether. The ether element is associated with the center of the circle (and hence with the core of our identity), so it helps us get centered. It also defines the periphery, the space in which activity takes place. It is the imaginative generator of experiences and possibilities, which define the outward limits of our dreams. Ether connects us to our spirits; when it is lacking, we feel dispirited.

The sense associated with ether is hearing: it challenges us to hear our own small, emerging, authentic voices, or, to put it another way, it allows us to march to the beat of our own drummers. In this way, ether is a key to finding our identities and vocations—what is most unique about ourselves. It is also, however, about singing the music of the stars, hearing and heeding the call of spirit to find our place and role in the universal harmony.

When we have gained the gift of the call, we are in tune with our own individuality. We then experience a lessening of our desire to sacrifice ourselves at the altar of social acceptance or career advancement. In fact, as Schaef makes clear, the more true we are to our individual uniqueness, the more likely we are to be loved and be successful. At this point we begin to be the advance team for a new and more magical age.

We do not even need to know the master plan. We just need to be true to ourselves, and our own inner knowing, in order to do our part to help that plan unfold.

THE EXERCISES

FOR INDIVIDUALS

- Describe a time when you have experienced a "call" to some endeavor, activity, or vocation.
- Write an obituary for yourself, describing a life that would be uniquely your own and about which you would have no regrets.
- Describe at least one time when you let go of concern for image, performance, or control to "trust your process." What was it like?
- With reference to your HMI results (Appendix B), what archetype is calling you right now?

FOR ORGANIZATIONS

- What enterprises have "called" your organization? (You can recognize a "call" when you do not need to do market research or a study to know if there is money in it. You just know it has to be done.) How did they work out?
- Write a newspaper article about the growth and development of your organization that captures its essence— what it is trying to do, what is unique about it.

Circle Two: Recognizing Your Bliss

THE STORY

Even before the Grail appears, Percival is practiced in answering the call. Raised far from court by his mother, a widow, who wanted nothing more than to keep her child out of King Arthur's army, Percival knows nothing of King Arthur or knighthood. One day several knights come by. Percival is so innocent he thinks they are angels, but nevertheless answers the call and tells his mother he must follow them. And follow them he does. He is equally quick to respond when the Grail appears in King Arthur's court. He has the confidence of someone who knows the difference between a call and a temptation.

THE LESSON

Mythologist Joseph Campbell offered the challenge to "follow your bliss." However, it is very difficult to follow your bliss if you do not know what your bliss is. I have seen many people respond to Campbell's call as if it were an excuse for self-indulgence, granting them permission to do anything. This clearly was not Campbell's meaning. He clarified "bliss" as that which deeply satisfies us because it connects us to our destiny. It is very different from a whim, self-indulgence, or an addiction.

Many of us do not know what we really want because we fear displeasing or hurting others. Percival's mother was so unhappy when he left for King Arthur's court that she died. The knights did not please King Arthur by their vow to seek the Grail. On the contrary, they saddened the man who was

---

THE GRAIL AS A CALL TO "SEPARATION"

Dolores Ashcroft-Nowicki describes the grail journey as beginning with *"separation,"* which occurs "the moment when the soul hears the inner call and realizes its need to seek out its source, to renew itself in the Grail of Grails." In the ancient mystery schools, she notes, people were initiated into the secrets of the Grail, but we can have these experiences in everyday modern life as well. Whereas in the ancient mystery schools the student was guided by his or her own personal mentor, today we more often rely on our own inner archetypal Magician.[8] The Magician archetype helps us heal, moreover, through the process of reconnecting us to ourselves as we deepen and grow.

---

responsible for their success and who had mentored them every step of the way.

Each one of us has chances to experience the cost of separation both ways: to take the risk and seek our own grail, even if it displeases those we love; and to watch as people we want to hold close separate and go their own way. The quest requires us to let go of the belief that it is our responsibility to protect ourselves and others from the pain of individuality.

The quest also demands a special kind of discipline and focus. It may seem odd to a modern sensibility that the Grail knights were expected to be chaste. One very mystical rendition of the Grail story clearly differentiates physical from mental chastity. Mental chastity is a state of mind, not of body. What does this mean? It means that the knight had to insist on the real thing—love, not just lust. The point was neither virginity nor monogamy. It was about learning to control passing urges for idle pleasures or possessions, to focus his resolve on finding ultimately more satisfying rewards. Percival resists sexual temptation, refusing to settle for anything less than his true love, just as he would resist the temptation to do anything unworthy of his true vocation—that of a knight.

Successful separation, therefore, requires the ability to discern the difference between a true call and a temptation or distraction. Many people ask, "How do you recognize a call when it comes?" When I directed this question to successful people one of my favorite answers came from a board member of a nonprofit organization I ran for a time. He told me he knew what to do by what he "vibrated into." By this he meant that as he went through life, many opportunities opened to him that were interesting and, on their face, made sense. Sometimes, however, when faced with a new option, he would feel an inner excitement, a quickening, that was almost like the vibration stimulated by sound. When this happened, he knew he should act quickly.

This is the same feeling described by people who "follow their hunches," making seemingly lucky investments, sales, or other business deals. They know how to listen in to those subtle body cues that tell them to take notice—something important is in the air.

This slight inner movement, which signals recognition, is what helps us choose a major if we go to college, just as it helps us choose a mate, a home, a vocation. We can learn how this works if we think of major moments in our lives when something suddenly caught our attention and set us in a new direction.

We can think back on times when we have had such moments of recognition. As children, many of us have premonitions of our true life purpose or work, just as Percival recognizes the knights and as Merlin has a vision of Camelot. For example, Joanna, an administrator at a prominent university, grew up in the South in the 1940s and '50s. The only work options she knew of for women were schoolteacher, nurse, social worker, or secretary. In college, seeing the dean of women (the only female administrator at the university) walk by, she experienced a moment of great identification, like an epiphany. She actually stopped and just watched this woman. For Joanna, this was a grail experience. Although she never even met the dean, seeing her changed Joanna's life by suddenly expanding her sense of what she, as a woman, could do.

These moments, which can stop us in our tracks, cannot be forced. They happen by serendipity. However, people who successfully create Camelot in their lives watch for such moments and allow themselves to be guided by them. We can miss them if we become anesthetized by addiction, worry, business, or simple preoccupation. Even if we experience these moments, it is easy enough to talk ourselves out of taking them seriously. Joanna, for example, could have talked herself into believing that if there was only one female administrator, her own chances were slim at best. People who think like that settle for second best and wonder why their lives feel shallow and empty.

Paying attention to such moments increases their frequency. Many people I interviewed talked about developing an inner sense of what was right for them. Some books, they said, looked mildly interesting; others beckoned. Increasingly, they read only those books that felt compelling. Some people talked of making consumer decisions based on whether a purchase felt as if it was theirs. Others talked about networking, and how they felt drawn to certain people, trusting there would be a purpose to the association. Some of the people they got to know this way were important to their business; others were important to their personal lives; still others just provided some valuable insight. What we call luck, people told me, can be learned by attentiveness.

To develop such powers of discernment, however, it also is important to notice when and how we get drawn into temptation instead of our bliss. On one such occasion, I was offered a job as a college vice president. I had a strong inner response to take it. After doing so, I learned it was not for me for a variety of reasons—some related to location, some to the job itself and its leadership aspects. I realize now that my desire to take on a new challenge (for I was bored) caused me to censor the more vulnerable feelings I had deeper down. I felt depressed when I thought about the job, but I chalked it up to fear of success.

It takes time and attention to differentiate the inner quickening that comes from fear, greed, ambition, or anxiety from the intense excitement generated by a genuine call. Doing so requires an attitude of conscious experimentation, not unlike that of scientists in a lab. Happily, I also have discovered that even when I get off the track, my mistakes ultimately feed my journey. In this case, the job in high-level administration required organizational skills I had not yet developed—skills that have been essential to me in subsequent endeavors.

Sometimes the career we chose may have felt right initially, but as we change, it no longer quite fits. In such cases, the grail comes to us first as a sense of restlessness, confinement, emptiness, ennui. The most magical people I interviewed *expect* change and welcome new calls, for they expect to be changing constantly. Peggy Williams, president of Lyndon State College, shared with me how much she loved her work—and almost always had. She said the secret, for her at least, was to live in what she called "chunks of time." She would think ahead in one-, three-, and five-year blocks, clearly envisioning what she wanted to do. She very consciously made decisions about whether to "reenlist and recommit" to what she was doing—or, if it no longer satisfied her, to leave and do something else. How did she know? She reenlisted if she still felt enthusiasm and energy for the work. She would let go if she felt no real energy for it, and would open her horizons to notice what work called her now.

In a rapidly changing society, organizational leaders can feel torn among seemingly infinite choices of new product lines, markets, and marketing and management approaches.

How can we decide what to do in the face of so much choice? Or conversely, if we are downsizing, how do we know what to keep (by any more qualitative measure than current profitability)? The Magician's answer is simple: Go toward new opportunities and safeguard old ones that still hum for you. Whether you are starting a business, buying stocks, or giving your money away, invest in what you care about.

James Gregory Lord, who advises philanthropists, told me, "We insure our cars, our houses, and our lives. We must also remember to insure our values." We do this by investing our time, money, and attention in the things that cause us to wake up internally and get excited. Lord talked about what happens when he asks potential investors in nonprofit organizations to discuss why they care about the project at hand. Over an evening, they get energized and inspired, and they feel intimate with one another because they have shared something that matters to them in a deep way. When you are honest about your deeply felt values, and when you let them guide your choices, your life feels—and is—meaningful.

Prosperity is more than money. We tend to feel wealthy when surrounded by people or objects or activities that we find meaningful. The more your business reflects the current state of your soul, the happier you will be. Some deep intuitive part of you knows this. The issue is to learn to access this reliable inner knowing. Doing so just requires attention and practice.

The Warrior and the Magician archetypes both experience sequential calls, but differently. To the Warrior, the call is to better oneself—to be more successful, to be more of a winner, or to measure up. The Warrior in us steels us for the next challenge and for pushing on stoically, toughing it out. The Magician in us opens us up and helps us try to stay attuned to our feelings and visceral reactions so we can respond to the inner hum that is set off when who we are inside matches an opportunity that presents itself on the outside. Whatever the opportunity—a job, an idea, a love, or a philosophical or spiritual path—the issue is not whether it is the best (by anyone else's standards) but whether it fits you.

In a fast-paced economy, we have little time to ponder. Therefore, it pays to practice making quick yes/no answers. Pay attention to your body cues. If your body quickens and feels awake and alive, it's a yes. If you suddenly feel tired and lacking in energy, it's a no. For many, the hardest challenge is trusting the inner sense of "no" when they cannot see a "yes" on the horizon. One of my trainees experienced a very trying time when she received one tempting job offer after another, but none felt right. Only by trusting her internal sense of "no" to all of them was she able to face the void of not knowing for well over a year whether the right offer would present itself.

When we settle for something that does not feel right, we are undercutting our belief in the existence of a grail for us. When we do this, we kill magic in ourselves.

I hasten here to say that this does not mean we should act like spoiled children, refusing anything that is not easy and instantly amusing. While writing this book, I took a new position at Mount Vernon College because I felt I should be there at least for a time. It is not always an easy place to be for a variety of reasons, including how financially strapped the college is. However, as I have become acquainted with faculty and staff, a surprising number of people have told me they also feel this way—that they are at the college because they are supposed to be. That feeling, of being in the right place for you, makes it possible to be calm and centered, even when the going gets rough.

Percival is successful as a knight specifically because he has a capacity for recognizing his bliss. He is sufficiently tuned in to know what will nourish him. When the Grail appeared to King Arthur's knights, it fed each the food he loved most. The test of whether a call is your bliss is whether it feeds and satisfies you over time. If you feel obsessed with it (as in addiction) and it brings you considerable grief, then it is not your bliss, no matter how much it attracts you. For example, many people mistake an addiction for their bliss. They light up when they drink, eat, buy, or work too much!

Finding our bliss is a lifelong discipline, requiring practice, attention, and skill. When, like King Midas, we become enamored with something—in his case gold—our lives can become waste lands. Remember the old saying "Be careful what you ask for; you may get it." In the 1980s many people fell prey to careerism, conspicuous consumption, and workaholism, thinking that money, achievement, status, and objects could bring happiness. Ultimately, our bliss depends on our values. For if we fail to live by them, our self-esteem plummets. Some things may be fun at the time, but they are not our bliss if we hate ourselves in the morning.

INTEGRITY CHECK FOR INDIVIDUALS AND ORGANIZATIONS

The integrity check of the call is simple. Ask yourself: Is this action in keeping with my own values and principles? You cannot thrive unless you can face yourself in the mirror. Whatever else happens in your life, if you live by your own principles and values, you have self-respect. No one can take that from you. In *The Genesis Effect*, Brian P. Hall argues that an inner ethical vacuum creates a void in the outer life. Well-developed humane values are reflected in responsible action in the world, resulting in a just society. He calls the magic of values the "genesis effect," which he defines as "the process whereby our internal images act upon and transform the world we live in. Values are those priorities which we act on that mediate those images and transform them into everyday behavior." As values evolve, society evolves.[9]

THE GIFT

Many of us think that certain people are just lucky, or intuitive, or unusually perceptive. However, all of us can be that way—if we listen to our hunches enough to learn the subtleties of what truly hums for us or beckons to us. Luck is learned, by the discipline of recognizing where we are supposed to be.

The Exercises

for individuals

- Practice noticing what hums for you. You will never notice the big calls in life if you are unable to respond to the small ones. Notice what foods please you and nourish your body. Notice what experiences and activities you love. If you practice with the small things, the big ones will follow. You will be able to recognize what work in what environment is yours to do if you learn to listen to your inner wisdom. Pay attention to body signals that are a yes or a no. Often you get a surge of positive energy for a yes and a loss of energy for a no. Keep a record of when you lose energy. How do you decide whether it is time to move on or to recommit and reinvent your work?

- Make a list of all the things, people, and activities that hum for you—that is, make you feel more alive and genuine. These awaken your own grail quest and help you find your life direction. To which of these can you truly commit? When have you had to separate from someone very special in order to go your own way? What was that like for you?

- Practice distinguishing between a bliss and an indulgence. This requires vigilance and consciousness. Record the result of saying yes to certain actions. Do they end up satisfying you in a deep way? Or do you feel good about them at the moment, then bad about them later? The resonance you are looking for comes from those experiences, activities, habits, loves, opportunities that satisfy not just at the moment but over the long haul. Keep a written record for a while of the feelings you have and the results you achieve when you follow them. Keep doing so until you can differentiate a call from a temptation consistently.

- Practice reverberating to what is good in the world. Do not deny that trouble, pathology, and evil exist, but discipline your mind so that you do not allow your attention to dwell on the negative or to be distracted by the drama of destructive events. Anxiety also produces a quickening or inner sense of energy. You can be seduced by this rush, which is produced by the body's fight/flight response rather than by positive anticipation. Make lists of things, people, and events that attract you and that seem genuinely positive.

FOR ORGANIZATIONS

- When has your organization had the courage to separate from others in its industry—to risk doing things differently?
- Are their times when the organization goes back to basics and reinvents itself? Describe some time when change was required and your organization dumped tradition and tried something new?
- How does your organization treat people who begin to follow their bliss? How is it supportive? How does it hinder them? What could it do to be more supportive while also conducting business in a responsible way?
- Does your organization encourage people to share their hunches, or does everything have to be proven before it can be proposed? If the latter, what might you do to allow freer expression of intuitive wisdom?

Circle Three: Entering the Waste Land

THE STORY

Percival cannot find the Grail until he enters the Waste Land, a kingdom characterized by its poverty, alienation, and despair. This kingdom is a Waste Land because something is wrong with its ruler. Legend has it that Percival will heal the Wounded King, allowing the Waste Land to bloom once more. Happiness and prosperity will be restored to the land.

Many versions exist of how the Wounded King (often called the Fisher King) received his wound and what it represents. One legend states that as a young man the Fisher King kept a vigil one night and saw a vision of the Grail in the fire. When he reached out to touch it, he was burned. The wound would not heal, so thereafter he lived in constant pain. The Wounded King lives in the Grail Castle. The Grail is there, and it nourishes everyone but him.

Percival is so self-conscious when he visits the Grail Castle that he censors his natural response and does not ask the questions that would have healed the king. For years he wanders, feeling inexplicably unhappy, until he meets Kundrie, an "ugly, misshapen, black-skinned hag" whose appearance scares everyone in sight. Kundrie explains to Percival that he had one chance and blew it. Her role is to make us understand that the Waste Land and the Wounded King are within as well as without. She is unmerciful in her criticism of Percival, but truth begins the process of integration, undermining his sense of in-

nocence. Paradoxically, when he recognizes that he is part of the problem, not simply an innocent victim, he reclaims his power.

THE LESSON

The story of Percival and the Wounded King is Camelot's most modern tale. Poet T. S. Eliot used the Percival story as the foundation for *The Waste Land,* the quintessential poem about the sterility of modern life. We all know the Waste Land in aspects of today's world, and we all have within us both a Wounded King and a Grail knight who can heal us so that our lives can blossom.

Many of us who work in contemporary waste land organizations are like the Wounded King. We have been taught to expect fulfillment in our work, but we may feel more burned out than nourished by it. We believe that we should have the power to create satisfying lives, but somehow things do not turn out as we expect them to.

I meet so many people who are suffering inside. On the surface their lives may seem fine, but inside they are tormented by the disjuncture between their high expectations and the way they actually are living, or by a sense that they are out of touch with themselves. We may feel especially like the Wounded King if we focus on external achievement and image to the exclusion of enriching our inner lives. We realize our grails exist, but it might as well not because it does us no good.

Such a sense of fragmentation often hits successful people in midlife. They begin yearning to contribute something that will make a difference, but they don't know how. They try to meet the challenge of the call with the strategies of trial by fire. For example, the Wounded King is burned trying to reach into the fire to get the Grail; fire is the way to find the gift of the sword, not the Grail. Many of us today are so fiery, focused, and achievement-oriented that we starve other parts of

THE MAGICIAN'S WOUND

Many times Magicians suffer from a significant physical wound that places them on a track different from that of their peers. Magicians' power to heal others comes from finding ways to heal themselves of such wounds or learn from them. Like the polio victim who runs marathons, the painfully shy individual who finds success on the lecture circuit, or the person with emotional or mental illness who becomes a great psychologist, many of us find our vocations through healing our own disabilities. Almost all of us become more empathic with others when we have suffered ourselves.

Some shamanistic traditions actually inflict wounds on budding shamans. In several of these traditions, would-be shamans are put into a trance, where they experience a vision of dismemberment—so real that when they awaken, they are astounded that their actual bodies are still intact. In my training class, I often lead guided fantasies that take people on a journey to find their inner Magician or Healer. Several trainees with shamanistic tendencies spontaneously, and independent of my instructions, have imagined being dismembered.

our lives. Perhaps we crave intimacy. Yet, out of habit or fear, we keep working so hard that we leave little time for our families or friends. One CEO confessed in an interview that he had a poet inside him in need of expression, yet every day he went to work in a high-pressure entrepreneurial firm and kept this poet locked up, silent. He could not yet trust himself enough to know he would not starve if he released a deeper part of himself.

People of any age experience a disjuncture between their inner and outer lives if they are trapped in a dead-end job that does not reflect their true talents or allow for the expression of their more noble qualities. When our work requires a discon-

THE WOUNDED KING AND MODERN SCIENCE

The ancient idea that the kingdom reflects the health of the king (and vice versa) may seem strange, but modern holographic theory offers a scientific analogy. David Bohm, a protégé of Einstein, asserts that the whole world has holographic properties. Any part of a holographic image can project the entire three-dimensional system. This is similar to magical lore, in which the macrocosm and the microcosm are directly parallel. In this system, the whole organizes the parts rather than the parts organizing the whole; everything mirrors everything else.[10] Nature reflects the Divine, and we reflect nature. Life is of a piece, and every part affects every other part. If this is true, then we can find no separate peace. When the kingdom is a waste land, some part of each of us is wounded. And, conversely, the kingdom is a waste land precisely because of the woundedness of its citizens—i.e., you and me.

Of course, we all know organizations that suffer because the CEO is shallow, mean-spirited, addicted, or inept. What we often fail to see is that each of us, regardless of our position, also affects the health of the organization. That is what it means to say that our kingdoms are waste lands when the ruler is wounded. We are all the rulers of our own lives.

nection from our souls, we suffer profoundly—or, over time, go numb—unless we can find some other way outside of work to express more of the truth about who we are. Unemployment, workplace anxiety, the sterility of many workplaces, and general social decline are all products of the modern waste land because they make us too fearful to trust the grail within us or to follow our own bliss.

In *Quiet Desperation: The Truth About Successful Men*, author Jan Halper speaks movingly about the many successful businessmen she has interviewed who, for years, have "been

subjected to rules and regulations about how they are supposed to be and what they are to do to succeed. They had to
suppress who they are and what they believed in, learning to
second-guess their bosses and tell people what they wanted to
hear." She found these men to be experiencing a kind of
"quiet desperation," leading to "a quiet revolution of men
breaking out of the straitjacket that had been harnessed on
them years earlier." These modern day Wounded Kings do not
want "to play the game anymore," yet they fear giving up the
status, income, and power this game-playing has provided.
Halper describes them as "silently suffering in the search for
new meaning and purpose: a search for their own truth."[11]
They do not want to be defined by others any longer, even
though doing so has made them successful in the world's
terms. Before they die, they want to have real intimacy and
make their most unique contribution to the world.

Such men have said yes to a call to achievement, risking
daily defeat in a competitive environment. But they are caught
in the waste land, wounded by having succumbed to the pressure to live inauthentic lives. As long as they surrender to this
temptation, they will not be able to be magical—or even
happy—though they may appear to be successful.

Similarly, women who responded to the call of liberation in
the late 1960s and early '70s quickly found themselves
trapped by the pseudofeminist image of superwoman. Psychologist Judith Duerk (in *A Circle of Stones*) reports that the career women she studied who had tried living in what she calls
a "masculine careerist mode" felt unfulfilled. It wasn't that
they wanted to return to traditional female roles. They did
want careers, but they also wanted to reconnect with their own
integrity as women. They found they were so locked into
achievement and living up to the image of the superwoman
that they were losing their authentic feminine values (just as
men in the men's movement today are sharing the wound of
having lost their own authentic masculinity). They wanted to

be successful in a fuller sense. Yes, they wanted to make money and to have interesting jobs, but they also wanted to treat others and themselves well and not lose the natural rhythms of life.[12]

The fact that so many men and women are suffering means that they are in the waste land. Wandering through this barren landscape, we may begin to think of ourselves as human capital or human resources to be managed or developed. We forget for a time that we are real human beings with yearnings for meaning and depth as well as acquisitions. Suffering motivates moral questioning, forces us to rethink our values.

Duerk concludes that we need to start talking about how awful it feels to pretend to be a performance machine—instead of a real person. "What is asked of us" is "to find a voice . . . to make us all attend to . . . that vast woundedness which has been so ignored, so denied . . . in hope and faith that it may heal." Both men and women, in different ways, are telling us they do not want to "gain the world" but "lose their own souls." People who feel like Wounded Kings and Queens can be found at all levels of an organization. They mean well; they try their best. They search for the truth that will heal, but instead they experience (at least temporarily) more suffering. It is their own knowledge—that their grail exists, that something is out there greater than what they currently have—that causes them to feel bored, alienated, or stressed. People who do not believe that their grail exists can go through life sleepwalking, just playing out roles and feeling vaguely dissatisfied. But when they know life and work can offer so much more, they suffer—that is, until they recognize their own woundedness and become healed.

Sometimes it is only when our bodies rebel, when we become ill, that we begin to grapple with the wounds to our souls and spirits. Such illnesses may be major or minor. Arthur W. Frank, author of *At the Will of the Body*, describes his own two bouts with serious illness. The first he dealt with simply as a

challenge to be overcome, and he bounced right back. Both
Frank and others were impressed with his ability to stay positive and fight for health. When he was diagnosed later as
having cancer, his initial response was depression; then he
reconsidered his values and changed profoundly. Like many
other people with life-threatening illnesses I have encountered, he began to place a greater value on intimacy, spirit,
and the joy of living in the moment. He is grateful for this
experience of wounding—a sentiment echoed by countless
others who have struggled against potentially fatal disease—
for it opened him up to spiritual values, to greater intimacy
with other people, and to a heightened sense of the extraordinary gift of living each day. In reality, Frank's illness revolutionized his whole worldview and changed his priorities completely. He sums up the learning he gained from the healing
wound by saying, "When I feel I have no time to walk out and
watch the sunlight on the river, my recovery has gone too
far."[13]

In the Waste Land, things get worse before they get better.
When the knights leave King Arthur's court, a degree of anar-
chy replaces a beautiful and noble order. And in the world
today, dogma and collectively held values are breaking down
as the old world is dying. The result is ethical confusion: old
standards do not seem to fit anymore and new ones are not yet
in place. Further, we have no guarantee that things will get
better. It all depends on us. Fragmentation can be part of the
creative process: an old order crumbles and a new one is
created. Or, things can simply come apart.

That's why it is so important that we learn to heal and that
we seek our grails. Alcoholism, drug abuse, and other addictions are epidemic, yet recovery programs are awakening millions to a life of spiritual integrity. Violence is rampant, social
injustice abounds, and pollution threatens the health of the
planet. Yet concern about these issues is awakening a new
awareness of our interdependence with one another and with

the earth. When we respond to the call, we sometimes see the waste land clearly, as if for the first time; we wake up to all the shallowness, pathology, and unethical behavior around us and in our own lives. During the grail search, we become aware of what is wrong with the world, so that we will take the responsibility to find our own grails, and with it our own values.

The grail lives in the transformation that occurs when people confront their wounds and begin the process of healing. The same call that awakens us gives us a heightened awareness of our woundedness. We cannot heal what we refuse to see. We are far more aware than in the past of the kinds of pathological behavior that used to be hushed up: rape, child abuse, incest, molestation. Furthermore, some harmful or even criminal behavior is likely to be seen today as evidence of mental or emotional illness and hence, at least in some cases, curable.

Everywhere we go we hear people complaining that they are working in dysfunctional organizations. Perhaps you have worked in such a place and know how awful it feels to be relatively healthy in an unhealthy environment. Psychiatrist and author Douglas LaBier (*Modern Madness*), for example, frequently is brought in by major companies when they have managers who are showing signs of stress or breakdown but are too talented and motivated to be fired.

LaBier discovered that often *the person showing symptoms is one of the healthier people in the system!* This phenomenon occurs typically in organizations where it has become normal to sacrifice one's personal life and one's ethical standards to career success; in such places people with deep-seated psychological problems or serious addictions often rise to the top —because pathology actually is a precondition for making the extraordinary personal sacrifices and ethical compromises required for success. Not only are LaBier's healthy individuals like the Wounded King, but so, in a less obvious way, are those with significant pathologies and those who have suc-

ARE YOU FINDING YOUR GRAIL IN THE WASTE LAND?

You are going into the waste land to find your grail right now if you are:

- In therapy or otherwise freeing yourself from limiting parental or societal messages;
- In recovery from an addiction, a compulsion, or other dysfunctional behaviors;
- Working for social justice or environmental awareness; and/or,
- Seeking or finding meaning and values in your life and work.

cumbed to cynicism. The latter may show less external distress—usually because some addiction is masking their pain —but the wound is deeper and their plight is ultimately sadder.

This means that if we are aware of our suffering, we can begin to seek the grail in order to find healing for ourselves and our organizations. It is tempting to despair when we see how shallow, materialistic, and unethical modern life can be. But we should take heart. In *The Grail Seeker's Companion,* John Matthews and Marian Green define the Waste Land as the "barren place where imagination, love, charity have ceased to function." Outwardly, it is "the grey world where possessions are all and love has died amid squalor and promiscuity . . . Yet the Grail exists at its heart . . ." Paradoxically, it is "both necessary and essential that we pass through the Waste Lands and see them clearly for what they are, for the potential which lies within them, for the opposite they represent, the perfect world hidden like a crystal inside a rough-hewn rock." They warn that it is "no use setting forth on the Quest filled with sweetness and light, believing that the Grail exists in some never-never-land . . . *The Grail is here, and it is now, and it is often hidden behind a surface of surpassing ugliness.*"[14]

The journey into the Waste Land usually begins with an error. Percival initially thinks of himself as a wonderful person. That's also how the rest of the world sees him. Moreover, he has had absolutely no problem rising to the challenge of battle. He is courageous, bold, and committed to doing right. He has all the virtues of the stage of trial by fire. I would imagine that after leaving the Grail Castle, he had no sense that he had done anything wrong. Imagine his surprise when Kundrie explains to him the significance of his failure. On the surface, all he did was be fairly quiet at a dinner party!

Why is it so important to raise our voices? Most of us have been at meetings or in classes where we sit on our own questions without raising them. When we do so, either the world is denied our critical input or we fail to learn. The older we get, and the more experienced, the more important it is to question everything. In fairy tales, magic typically occurs only when the hero or heroine asks a magic question. Force, or blundering one's way through, simply will not do.

Many explanations have been offered for why Percival did not ask the questions he yearns to ask. Some say that he was sleepy; others that he did not want to offend the Wounded King with inappropriately prying questions, while still others guess that he was concerned with his image—and had been told that good knights do no ask unnecessary questions.

But what seems most likely to me is that he was censoring himself and repressing his spontaneity. That is what we all do when we want to be good, appropriate, in control, or professional. All of Arthur's knights are sworn to uphold the good, so they are very attached to appearing virtuous. In fact, in several rather touching stories in the Grail legends, Percival and

Galahad are attacked by rival knights, whom they defeat with great relish. Sometimes they express nervousness after the battle about the victims of the massive slaughter they have waged. Invariably, though, they discover they have killed very evil men and in the process liberated vulnerable but worthy victims of tyranny.

In this way, knights lived according to the worldview of the Warrior, seeing good and evil as quite separate, identifying with one and battling against the other. Now, seeking the Grail, Percival must change his archetypal stance and confront parts of himself he would rather not see. Percival always has identified with success, but here he has to see that he has failed. He always has identified himself as a compassionate rescuer of people in need; now he has to realize that he was so preoccupied with himself that he could not help the Wounded King.

It is dangerous for any of us to identify too strongly with being good, successful, or right. Total Quality Management, for example, is such a powerful concept that it revolutionized the Japanese economy after World War II. However, its very name suggests the danger implicit in identifying completely with quality. Florida Power and Light was the first American company to win the Deming Award for quality. In the process, however, two of its managers suffered heart attacks and internal staff relations were ruined. What this meant was that in identifying completely with quality, it was not OK to make mistakes—that is, to be human. People were sick and quarrelsome—and dying! The desire to do the task perfectly created a Shadow in the human domain.

The Shadow is formed by the perfectly human traits we judge and hence repress, and once it is formed, it takes us over to get our attention. At Florida Power and Light, people could not sustain being perfect. They had to face their human vulnerability, evidenced in illness. The next CEO completely stopped the overly strenuous quality efforts that had been put

ROBERT JOHNSON ON HOW THE SHADOW ORIGINATES

"We are all born whole and, let us hope, will die whole. But somewhere early on our way, we eat one of the wonderful fruits of the tree of knowledge, things separate into good and evil, and we begin the shadow-making process; we divide our lives. In the cultural process we sort out our God-given characteristics into those that are acceptable to our society and those that have to be put away. This is wonderful and necessary, and there would be no civilized behavior without this sorting out of good and evil. But the refused and unacceptable characteristics do not go away: they only collect in the dark corners of our personality. When they have been hidden long enough, they take on a life of their own—the shadow life . . . If it accumulates more energy than our ego, it erupts as an overpowering rage or some indiscretion that slips past us; or we have a depression or an accident that seems to have its own purpose. The shadow gone autonomous is a terrible monster in our psychic house . . .

"It is also astonishing to find that some very good characteristics turn up in the shadow. Generally, the ordinary, mundane characteristics are the norm. Anything less than this goes into the shadow. But anything better also goes into the shadow! Some of the pure gold of our personality is relegated to the shadow . . ."[15]

in place, recognizing that the organization's goals needed to be expanded to include issues of quality of work life, not just quality results. Today many Japanese organizations are concerned about the rising number of executives who literally work themselves to death.

I read about one Japanese firm that learned how to respond to human errors in a light and fun way. A family came home and found they had bought a VCR that was completely missing its inner parts. The firm, upon hearing about this problem, sent over a car with four executives, who delivered not only a new VCR but balloons and a bottle of wine as well. Instead of identifying completely with quality, the firm had planned how to make it fun when mistakes inevitably occurred. This is a great example of anticipating the Shadow, which is an inevitable side product of a commitment to total quality—that is, planning ahead for the inevitable screwups that are part of life. The more we pretend to be gods, the more that Shadow will take us over as burnout, and eventually the more mistakes we will make.

It is only human to be imperfect. When we recognize this, we can try to act as well as possible. When we refuse to admit to having problems, however, we may become guilty of scapegoating. Hitler's treatment of the Jews was a classic example of Shadow projection. The German people did not want to face the fact that their humiliating defeat in World War I had anything to do with themselves, so they found a group to blame.

People do this all the time. For example, in one horribly sick organization, the CEO refused to face his own culpability and just kept firing one person after another—every one of whom he blamed for the problems of the company. The firm finally did go under; however, it lasted longer than might have been expected, leading to suffering and considerable demoralization for a majority of the employees. Today it is quite fashionable to act like the victim and blame society, your family, or some other group for your problems. Scapegoating works to deflect blame for a while, but it never solves the underlying problem.

Moreover, organizational leaders frequently are victimized by their own organization's Shadows. For example, I was brought into one company by a CEO who had a very caring and civilized manner. He worked in an organization that also prided itself on how sophisticated, compassionate, and rational it was. However, it provided little leeway for lesser human qualities—like being aggressive. Competition was forced underground. Conflict tended to be suppressed. Everyone tried to appear tolerant and kind all the time.

Since they could not assert openly, employees became passive-aggressive. The second-in-command frequently would agree with the CEO and then go out and do something different. In fact, he would agree with everyone and then do what he wanted. The CEO would put up with this, trying to be nice, until he would blow up. Then the people who worked for him —who never confronted him to his face—eventually went to the board and tried to get the CEO fired because of his erratic behavior and his temper. Up to this time the CEO had felt long-suffering and blameless. However, with his job on the line, he was willing to take responsibility for his Shadow side. When he did so, he changed and thus was able to save his job.

When the Shadow has us in its grip, we do not recognize ourselves as part of the problem. That's why we need to listen to others, who may see us more objectively than we see ourselves. A similar CEO, when talked to about her problem, realized that she simply had to learn to confront her employees and demand accountability. She took assertiveness training courses and learned to surface conflict so that it did not go underground. When she did so, the employees who reported to her soon settled down, stopped being passive-aggressive, and did their jobs (or left).

Anyone in leadership needs to understand the Shadow. Otherwise, it will control him or her. Magicians learn to take split-off parts that threaten to control them in negative ways and integrate these parts so that they can make a positive contribution to their lives.

In Ursula Le Guin's *A Wizard of Earthsea*, Ged, a young Magician who is showing off his powers, inadvertently lets loose upon the world a dark and dangerous creature. Ged is a responsible man, so he begins a quest to find and subdue this creature—a quest that takes him over many lands and years.

THE GIFT OF THE WOUND THAT IS ALWAYS THERE

In *Power in the Helping Professions,* Adolf Guggenbuhl-Craig
warns that any time such professionals see themselves as completely healthy, assuming that only their clients are wounded,
the potential for abuse of power exists. Healers who can connect with their own Shadow, their own wounded part, have
greater empathy. In fact, by acknowledging their own woundedness, magical healers help clients gain access to their own
inner healer.

When we deny complementarity between health and sickness, Guggenbuhl-Craig argues, we get stuck in roles that allow
the healer to become self-important while the patient becomes
disempowered. Similarly, teachers who forget that they are also
learners dry up and become dull and ineffective. Change
agents who forget they also have a vested interest in the status
quo become out of touch and irrelevant. Managers who are not
willing to be managed by their employees become autocratic
and cut off. And so on.[16]

When Ged finally finds the monster, he suddenly recognizes
that the creature is his own Shadow:

> Aloud and clearly, breaking that old silence, Ged spoke
> the shadow's name and in the same moment the shadow
> spoke without lips or tongue, saying the same word:
> "Ged." And the two voices were one voice. Ged reached
> out his hands, dropping his staff, and took hold of his
> shadow, of the black self that reached out to him. Light
> and darkness met, and joined, and were one.

Ged's friend Estarriol looks on with horror, not understanding
what has happened to Ged, until Ged reassures him, saying,
"The wound is healed . . . I am whole, I am free."[17]

When we accept our Shadow sides, we feel less virtuous but also less one-dimensional. We cannot be magical unless we are willing to let go of trying to be perfect, embrace our own Shadow, and, like Ged, become *whole*. Whatever it is we are most attached to being or becoming—competent, wise, kind, powerful—is our major danger. This desire or attachment often breeds its opposite (which in the Shadow will be expressed as a negative—being or becoming incompetent, ignorant, cruel, impotent). If we are willing to face our Shadows, they can appear not so much as opposites but as *complements*. Competence and wisdom are complemented by a healthy sense that we have more to learn. Kindness is complemented by setting personal boundaries and saying no. Being powerful is complemented by being appropriately intimate and vulnerable.

Organizations can benefit from recognizing the Shadows of their dominant values when they go about establishing structures. For example, a consulting firm founded by rugged individualists made no provision for any kind of security or benefits for its associates, who soon started acting very dependent and insecure. A liberal arts college redesigned all academic and student services in accordance with the high value it placed on caring. The result: the faculty and student-life staff were nurturing the students but backbiting one another. A food co-op set up to be run by the consensus of a leaderless group found that much time was being wasted by group members jockeying for informal leadership.

THE GIFT

Such individuals and organizations are transformed when they make a place for their Shadows. The consulting firm adopted health benefits and retirement plans. The college instituted a competitive merit pay system based on performance. The food co-op designated different people to take on various aspects of the leadership task so everyone would feel important and valu-

able. In each case, the organizational Shadow called into play
a greater sense of balance. What the organization valued was
good, but too absolute.

When Percival understands the implications of his failures,
he stops feeling depressed and starts feeling remorse. In some
ways, being guilty is better than being powerless: at least his
actions matter. When we are attached to being virtuous and
things go wrong, we feel powerless and victimized. If we face
our culpability, paradoxically we are empowered to act—to
seek healing and health.

Moreover, we are freed from the compulsion to be perfect,
so we recognize that it is OK to be human—we can redefine
success in a way that makes room for all of who we are. Poets
and artists are known for being wild and sometimes even im-
moral. If we want to create, we cannot be timid. As Martin
Luther is said to have urged, "Sin bravely so that grace may
abound."

THE EXERCISES

FOR INDIVIDUALS

- List things you notice about your organization that seem
  unhealthy or dysfunctional. Then, expand the list to include society as a whole. Finally, write down ways in
  which you either contribute to these problems inadvertently or feel forced to act less than positively. (For example, you may feel critical of the way organizations put
  pressure on people to work so hard and long that they
  have little time for family, community, or self. At the
  same time, you may be acting in this way yourself as a
  response to the pressure to measure up.)
- List any ways in which you feel low in energy or dispirited or in need of healing. Imagine what Percival might
  look like in your life. Why would he fail to ask the questions that would heal you?

- Make a list of your major values and then balance it with a list of their opposites. This is likely where your Shadow resides. Find ways to integrate these qualities into your self-concept.

FOR ORGANIZATIONS

- List things you notice about your coworkers that seem unhealthy or dysfunctional.
- Make a list of the organization's major values, then balance it with a list of their opposites. This likely is where your Shadow resides. Find ways to contain the Shadow so that it does not sabotage your success.
- Make a list of everything you dislike about the society around you. Then list ways your organization may inadvertently be contributing to (or reflecting) those problems.

Circle Four: Healing the Ruler

THE STORY

After Kundrie accosts Percival and tells him how he has failed himself, the Wounded King, and the Waste Land, Percival wanders for a long time, feeling contrite and wishing he knew what to do. Finally, a hermit ministers to his soul, and Percival makes his peace with God and vows to go back and heal the king. The hermit says, "No. It is too late. The legend said you must heal the king spontaneously and in innocence." Yet Percival goes back, asks the questions "What ails you, Uncle?" and "Who serves the Grail?" and heals the king. As a result, the Waste Land blooms once again.

THE LESSON

Although the legend has said that Percival can heal the Wounded King only in innocence, he does not do so until he is thoroughly disillusioned with life. Advised (as we often are) to accept the necessary losses of life and come to terms with the disparity between his own great aspirations and his dismal performance, Percival chooses instead to trust his heart. The result is a miracle.

What are the magic questions he asks? Remember, they were questions that might have burst from him spontaneously when he initially visited the Wounded King and the Grail Castle. The first is "What ails you, Uncle," an expression of compassion and concern for the king. The second should have been asked when the Grail mysteriously floated through the castle: "Who serves the Grail?" These two questions are the

Grail-legend equivalent of two very ancient magical queries, "What binds you?" and "What do you hold sacred?" As the first opens the way for healing, the second brings us back to where we started in this chapter: our grails help us find what is *sacred* to us.

Imagine the second meeting between Percival and the Wounded King. Percival is full of self-recrimination. He has failed in his task, and he, the Wounded King, and the whole Waste Land kingdom have experienced untold suffering. The king undoubtedly is full of self-blame for his failure to maintain a peaceful and prosperous kingdom. Although Percival is supposed to heal the king in the purity of youth, the way he actually does it makes better psychological sense. Had he asked the king the magical question "What ails you, Uncle?" the first time, the arrogance of his youth likely would have made him feel judgmental: that is, he'd have said, "What's wrong with you, old man?" But after he has experienced his own failure, he has no judgment, only empathy. When he poses the question, the emphasis is on "Uncle," for he sees the king as kin.

Joseph Campbell, when telling this story, delights in the unexpected ending, recounting how a hermit tells Percival, "You, through your tenacity of purpose, have changed God's law." According to Campbell, "That's big talk. The god within us is the one that gives the laws and can change the laws. And it is within us."[18]

Michael Higgins, executive director of the Foundation for Free Enterprise Development, was asked to speak at his class reunion at the Harvard Business School. Instead of providing the expected inspiring words, he talked about a recent business loss. Before taking positions at the Aspen Institute and later at the Foundation for Free Enterprise Development, he had painstakingly built another institute, which he then, for a variety of reasons, had to shut down. It was a very painful thing to do, because he had invested so much of himself in it.

He spoke to his classmates of what had happened and its impact on his own self-image, and wondered aloud about the ways in which business schools prepare students for success but not for dealing with failure.

According to Higgins, the room suddenly came alive. People seemed free from the pressure to act so successful. They started sharing their failures as well as their successes. Although they did not achieve consensus on what business schools might do to prepare the next generation to meet such setbacks, healing happened that day as they shared their wounds and learned they were not alone. As they spoke, they changed the old laws of the gods—the ones that said that such illustrious graduates could share their triumphs but had to be alone with (and, typically, ashamed of) their failures. Suddenly failure was restored to its rightful place as just a part of business—and of life.

In one of my interviews, a training director at a major multinational corporation said that those of us who heal others cannot heal ourselves. Such vulnerability can be a gift, for it forces us to experience our interdependence with others. I know that at the time I strongly related to what he said because that had been my experience as well. However, since then I have realized that this is the case only if we have compassion for others but not also for ourselves. We *can* have empathy for our own inner Wounded Ruler, just as we would for anyone else—and doing so is profoundly healing.

If we are called to magic because we are experiencing a waste land within or without, transformation begins the moment we have the self-compassion to acknowledge that things are not working. Then we can reach out to ask others for help. Remember, we do not have to have it all together. The Warrior ethic taught us to keep on keepin' on no matter how wounded we might be. The Magician ethic encourages us to acknowledge and learn from the healing wound. The irony is that accepting the truth about our human limitations is a key to

THE MAGIC OF EMPATHY

Example One: Koh, the Korean Magician, was observed talking in a very respectful manner to a young boy who had just been caught stealing a wallet. Instead of using the familiar form of Korean, Koh used the most polite sentence structure possible. Asked what he said to the boy, he replied that he told him he should never be ashamed of himself. Koh explained that the boy already had too much shame—that's why he would break the law. Shaming him only would make his self-esteem worse. "I told him if he gives back the wallet then the shame can reduce. He has to respect himself more—not be so much ashamed himself every day. If he has respect for himself, such a boy cannot steal. You know how these boys think themselves? The most low people. They are too ashamed themselves already. That's the problem."[19]

Example Two: Tia, the heroine of Lyall Watson's *Gifts of Unknown Things*, develops healing and psychic powers after she chooses to show compassion rather than following the rules of her culture. A whale has been washed ashore and is dying. Although she had been warned by the religious authorities that it is unlawful to touch anything unclean, she risks punishment and her status in the community to sing to the whale and keep it company as it dies. She cannot save its life, but she can save it from dying alone. From then on, her life is never the same. She has become a Magician.

finding our grail—that is, to reconnecting with our souls and our full integrity.

At the end of Arthur's story, he is taken to Avalon to be healed of his wound. Stories of rulers being wounded recur throughout the Camelot narrative. Very likely the Wounded King is Arthur's Shadow and double. Arthur is a great leader, but he certainly is wounded in his relationships. His wife is having an affair with Lancelot, his best knight and best friend. His knights all leave his court to seek the Holy Grail. His son leads an uprising against him. Arthur reminds me of many successful executives who find in midlife or old age that their neglect of relationships has left them lonely at the top.

Psychiatrist and consultant Lindbergh S. Sata, M.D., has immediate and touching empathy for people who feel marginal to society. Born in this country of Japanese ancestry, Sata considered himself an American when he was a boy. However, when he was thirteen and the United States went to war with Japan, he and his family were herded into internment camps, "for their own protection." He explained to me that he believed this explanation until, as he entered the camp, he noticed that the guns along the barbed wire fence were pointing in, not out. In the camp, he was given a very inadequate education and was frequently terrorized. Once, he remembered, a guard opened fire on him and his friends because they were cutting up. Although the guard most likely meant only to scare, not kill them, no child needs to be scared like that.

When Sata entered college, the advisor to whom he was assigned took one look at him and told him if he ever saw him again, he would have him thrown out of school. With no advisor, it took much longer for him to graduate. As a result of such experiences, Sata has a visceral understanding of what it can mean to be a "hyphenated American." Although he has achieved distinction as an academic psychiatrist, what excites him most is his work with the marginalized people of society, whether they are American Indians or police officers. As president of the Seattle chapter of the Japanese American Citizens' League, Sata funded an audiotape about the internment camps that was circulated among chapters throughout the nation, leading eventually to the movement that called for reparations to camp survivors.

These audiotapes asked the equivalent of the magical ques-

tion "What ails you, Uncle?" As people listened, they began
to share their own stories, stories many had not told even to
their own children. As they shared these painful memories,
their compassion for themselves was released and they began
to heal. And as they healed, they were able to mobilize. The
result of their efforts was an apology from the U.S. government
in the form of reparation payments.

The question "What ails you, Uncle?" calls us to empathy
and service to others, especially those hurt or in need. Many of
the knights traveled (chastely, the legends say) with female
questors. On one of his journeys, Percival travels with his
sister, Dindraine, who is asked to sacrifice a bowl full of her
blood to heal the virtuous but leprous queen of another ailing
kingdom. Legend had it that the queen could be healed only
by the blood of a virgin born of royal parentage—like Percival's sister. Percival tries to stop Dindraine from complying
because he knows that giving so much blood will kill her.
Nevertheless, she agrees and, in what today we might regard
as an excess of empathy, gives her own blood that the queen
may be healed. The queen is healed and Dindraine's body is
sent to the Holy City of Sarras, where she is buried in the
temple beneath the Grail.

Dindraine also is known as the Grail Maiden, for she carries the Grail in the ritual procession in the Grail Castle. She
does not just seek the Grail, she holds it—regularly. She can
do this because she lives a life completely devoted to service.
She gives her life so that others may live.

Scholar Jessie Weston connects the Grail and these blood
mysteries to communion, wherein the worshipper partakes of
the flesh and blood of Christ to become one with God, "receiving thereby the assurance of eternal life." The Grail stories,
she argues, are a literary record of "ancient Ritual, having for
its ultimate object the initiation into the secret of the sources
of life, physical and spiritual." This ritual concerns not only
the processes of nature but "high spiritual teaching concern-

ing the relation of Man to the Divine Source of his being, and the possibility of a sensible union between Man and God."[20]

Percival's second magical question—"Who serves the Grail?"—provides a key to these higher mysteries. In this case, the answer must be "I do." To serve our own grails is to commit to our own values and to whatever is sacred to us. When we do so, we are no longer fragmented. We come together and are healed.

Lindbergh Sata also knows how to move people to understand this second question. He shared with me a beautiful letter he wrote an American Indian who was seeking information about his tribe, the Ojibwas. Sata himself tried for six months to research the tribe, but he found little or nothing. In his letter he shared his sadness that a whole cultural history had been wiped out, his understanding of the pain of never belonging anywhere, but also a vision of a postmodern approach to community and culture.

As alienated as Sata feels, he also sometimes finds people —who may be from any culture or race—"who feel as I do." In these cases, "I almost experience our hearts beginning to beat together." According to Sata, culture is "always evolving. In this era, you have an opportunity to create a new culture through your eye and your experience coupled with the experience of others in your group." In the In-Between, all cultures —whether dominant or minority—are inadequate in some way. That's why we have to serve our own grails. When we do so, we create new cultures and transform our worlds.

Douglas LaBier uses his version of the Grail questions with executives and executive teams. Most people who rise to a level of power are at midlife and, as such, in the In-Between in their own lives. In midlife, people begin to ask "What is the meaning of my life?" or, to use Camelot language, "What Grail do I serve?" At the same time, they yearn for greater connection and relatedness. Hierarchical, performance-based, and role-defined relationships no longer are satisfying. These executives want greater mutuality. In this way they are prepared to ask one another "What ails you?" while sharing their own pain and vulnerability.

LaBier teaches executive teams how, when we fail to ask these questions of ourselves, we may well "derail" our work life and our relationships. Ironically, we tend to trade intimacy and meaning for success, and if we do so, success eventually runs like sand through our fingers. Healing comes when we are willing to question our values and commitments, so that we serve a grail that is worthy of our best selves. This requires an expansion of vision, so that "success" becomes more than money and power. LaBier helps members of teams reinforce for one another the idea that success includes high quality of life as well as high productivity.

Organizations often can go through a sort of crisis when they forget to ask the ultimate questions—or when they give up their values in the hurry for the next sale. Organizational values are the "unifying field" that defines the organizational culture, just as one's own values define one's own character. In the In-Between, old values are breaking down. It is tempting to forget values altogether and simply focus on making money—which, of course, demeans the spirit and undermines our lives.

Margaret Wheatley says that an organization's guiding values are always critical: space is never empty; "values create the 'cornucopia' of structure in the organizational field."

. . . if we say one thing but do another, then we create dissonance in the very *space* of the organization. As employees bump up against contradicting fields, their behavior mirrors those contradictions. We end up with what is common to many organizations, a jumble of behaviors and people going off in different directions, with no clear or identifiable pattern. Without a coherent, omnipresent field, we cannot expect coherent organizational behavior.

What we lose when we fail to create consistent messages, when we fail to "walk our talk," is not just personal integrity. We lose the partnership of a field-rich space that can help bring form and order to the organization.[21]

THE GIFT

The kingdom of our own lives and our own organizations is transformed as we identify what ails us and then clarify and live by our own values. John Scherer ends his book *Work and the Human Spirit* by telling how a manager of a hotel world-famous for its customer service explained to him, "We hire people very carefully. We can teach people what to do. We can't teach them what to be."[22] We heal ourselves when we let go of all the limitations, pathologies, and blocks that keep us from living up to our finest potential. Then we become the kind of people whom organizations can trust enough to hire. Training can go only so far. You can teach people skills, but you cannot teach them virtue. The transformation of the business world today depends less on doing than on being—being true to our deepest and highest values. When we hold to these values, our collective kingdom certainly will be transformed.

THE EXERCISES

FOR INDIVIDUALS

- Answer the question "What ails me?" How might you enlist help to remedy the problem? How and where might you be more open and vulnerable with others?
- Ask yourself, "What do I believe in? What are my values? How can I better live up to them?"
- When you feel judgmental about another person, try to find some way to genuinely empathize with him or her. (It has been said, "If you cannot love Hitler, you cannot love anyone." You can begin by thinking about him as a little

boy being brutalized by his family. This does not require excusing his extraordinary cruelty, it simply acknowledges such inhuman behavior as a symptom of a sick and damaged mind.) Practice expressing empathy for others, showing concern for and interest in their situation. (Be careful that you express empathy, which comes from an equal position, rather than sympathy, which generally reflects a one-up position.)

FOR ORGANIZATIONS

- What strategies does your organization have in place to discover "what ails" its employees? What help can or does it provide them? Develop organizational plans (if you do not have them already) to address dysfunction immediately, both in individuals and in the organization as a whole. This includes, of course, addictiveness, abuse of power, unethical behavior, and punitive or inhumane policies of all kinds.

- What are the values of your organization? What are the blocks to the expression of those values? How could the blocks be removed? Are the values clearly stated and available?

- What about employees with values different from those of the organization as a whole—values that have their own validity? How are they handled? Do employees get an opportunity to be involved in defining or updating organizational values?

- What processes are (or could be put) in place to monitor departures from these values? Can people point out failures in this area with impunity? If not, what protections can be given to ethical whistle-blowers?

Circle Five: Finding the Grail

THE STORY

Some few knights and at least one lady in the Camelot story succeed in finding the Grail. Lancelot reaches out to steady the Grail when it appears to be in danger of being dropped, and he falls senseless to the ground. He lies motionless for twenty-four days while he integrates the power of what he has learned. Galahad finds the Grail and returns it to Sarras (where Joseph of Arimathea had found it and taken it to England) and becomes king of this Holy City. Soon, however, he chooses to die because he wants to experience the awe and wonder of the Grail all the time. Dindraine carries the Grail in the nightly procession within the Grail Castle, and she is buried beneath it in Sarras. She, of all others, embodies its mysteries in action. Several different stories are told about what Percival does after he sees the Grail. In some, he retreats to contemplate its mysteries for the remainder of his life; in others, he becomes the king of the Grail Castle. Bors, the most practical and grounded of the knights, reaches enlightenment when he sees the Grail, and then simply returns to Camelot, as he had promised, to serve King Arthur.

THE LESSON

Joseph Campbell loved to tell how each of the Grail knights entered the forest in a different place because he believed that to go where a path existed was to give in to a shameful temptation to follow in another's footprints rather than finding one's own way. Yet Campbell also stressed that the purpose of going on this quest was to find something common to us all. This means that any of us, no matter how circumscribed our lives, can find the Grail inside ourselves. Campbell reflects, "When you have found the center within yourself that is the counterpart of the sacred space, you do not have to go into the forest. You can have a technique for extracting your own repose from that center. You can live from that center, even while you remain in relation to the world."[23] Finding this place of "inner repose" makes it possible to stay sane even in a high-pressure, fast-paced world.

Chaos theory holds that every point in a system is as much the center of that system as any other point. Round-world thinking also reinforces this point. On the old maps depicting a flat world, our hemisphere often was drawn in the middle, reinforcing a sense of the United States being at the center of the world. On a globe, however, there *is* no center—or, conversely, we could say, any point is the center.

If the center is everywhere, we each have only to claim it to reclaim our power. In the Hawaiian shamanistic tradition, says practitioner Serge King, Magicians see themselves as spiders "at the center of a three-dimensional web, stretching out in all directions to every part of the universe." The shaman can send out "vibrations along the web and consciously affect anything in the universe, according to the strength of his *manna.*"[24] You might imagine yourself as the magical spider in the midst of a web consisting of invisible lines connecting you to everything that matters to you. Linking yourself to the things, people, places, and experiences that quicken your life energy charges up your magical batteries. It is through these webs that magic happens.

The more centered we are, the more "manna" (magical power) we have. The term "centering" comes from pottery. If you ever have tried to throw a pot, you know that first you must center it on the potter's wheel or it quickly will become lopsided and collapse; to do this successfully, you must remain quiet, calm, and focused. Success is not so much about working hard as it is about working smart. To put it another way, when you hit a home run, you can run around the bases very slowly.

When Galahad sees the Grail, he gives thanks for seeing "the source of valor undismayed, the spring-head of endeavor."[25] Galahad discovers that at the core of each of us is the power of creative imagination, which helps us prevail over whatever befalls us. Therefore, we can have courage in the In-Between, no matter how many times we must re-create our lives and work.

In a holographic universe, change anywhere produces change everywhere. Systems theory tells us that whenever one person in a system changes, the whole system has to adjust. For example, in an organization that shies away from conflict, disagreement often gets aired unproductively as griping in the halls rather than in meetings. If one person breaks this pattern and begins naming the conflict in the appropriate forum, either the old dysfunctional pattern is shattered or the truth-teller is fired.

When Martin Luther King delivered his "I have a dream" speech to the world, his words had an electrifying impact. Why? First, because he articulated a dream of freedom and justice that connected with the nobler, better part of his listeners. Second, he knew how to move to the center. When King wrote his famous "Letter from Birmingham City Jail," he was, in fact, an African American in a segregated city that was not even his hometown. He could have thought of himself as an outsider, someone on the periphery. Instead, he made an appeal from the center. He talked from the heart about how it felt to live under segregation, then appealed to the American values of dignity, justice, and compassion. Rather than portraying himself as a victim, he spoke as a national conscience, calling on all Americans to protect the rights of life, liberty, and the pursuit of happiness for *all* citizens.

TECHNIQUES FOR FINDING YOUR OWN GRAIL

The grail within calls us to center by listening to our own inner truth. Here are some ways that work:

- Silence (meditation, contemplation, prayer, quietly listening to music)
- Keeping a journal to record your insights
- Creative expression: writing, singing, drawing, dancing, etc.
- Noticing your dreams, daydreams, and doodles; active imagination exercises

Such change is not about power struggles, victimization, or who has done what to whom; it is about living up to our noblest dreams and our fondest hopes of what it can mean to be human. Finding the grail inside us is about connecting with what is best in ourselves and about discovering that we are not different. When we are most truly ourselves, we also can experience oneness. Then, all win/lose solutions lose their appeal. If any of us loses, we all lose. That is why Galahad recognizes the Grail as a guide to the mysteries of enterprise, as a call to action.

John Scherer, a management consultant and former president of the Association for Creative Change, as well as author of *Work and the Human Spirit,* spoke with me about his commitment to helping executives connect with their centers and, in so doing, with their spirits. Many people today, he says, believe that we need to return spirit to business. Scherer believes, however, that spirit is always in business—his job is just to remove blocks to its expression.

Scherer comes from six generations of Lutheran ministers. A successful Lutheran minister himself, he felt called to expand his ministry by giving up his church so that he could minister to executives throughout the world. Executives are important, Scherer feels, because they "are in a position to change the world." Moreover, most of them care more and carry more of a burden than other people realize.

In his popular executive leadership seminars, Scherer empathizes with the executives' pain, then seeks to identify and remove whatever is blocking the expression of their higher or deeper selves. To be certain that he is centered enough to do this work, he begins each morning with a meditative run and yoga. During the day he takes time to center himself frequently by using sound. He has a chime on his desk. By the time the sound ends, he finds, he is centered.

In his seminars, Scherer helps participants find the witness or spirit within them that is not hooked to their personal issues. He accomplishes this by teaching them to center, showing them how to stop and breathe deeply. When any of us gets hooked (with strong positive or negative emotion) in any situation, he says, "we are history." That is, we are responding out of something that has happened in the past. We get free from being hooked—so that we can live authentically in the present —when we stop and pay attention to the situation triggered from the past. Then we can share it and let it go.

Scherer offers an example. He is at a staff meeting where someone does not like one of his ideas. He feels immediately put down and defensive, and therefore is unable to listen to important alternative ideas. He stops, breathes, and remembers a series of events in his youth, when he was elected vice president of his class, not president, because he was seen as an idealistic idea person but not someone practical enough to get things done. When he realizes that his current reaction is coming from the past—and today he is the respected president of his own firm—he can return to the matter at hand and take in criticism as a gift that gives him new insight. Breathing is important at these moments, he says, because "fear cannot coexist with oxygen."

When we breathe, we relax. When we connect with the creative source, or grail, we learn we can trust our own authentic responses. Scherer has decided, based on his own experience, that all manipulation is evil sorcery. He began to realize that anytime he got his way by controlling others, he was left with a bad taste in his mouth. Now, instead of wanting his way, he simply wants to learn by finding the truth in any situation. The truth is the gift. With this in mind, he goes into difficult interactions holding a clear intent that they will work. Then he allows himself to be completely authentic and spontaneous.

Should he fight with his wife, he thinks, "This is how the greatest marriage in the world is manifesting itself right now." When his business "hits a blip," he thinks, "This is another way a world-class business looks."

THE GIFT

Noted Camelot scholar Caitlin Matthews sees the call as not just about finding, but *becoming* the Grail, which means allowing consciousness to be transformed so that we can express our highest and best selves in our lives and work. "For the essence of the Grail quest is not to disappear into a never-never land of no return; our duty is to return bearing the gifts of the Grail within ourselves, that we might be a cup, a means of regeneration and remembrance to every living creature. We become the Grail that others might drink; for to find the Grail is to become it. Unlike Galahad, Perseval returns from his Grail quest to become king of the Grail castle. The Wounded King finds his sovereignty once more and is healed . . . The Grail itself ceases to be an object and becomes a living reality."[26] In becoming the grail, we take our places at the center of the cosmic web of human interaction. From there, we are placed strategically to begin turning the wheel and, in so doing, to transform the world in which we live.

THE EXERCISES

FOR INDIVIDUALS

- What strategies work for you to help you get centered? Experiment with a variety of strategies to quiet your mind so that you can connect with your creative source.
- Experiment with thinking of yourself as at the center of your organization. If you thought this way, what would you do differently?
- Have you ever had a mystic experience? If so, what was it like? How has it affected who you are?
- What is sacred to you? How do you (or could you) express spirit in your workplace?

FOR ORGANIZATIONS

- To what degree do employees have the opportunity to stop and center in your workplace? What could the organization do to encourage such centering practices?
- What would it mean to act on the belief that your organization is at the center of your industry or field? What would it mean to believe that your organization is at the center of society? How might your organization (or does it already) act to change both?
- What is the organization's grail? That is, what is sacred to your organization? How is spirit expressed?

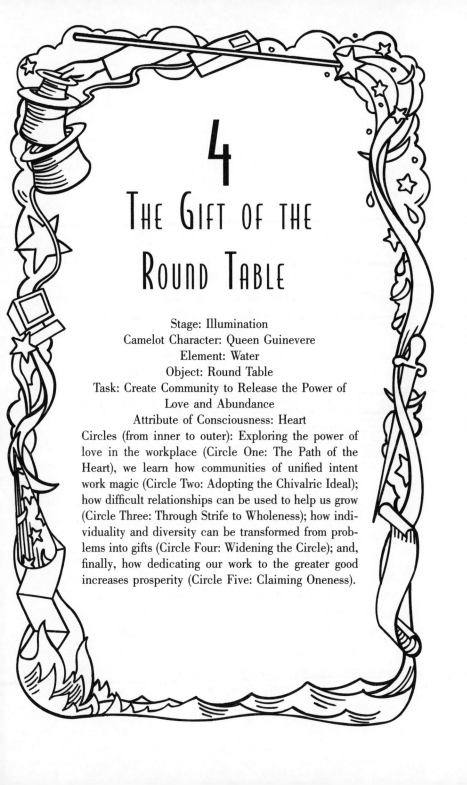

4

The Gift of the Round Table

Stage: Illumination
Camelot Character: Queen Guinevere
Element: Water
Object: Round Table
Task: Create Community to Release the Power of
Love and Abundance
Attribute of Consciousness: Heart

Circles (from inner to outer): Exploring the power of love in the workplace (Circle One: The Path of the Heart), we learn how communities of unified intent work magic (Circle Two: Adopting the Chivalric Ideal); how difficult relationships can be used to help us grow (Circle Three: Through Strife to Wholeness); how individuality and diversity can be transformed from problems into gifts (Circle Four: Widening the Circle); and, finally, how dedicating our work to the greater good increases prosperity (Circle Five: Claiming Oneness).

Circle One: The Path of the Heart

THE STORY

In the earliest Camelot legends, Guinevere is a goddess. Came-
lot scholars Caitlin and John Matthews see Guinevere as the
"British Venus" and as one of the mortal women who manifest
aspects of the Lady of the Lake, the goddess who determines the
destiny of the major characters in the story. In such stories
Guinevere also is seen as arising from the otherworld through
the lake, just as the Lady of the Lake appears out of the lake to
give blessings and boons. In the more recent and best-known
versions of the story, Guinevere is mortal, but, like Merlin and
Arthur, of mythic proportions.

When Arthur is enjoined by his people to marry, he is at-
tracted to Guinevere because she is "the most valiant and fairest
lady" he has seen. He persists in his choice even though Merlin
warns him about Lancelot's destined love for her. Guinevere
returns Arthur's affection and agrees to marry him. As her wed-
ding gift, she brings with her the Round Table.

At Camelot, Guinevere is the glue that holds the court to-
gether. She hosts wonderful rituals and celebrations, renowned
throughout Europe, and is the primary author of the code of
chivalry. She presides over the Court of Women, advises and
accompanies Arthur on his adventures, and inspires love and
loyalty from the assembled knights. She seems to hold in her
own person the honor of the king and the values of Camelot.
The knights—especially Lancelot—spend a good bit of time
rescuing her or defending her honor, for she is frequently ab-

ducted or insulted. *Defending Guinevere is the way the knights show their fidelity to the ideals of Camelot.*

Guinevere also has been likened to the Flower Maiden, a ritual figure symbolizing the arrival of spring. *In this guise she is associated with the holiday of Beltane, celebrated by bonfires and sexual license.* For this day only, all rules about relationships are off, and people can respond to the authentic desires of their hearts.

Guinevere is therefore the Camelot character most in charge of relationships and of happiness and fruition. *Guinevere embodies a morality very unlike that usually expected of a medieval queen. Coming from the otherworld, she lives by a code that values authentic eros much more than chastity or constancy. Her love affair with Lancelot, however, is complicated for her because she seems genuinely in love with him, as she is also with her husband, Arthur. Furthermore, Lancelot is Arthur's favorite knight and best friend. Arthur knows Lancelot is "her knight" and expects him to fight for, rescue, and defend her. However, Arthur is not prepared to allow adultery. Eventually, Guinevere and Lancelot are caught together and Arthur sentences her to death by burning (only fire was seen as capable of killing a goddess).* However, Arthur loves Guinevere so much he allows Lancelot to rescue her.

When Arthur leads the expedition to Rome, he leaves Mordred in charge. Mordred decides to take over the throne and marry Guinevere to cement his position. Guinevere escapes to a convent, however, and lives the rest of her life in prayer and contemplation.[1]

THE LESSON

Queen Guinevere illustrates the illumination stage of the Magician's journey. Guinevere brings love, commitment, and community to Camelot (Circle One). When she marries Arthur, she brings with her the Round Table and establishes the chivalric ideal (Circle Two). Guinevere presides over the Court of Women, helping those who come before it learn to respect others (Circle Three). Guinevere's individuality is asserted when she falls in love with Lancelot, thus raising the question of how (or if) individual desires can be supported within the court community (Circle Four). Finally, Guinevere escapes to a convent and dedicates her life to the love of God and humanity (Circle Five).

Guinevere, as the British Venus, arises from the lake, just as Venus arose from the sea. Her life exemplifies that path of love. Thaddeus Golas, the author of *The Lazy Man's Guide to Enlightenment*, contends that while there are many complicated paths to enlightenment and many esoteric practices, they all come down to one thing: learn to love and forgive more —beginning with ourselves. Every moment we are faced with a choice. We can act out of fear and flee from experience, or we can engage and love more. Love is the ultimate reality. When we tap into oneness, we tap into love. The decision we make daily—to contract out of fear or to open to love—is like the spigot on a water tap, connecting us to others or separating us from them.[2]

The leadership development text *Managing from the Heart* tells the story of a hard-driving manager who is told by a celestial guide after near death from a heart attack that he can go back and live out his life if he learns to love. When he agrees, the guide teaches him five attitudinal laws that first transform his communication skills and then transform his life. He changes his workplace from one in which people live in fear to one where people's faces shine with happiness. Anytime we improve our ability to appreciate and understand others, we are making the world a safer and better place.

King Arthur, with Guinevere's help, spends about as much time arranging marriages—to solidify relationships between warring lords—as he does fighting battles. When people become family, they have a vested interest in one another's successes. That's why successful people in business today en-

MANAGEMENT FROM THE HEART

The modern love potions, or communication laws, described in *Managing from the Heart* are:

Hear and understand me.
Even if you disagree, please don't make me wrong.
Acknowledge the greatness within me.
Remember to look for my loving intentions.
Tell me the truth with compassion.[3]

Applying these communication skills in your work can change your life. Try practicing these just for a day in your interactions with others and see what happens.

courage customers and employees to feel they are part of the organizational "family." Mutually beneficial solutions are easier to find and people are more willing to resolve conflict if they believe they matter to the organization and one another.

The Camelot story is also, among other things, a love story. As Gerald Jampolsky (*Love Is Letting Go of Fear*) so eloquently demonstrates, the opposite of love is not hate, it is fear. When we are afraid, we can't really love. The ecological sciences teach us that plants and animals are not "good" or "bad." Everything has its part in the ecological chain. Similarly, each person also has his or her part. The more behaviors we can appreciate in others, the more we can honor in our own lives. As we love others more, our own self-esteem grows. As our self-esteem grows, we can love others more. *It is a virtuous circle.*

Anytime we honor both ourselves and others, we create a context of emotional safety. This safety means that people— perhaps on a work team—do not have to be afraid to risk sharing a new idea or a vulnerable feeling. As a result, they have an ease with others that allows them to be part of a synergistic flow of ideas. They may disagree, fight, or work things out, but eventually they can reach consensus, so that magic results. They are able to connect not only at the surface level but from their depths.

The power of this is amazing. Canadian consultant Laureen Rama characterizes this synergistic process—when people are committed to the same ends and "share ideas, build on others' ideas"—as "fast, fun, exhilarating, and fulfilling." Most of all, she says, they "feel bigger afterwards." Fully connecting with others in the synergy of a planning process not only creates results greater than the sum of the ideas that produced them but expands the potential of everyone involved. When you are fully engaged in such a process, you never again will be the same. You forever carry with you a bit of the magic of each of the people you've touched and who have touched you. You realize you are truly "a part of all you have met."

A CASE STUDY

Organizational consultant Edith Whitfield Seashore has been committed to helping people create community since she was a senior at Antioch College and was voted community manager (the equivalent of the student body president). She worked closely with then president Douglas McGregor (author of *The Human Side of Enterprise*). Hearing him speak about principles of organizational development, she knew immediately what she wanted to do with the rest of her life—help people learn to form groups and communities and to work together productively. One way she now accomplishes this is by helping people gain complex caring skills—one-on-one, in small groups, and in whole organizational settings.

Her own story has been one of committed and sustained partnership—with her mentor; with her husband and consulting partner, Charles Seashore; and with the NTL Institute for Applied Behavioral Science. Clearly, her own sense of self is so clear and strong that she does not need to be separate from others to know who she is.

President McGregor, one of the founders of the field of organizational development, took a sustained interest in Seashore at Antioch, encouraging her personal and professional development. McGregor saw such great potential in Seashore that he sent her to the then three-year-old National Training Laboratories (NTL) in Bethel, Maine, after her senior year—so quickly that she missed graduation ceremonies at Antioch.

That summer the NTL associations participated in a sociogram as part of a research project: they drew arrows diagramming the influence pattern of the organization. More arrows pointed to Seashore than to any other person. That's why—she explained to me in an interview—they asked her back. It is also why she is an effective designated leader—because when formal power reflects information power, developing group consensus around common goals is much simpler. (Otherwise, formal leaders spend endless hours either courting or competing with the informal leadership.)

At NTL, Seashore took everything they offered about T-groups, group dynamics, and organizational development. In fact, she said with a laugh, they did not know what to do with her—as a woman—so they just kept training her. As a result, she became one of the best-trained people in the field. Finally, all the men who had been her teachers voted her "into the club," making her one of the first NTL female fellows.

Some years later, when NTL was in serious financial trouble, the outgoing president asked her to be part of a team of four charged with developing a plan to save it. Seashore and her colleagues decided that the source of NTL's financial difficulty was its tendency to act like a consulting company, causing the loss of its membership base and hence its supportive community. They selected seventy-five leading consultants, making sure they were a racially diverse group, and asked them to commit to giving the organization a week of their time every year. Each consultant taught a course gratis over a two-year period, generating a total of approximately $150,000. NTL then leveraged this commitment by going to foundations and corporations, raising the additional funds necessary for the organization to thrive. To make certain that the key consultants knew that their input was valued, Seashore and her colleagues gathered all seventy-five of them in a hotel for two days to set a new direction for the organization. It was after this gathering and the selection of a multicultural board of directors that Seashore was selected as the new president.

In my interview with her, Seashore radiated joy and confidence while sharing how she helped develop several academic programs, chief among them the American University/NTL Institute Master's Program in Organizational Development. Although NTL had considered setting up its own master's program, she recognized that arranging a partnership with an established credit-giving institution would be more efficient for both parties.

Clearly grateful for the mentoring she has received, Seashore makes passing it on a high priority. She develops curricula to teach others, as well as taking time to mentor individuals. A sought-after lecturer and consultant, she amazes others by giving away her training designs—literally presenting them in huge lecture halls. She consciously lives in an abundant rather than a scarce universe, trusting that she need not hold tight to what she has. This generosity stems from confidence and altruism. She knows she always will have other ideas. She also is committed to disseminating her ideas, and expanding their influence, because she believes in their importance.

After only an hour and a half with me, Seashore again was expressing her generosity, moving to the phone to arrange interviews with "magical" people who would be "just perfect" for this book.

THE GIFT

Leaders in the illumination stage illustrate the gifts of water. Water is flowing and generative. A fertile and prosperous area can become a waste land when it endures a drought—literally and metaphorically. It is restored to health when the rains come. In the physical world, water is a connector of energy. That is why it is so dangerous to stand in a puddle during a lightning storm! In our workplaces, water presides over connections between people.

Leaders who demonstrate the gifts of the water element are comfortable in the realm of human relationships. Intimacy and trust come easily to them, and they tend not to lose themselves in relationships. They know who they are, and they are not threatened by others' being different. In fact, difference is exciting. As we let in others' realities, we become more capable of finding adequate solutions to our workplace problems.

We tend to prosper, individually and organizationally, when we are part of a community that recognizes our own value and wants us to do well. Indeed, success is a result of consensus— a consensus of affected individuals who believe in us and what we do. Moreover, leaders who demonstrate the wisdom of water trust reciprocity: they "throw their bread upon the waters," expecting that if they do so, good will come back to them.

The water element provides the bonding that is necessary for good working relationships. The lake, the pool, and all watery realms represent the mysteries of the deep, the unconscious. If we remember that Venus arises from the sea, just as the Lady of the Lake also arises out of the water, it is easy to see that love emerges from, and reflects, what Jung calls the unconscious. Stage four of the Magician's journey, the stage Richard Ellwood calls "Illumination," opens our hearts so that we feel the reality of oneness.

The sense associated with illumination is touch, as used in

the phrase "high tech, high touch." Moments of illumination are typically "touching," and also put us "in touch" with our deeper selves and with each other. When the water element is active in a healthy and positive way, it feels natural for people to touch each other while communicating—and doing so is not a violation of boundaries, because it is respectful and caring.

In *Cat's Cradle*, novelist Kurt Vonnegut offers the lovely idea that we all have a "karass"—people born with the same sort of mission we have. Finding our own karass not only helps us fulfill our destiny; it also gives us a sense of personal support and make us feel as if we were coming home. We can see Edie Seashore's magic as resulting from the combination of an inner clarity about her own mission and a genius for recognizing her natural individual and organizational partners.

Most of us have had the experience of feeling inexplicably connected to a person, an organization, or even a place. The gift of illumination helps us find and honor such special connections while simultaneously identifying with the good of the whole. We experience a sense of oneness that decreases our sense of separation. When we feel separate, we defend against others. When we feel like part of a group or an organization, we can let down our shields and empathize with others. In doing so, we become willing to open our hearts with compassion and work for the good of the whole, as the well-known story of "The Long Spoons" illustrates:

A woman who had just died was first taken to hell. Her guide brought her into a room where an untold number of people—as far as the eye could see—were sitting at a banquet table. Unfortunately, they were starving and miserable despite the wealth in front of them because they were forced to eat with very long spoons—much too long for them to successfully get even a morsel of food into their mouths.

After she could no longer stand watching this torture, the woman was then taken to heaven where she was stunned to see exactly the same arrangement! There everyone was, seated at a bountiful banquet table laden with food of every type. Even more startling was the fact that everyone had the same long spoons with which to eat, yet each person looked happy and well-fed. The only difference between heaven and hell was that in heaven the long spoons were used to reach across the table and feed another person.

This section describes the heart of the matter. The following sections are like concentric circles, emanating outward to explore the full development of love in our lives. Guinevere's story provides the frame. Following the events of her life, we explore love in the workplace as it is expressed through the marriage of the feminine and the masculine, and then through three kinds of love: eros (life force, relational energy), amore (personal affection for another individual), and agape (love for humankind, a love feast, generosity).

THE EXERCISES

FOR INDIVIDUALS

- Who are the people in your work life that really matter to you?
- What sorts of partnerships do you currently have—with people, organizations, groups?
- If you were to open your heart further in your work life, what would you change?

FOR ORGANIZATIONS

- Describe the networks of care in your organization. Draw an organizational chart about who influences whom. You might want to have plain lines for respect and liking, dotted lines for people prone to feuds or disagreements, people who influence each other negatively ("I wouldn't be for anything he suggested!").
- What community or civic partnerships does your organi-

zation have? Is there a community that cares about it? If so, who is a part of that community?

- How does the organization show people it cares about them? Do people feel that care? If the organization were to open its heart further, what might it do differently?

Circle Two: Adopting the Chivalric Ideal

THE STORY

When Guinevere marries Arthur, she is accompanied by four queens and brings with her the Round Table, a wedding present from her father, Leodegrance. At the wedding breakfast a white hart (a male red deer) appears in the hall, followed by a white hound and thirty black hounds. Then a lady rides in and demands the return of her white hound. A strange and evil knight appears and takes the woman and her hound away.

Arthur is annoyed at this interruption of the ceremonies, but Merlin tells him not to shirk this adventure. Therefore, Arthur dispatches Sir Gawain to rescue the woman and punish the knight. Gawain follows the hart into a castle and then kills it. Ablamar of the Marshes, a rival lord, emerges from the castle and kills two of Gawain's hounds. Gawain "beats Ablamar to his knees" and is about to behead him when a lady suddenly appears and throws herself under Gawain's sword so that he accidentally beheads her instead. As punishment for killing a woman, Gawain is then made to carry the dead queen's head around his neck as he returns to Camelot. By ordinance of Queen Guinevere, Gawain is then charged with the chivalric ideal: "to be with all ladies, and to fight for their quarrels; and . . . be courteous, and never to refuse mercy to him that askest mercy."[4]

THE LESSON

What a strange story—it seems psychedelic, surreal. It makes sense only if we remember that medieval literature teaches through symbols. We can analyze these symbols as though we were interpreting a dream.

1. The four queens. The number four is associated with the mandala, the traditional symbol of wholeness. Thus, we are alerted that Guinevere's appearance at court introduces feminine wholeness to Camelot. The next four symbols elucidate what this means.

2. The Round Table. By itself, male culture is hierarchical and competitive—fiery. Before the appearance of the Round Table, the knights were always vying for dominance. Female culture emphasizes intimacy over hierarchy, for intimate relationships are inherently equal and interdependent. The Round Table provides a balance—enough equality to allow the group to operate as one team; enough hierarchy to allow for quick decisions and action. This is why it is so important that the Round Table has come to Camelot with Guinevere, who represents and exemplifies feminine values and ways of being.

3. The white hart. This symbol is a pun. It is about the sudden appearance of the white, or pure, heart. The chivalric ideal is about opening the heart, so that its expression is healthy and pure.

4. Gawain wearing the woman's head. This is the strangest part of the story. Eros is let loose in the court and in the land, and it first causes commotion and strife. Then people begin to lose their heads. However, the hoped-for result is symbolized by Gawain's two heads—one a man's (his own), the other a woman's. In other words, the story teaches us the wisdom of developing an androgynous consciousness.

5. Guinevere's ordinance. As judge of the Court of Women,

Guinevere presides over all matters of relationship. She declares that members of the court must honor the feminine and learn to show mercy as much as they previously have demonstrated courage.

Jung predicted the "rise of the feminine" in the twentieth century, making it possible once again for a truly androgynous consciousness to emerge in our culture. As we reestablish the balance between masculine and feminine, we create the precondition for restoring magic to society. Today patriarchal gender arrangements are breaking down in ways that have not only fundamentally changed the definition of family but also revolutionized our expectations about how men and women relate in the workplace. The scope of this transformation is generally underestimated. People have assumed, for example, that it would be possible to change sex role patterns without disturbing anything else.

Warrior society depended on an archetypal role split. Men carried the Warrior archetype, predominantly in the public world of enterprise. Women carried the complementary Caregiver archetype, predominantly in the private world of nurturance. The Magician archetype demands the achievement of internal psychological androgyny—a much more complex inner dynamic. It also requires a massive change in relationships between people. In a Warrior society, people could relate to others primarily as defined by roles. When we want magic to occur, we have to honor the full complexity of others, which means that we need to know them and let them know us.

The transition from the Warrior to the Magician archetype stimulates a simultaneous change in politics, economics, family relationships, and consciousness. *For they are all of a piece.* To do magic, we must understand individual and group psychodynamic processes. We cannot just act as if people were machines.

Jung saw the feminine as defined by eros—the relational

side of life. Mrs. Ramsay in Virginia Woolf's *To the Lighthouse* illustrates these traditionally feminine gifts. Mrs. Ramsay presides over her home with the dignity of a queen. Her gifts are supremely demonstrated when she hosts a dinner party. People come to the table feeling alienated and separate; as a result, they are prone to be competitive and brusque. Mrs. Ramsay chats away charmingly. Many of those at the party view her fondly, but without taking her very seriously. Eventually, it begins to dawn on people that she is performing a kind of magic, made no less impressive by the fact of its everyday domestic quality. At just the right moment she invites the children to light the candles. By doing so, she brings her guests together, their separate egos melting away as if by magic. They are suddenly unified, one group, sharing an experience that can be seen as a kind of illumination, an experience so powerful that one distinguished male diner stands up and bows to Mrs. Ramsay in tribute to the miracle she has inspired.

Edie Seashore told me about an award dinner that was held in her honor with a Mary Poppins theme. Like Mrs. Ramsay, Mary Poppins creates family where only separation existed before. Poppins floats down with her umbrella to help a family in which the father is a workaholic, the mother is caught up in the feminist cause, and the children are left to fend for themselves. By the time she leaves, the family is happily flying kites together, remembering that love and connectedness are at least as important as achievement. What Mary Poppins achieves is what Seashore and other consultants who do team or community building also aspire to. They try to help groups of separate, distrustful people find the magic of becoming one group, one family, or one community.

Organizations that configure themselves as machines have no capacity for magic. They are inorganic, treating people like endlessly exchangeable cogs. In this inhuman world, relationships are defined entirely by roles, and people are expected to act as if they had no feelings. However, feelings (and the imagination) are the realm of magic. We often know if a love relationship is here to stay by whether there is "magic" in it. When eros is expressed appropriately in our organizations, they can feel magical too.

Guinevere's magic has to do with bringing love, loyalty, and compassion into Camelot. The knights and ladies create magic out of their devotion to their mission and to Arthur, Guinevere, and each other. They also make the chivalric commitment to compassion and mercy—to the opening of the heart. This means that they are not just of one mind or of one intent, but of one heart. As a result, the magic of eros unfolds.

In her groundbreaking essay "The Uses of the Erotic," poet Audre Lorde says that our culture so fears eros that we allow it only in genital sexuality. Actually, she argues, eros is the "life force" and should be there anytime people are creating or working together.[5] One of the reasons for sexual harassment is this fear of eros. Eros is about the vulnerability of caring about each other—or even just caring about what others think of us. The easiest way to escape from that powerless feeling is to lord it over the other person, using eros to demean rather than to cement interconnection.

In a culture that fears eros, it is easier to keep men and women away from each other or to keep their relationships defined by hierarchical roles. Today not only have women entered the workforce, but they have brought with them what Jung calls "the feminine"—eros. People spend so many hours at work that the workplace is now a primary setting for social life. People find friends and mates there. Increasingly, they also expect genuine and authentic relationships with coworkers. Therefore, insights from the private world of romance, friendship, and family—a world that has been the province of women and that opens up a Pandora's box of deep feelings— are now critical to the adequate functioning of the public world of work and politics.

Some people are deeply threatened by eros, and their fear can give rise to behavior like sexual harassment. The answer, however, is not a new puritanism. Instead, it is learning to respect and understand erotic energy that is not primarily about sex but about bonding. When people have integrated the masculine and feminine within, they can feel this energy and allow it to feed the enterprise without getting confused by it.

The Grail stories have much to teach us about this integration of masculine and feminine accomplishments. Remember the Ship Draped in Silk that tempts King Arthur and that also carries Dindraine, the Grail Maiden, to the Holy City of Sarras. This ship was built by King Solomon and his wife out of wood from the Garden of Eden's Tree of Life. Even King Solomon, with all his wisdom, had difficulties; he disapproved of his wife because she was always playing politics.

When Solomon complained to his court advisor, the latter comforted the king by announcing that he would have a descendant who would be the perfect man, integrating wisdom with enterprise. Solomon determined to get a message to this descendant, to let him know that Solomon's achievement had preceded his and made it possible. The king's advisor suggested that he ask his wife what to do, for she was a very practical woman. When his wife came up with the idea of building the Ship Draped in Silk, which would sail through the ages to this descendant, Sir Galahad, Solomon recognized her value. In this story, then, the feminine power of eros is seen as presiding not only over the personal relationships of the home but also over the public realm of politics. Solomon at first looked down on his wife's politicking; only later did he recognize its value.[6]

Galahad's ability to integrate the most positive qualities of both the masculine logos (wisdom) and the feminine eros (relatedness) requires a respect for women and their historical achievements. Even when women have held no political power, they have played an important role in cementing social relationships—being the glue that holds civilized society together. A respect for women and the feminine is the consciousness that Guinevere's chivalric code—which requires the knights to honor and protect ladies—is designed to foster.

Many people today cold-bloodedly see networking as a way to build connections and use people. The most effective politicians (whether male or female), however, network as a natural outgrowth of their genuine regard for people. They also understand that good relationships are the prerequisite for getting things done. When he first came to Washington as a young intern, former President Lyndon Johnson lived in a boarding house with other up-and-coming young politicos. The group shared a bathroom, where Johnson spent far more time than necessary to shave and shower. While there, he chatted with everyone who came through; eventually, he was the only person in the house to *know* everyone.[7] Effective leaders take time to know people and really connect with them. They have a knack for letting others know they care. Former President Bush was famous for remembering everyone and writing wonderful notes acknowledging people's triumphs and pains.

Sally Helgesen, author of *The Female Advantage: Women's Ways of Leadership,* found that successful women workplace leaders envision themselves at the center of a network, or "web," rather than at the top of a ladder. Their offices, moreover, are information-central. Instead of hoarding information to gain power, they see the need to disperse it so that people can do their jobs more successfully. Not only do these women have an open-door policy themselves, but they encourage others to interact with one another across hierarchical lines. To the degree that information is shared, the collective intelligence increases. Such women have integrated the traditional female virtue of promoting harmony through communication with the male virtues of ambition and assertion.[8]

I often have challenged people to recognize that God did not make a mistake in creating two sexes. The genders have been specializing for thousands of years, perfecting two complementary ways of being. Magic is possible in our lives today in part because these two traditions are coming together—like two chemicals in a test tube, creating a synergistic reaction greater than the sum of its parts. One sign of our readiness for this advance is how men and women today see traditional sex roles as confining. Perhaps for the first time in human history, the majority of people are cognitively complex enough to be functionally androgynous. Contrary to popular conceptions, androgyny is not a sexless, neuter condition. Its very complexity comes from an ability to exemplify the qualities of both genders—and then to integrate them into a unified individual consciousness. This is demonstrated by an equal facility for dealing effectively with both men and women, individually and in groups.

I am not implying here that men and women are intrinsically so very different as individuals. Moreover, when Jung talked about the "feminine," he was referring to the relational side of men as well as women. Moreover, works such as Jean Bolen's *Goddesses in Everywoman* and *Gods in Everyman* greatly expand Jung's notion of the masculine and the feminine. Thus for Bolen, Artemis, goddess of the hunt, is every bit as much a part of the feminine as Aphrodite. Nevertheless, because of sex role patterns and the qualities they reinforce, Jung's simpler formulation still is useful.

Professor Morley Segal, cofounder with Edie Seashore of the American University/NTL Institute Master's Program in Organizational Development, for example, described to me the conscious development of his own feeling qualities. Working with group processes in NTL, he said, helped him "develop his feminine side." This experience "opened the door to being creative enough to structure a program many have described as magical." This was his way of "turning the lead of the university into gold."

I asked Segal what was magical to him? In response, he

defined "magic" as the capacity to use natural laws that have not yet been discovered. "For example," he explained, "no one wrote about group processes until the 1930s." Of course, this did not mean that they hadn't existed until then. Anyone who understood them would have appeared to do magic. It is no accident that awareness of group processes has entered the academic and business worlds in the twentieth century as sex roles are changing.

Group processes exist in the affective domain: they are matters of the heart that affect the decisions of the mind. Today we can all be magical by coming to understand how groups function. We then can move beyond work as a war of separate egos, so that we can work real magic together.

Genuine dialogue is not possible in whole organizations or work teams unless people bond in ways that inspire trust and emotional risk-taking. On typical work teams, discussion of issues is mere posturing. People defend their positions against assaults from others. This means that information is hoarded and counterviews are seen as threats. When a group has truly gelled to become a community, it can begin to explore what Peter Senge calls "the large pool of meaning" that the water element offers.[9] Doing so requires emotional vulnerability and risk: sharing ideas we have not developed completely, building on others' ideas even when we do not know where they are going, allowing the expression of feelings as well as thoughts. The result, however, is a kind of synergy that creates an abundance of high-quality ideas.

This kind of bonding also greatly improves the quality of work life. People who like to work do so not just because it enables them to make a living (or even just because it allows them to achieve) but because it provides a chance to socialize. Second on Abraham Maslow's Human Hierarchy of Needs is "belonging." According to Maslow, the need to belong comes right after issues of security and survival. The greater the sense of community, safety, and connection in the workplace, the higher the job satisfaction. Modern-day Guineveres help people link hearts and minds around a shared task.

Jesus Christ promised that "when two or three are gathered in my name," prayers would be answered. Ancient Magicians created rituals to galvanize people together so that they would be of one heart and one mind. The magic circle was constellated when people created sacred space in which they agreed to become one unified group with a single intent: healing, perhaps, or restoring fertility to the land, or envisioning a hoped-for boon. Often they would chant, drum, and dance together to make the sense of connection tangible and felt, as individual egos gave way to a shared experience. In the workplace today, we sometimes similarly forget our own egos when working together toward a shared goal. The feeling can be as ecstatic and joyful as that experienced by indigenous people dancing around the tribal fire. Both ways of creating a magic circle are equally valid, and equally effective.

THE GIFT

The water element teaches us that we are the magic circle—as we bond with one another. The Camelot symbol for this bonding is the Round Table. It is, therefore, no accident that the Round Table enters Camelot with Guinevere, or that she is the British equivalent of Venus. She arises out of the water element to teach us that eros is not just about the bonding of romantic love or even about the visceral bonding of parent to child. Eros is also about the deep bonding that work teams can have when they believe in the work they do and when the team members take the time to know and trust one another.

Work teams that experience even transient moments of bonding know a kind of time-bound illumination. Sometimes it is confusing that such a connection can be at once so deep and so limited. The connection typically passes—in a work team or in a workshop—as soon as the task is complete; someone breaks the bond of trust, or it is simply time to go home.

The relationships involved do not necessarily have any life outside the work or workshop context.

Yet even if you have this experience only once in a lifetime, you will not forget it. Moreover, the more such moments you have, the more likely you will be able to replicate them. Replication is not the point, however. Knowing what it is like to be completely true to the highest and best in you while also working with others in a highly bonded team effort—this is what the illumination stage is about. It teaches us that when we are most true to ourselves, we are most able to bond intensely with others.

THE EXERCISES

FOR INDIVIDUALS

- Describe your perfect man and your perfect woman. Describe yourself as you might be if you integrated the qualities of both.
- What is the best experience you have ever had working with other people? What made it so special? How might some of the quality of this experience be replicated in your present or future work team(s)?
- Draw your work team. Referring to the heroic archetypes in Appendix B, notice what archetypes are present in your work team. Notice which people you get along with and with which you have trouble. Notice whether your individual HMI scores (Appendix B) are related to the archetypes of your work team.

FOR ORGANIZATIONS

- In your work teams, consciously do team building that helps people bond with one another. You might have them learn about their Myers-Briggs types (using the Myers-Briggs Type Indicator) and their heroic archetypes, and/or have them talk personally about their lives and what they want out of work.

- Experiment with honest dialogue—encourage people to talk freely about their thoughts and feelings without making anyone else wrong or to blame. Encourage active listening and feedback. Make communication skills training widely available to help people communicate in clear, direct, tactful, and nonblaming ways. (Without skills development, encouraging more honest communication can lead to bruised egos and increased tension between people.)

Circle Three: Through Strife to Wholeness

THE STORY

When one of Arthur's knights rapes a young damsel, Guine-
vere's Court of Women claims jurisdiction in the case. Guinevere
gives the man twelve months to find the answer to the question
"What thing is it that women most desire?" If he fails, he will
be beheaded. The knight asks everyone, but no one has a con-
vincing answer. Finally a hag, the Hideous Damsel, offers him
the answer to the riddle if he promises to marry her. In despera-
tion he agrees. When he gives her answer—"Women desyren to
have sovereyntee"—Guinevere compliments him on his wisdom
and begins to prepare the wedding. At the feast the Hideous
Damsel appalls those present with her grotesque appearance
and behavior. When she and the knight retire to the marriage
bed, he kisses her and she suddenly becomes quite beautiful. He
is, of course, delighted, but his joy turns to perplexity when she
tells him she can be either beautiful for him at night and ugly
for the court, or beautiful for them and ugly in bed with him.
He tells her she should decide to please herself. When he does,
she exclaims that since he has granted her sovereignty, she will
be beautiful by day and by night, for the court and for him.

THE LESSON

In *Ladies of the Lake*, Camelot scholars Caitlin and John Matthews explain that "the Grail quest is undertaken in order 'to
free the waters'—to cause the lustral waters of the spirit to

flow in the land. However, after its achievement, the waters flow only too readily: emotions run high, quarrels erupt, jealousy is plumbed, and the fall of the Table is brought about."[10] When eros is first released on the land, its expression is not "pure" or "clear." Baser emotions abound—not only jealousy but lust and the desire for conquest and power.

Rape is a crime against eros—the attempt to gain the pleasures of relationship through force. In "The Story of the Well-Maidens," girls from the otherworld offer water from a well in golden cups to travelers—until King Amangons and his men rape the maidens and steal their cups. From that time on, this legend explains, the power of the Grail is withdrawn from the land. The Waste Land as described here results from a drought both of literal water and of eros—loving and pleasurable connection between people. Drinking from the Grail heals and restores.[11] Sound like communion? It is. However, this is the everyday psychological equivalent of the religious ritual. When we are able to drink from the cup of mutually bonded interconnection, fertility and joy are restored to our lands—our homes, our organizations, our society.

Why do people rape? They do so, at least in part, because they want a sexual experience without the vulnerability of true intimacy. Rape in the Camelot story is a metaphor for all the violations of the human spirit where we objectify or use people. The return of the Grail allows us to be in genuine relationship with them.

Relatedness, however, throws us into the murky and complicated arena of interpersonal relationships where neither the course of true love nor the course of true colleagueship runs smooth. Relationships tend to be messy and mysterious. Work relationships sometimes are complicated by our deep feelings, conflicts, and loyalties, as well as by childhood traumas projected on the present. To understand all this, we must develop a relationship with the unconscious—or what Jungians often call the soul. Our current relationships are triggers that uncover parts of the unconscious that may or may not be pleasant. Magical leaders do not shy away from psychological complexity. They welcome it as a chance to learn.

Many of us have trouble with people very different from ourselves, especially those we dislike. The Arthurian story "The Knight and the Hideous Damsel" and the well-known fairy tale "Beauty and the Beast" both tell us in different ways that when we see beyond appearances to the often hidden qualities of a person, she or he may turn in our eyes from a beast into a prince or princess.[12] Even more important, dealing with people who are difficult for us can make *us* more beautiful.

In a Magician's view, each of us is a microcosm of the whole. That means everything we experience outside ourselves has a parallel aspect within us. So when we experience distance from another, it mirrors an inner distance between parts of ourselves. A knight who is capable of raping a woman already has "raped" and objectified his own relational, feeling side (what Jung calls the male "anima," or woman within). To objectify anyone, of either sex, we first must objectify a part of ourselves. The knight does not move from being a rapist to giving his wife sovereignty without an intervening process. Perhaps this is why Guinevere gives him a year to seek the answer to the question. The rapist's fantasy is about invulnerability. Knowing he is going to die in a year if he does not find someone both wise and willing to help him, the knight learns vulnerability. Moreover, he also learns that in order to get something, he has to give—in this case, be willing to marry someone so ugly she has no other prospects. Something about experiencing his own neediness allows him to empathize with hers. Hence, he can kiss her and also allow her to make her own decision in what appears to be a win/lose situation.

It would be wonderful if illumination occurred primarily as a positive, ennobling experience. However, we generally learn more, at first, through the kinds of painful relationships that make us feel trapped. When we deal with very difficult relationships, we discover parts of ourselves that are in need of development or healing.

Often the people we most dislike have qualities that we have underdeveloped and devalued in ourselves. For example, if you are a creative free spirit who is not very organized or precise, you may be driven crazy by a coworker who is a compulsive perfectionist—at least until you come to honor and develop that part of yourself. Mr. Warm and Wonderful may be driven crazy by a boss who seems like the Ice Queen, even though she is much better than he is at setting boundaries, making tough and objective decisions, and doing what is required to get the task done.

The Magician within you knows that every time anyone drives you nuts, chances are good that his or her presence and example are activating a repressed part of yourself. You know many people who do not behave well, but most of them do not inspire much reaction in you. You may think they are incompetent, crazy, or just real jerks, but you do not have deep feelings or conflicts about them. If you are their boss, you just fire them, refer them for employee assistance, or provide feedback or additional training that gives them the chance to improve their attitude or performance. However, the people who call you to growth are the ones resembling fingernails on the blackboard. In attempting to deal with your frustration in working with them, you often learn to awaken the part of you that is like their more positive potential. Then, and only then, can you empathize enough to communicate with them effectively. In some cases, this requires making friends with your own Shadow.

Whatever part of us is wounded and not getting our attention may force itself into consciousness through projection onto someone else in our lives. When we ignore the cries of our own inner wounded child, we may obsessively rescue others without recognizing why they have such a hold on us. For example, a banker who was very successful in her chosen profession made a bad career move. Although she was miserable in her new job, she was too proud to show it; in retrospect, she realized she had distracted herself by trying unsuccessfully to rescue an alcoholic boyfriend. Eventually, she got herself to Al/Anon and to a career counselor and found a new job.

In her new position she supervised a man who could never say no to his employees. She could now see that his inner child was so vulnerable, neglected, and in need of love that he feared alienating anyone. The more people ran all over him, the worse he felt about himself and the less he was able to demand accountability. Because she had learned to be kind to herself, she did not have to judge her employee. Instead of firing or rescuing him, she told him her own story. Then she sent him to a management consultant (to teach him more effective management skills) and a counselor (to work on inner child issues). The result? He and she became a magical team. Healed of a similar wound, they had tremendous empathy and trust for one another, and over time they rose to prominence together in their organization.

It is amazing how many times we will gravitate into workplace environments and relationships that reenact whatever was most difficult in our childhoods. Such situations give us an opportunity to heal wounds that were too overwhelming for us to deal with when we were young. Reba Keele, dean of undergraduate studies at the University of Utah, reported that when she was a professor at a different university, she had a very difficult relationship with a younger male colleague—so difficult that virtually any faculty meeting could end up as a "shoot-out at the O.K. Corral." Despite the fact that everyone saw them as enemies, her department chair made her the head of this man's professional review committee. Striving to be objective and fair, Keele worked hard at understanding her colleague; she read his writing and immersed herself in the information available about him. At the same time, she ran across a picture of her older brother, who had abused her as a child. Suddenly she realized that her colleague annoyed her because he looked like her brother!

Realizing this led her to view her faculty nemesis very differently. All of a sudden she felt like an adult when dealing with him. True, he and she still disagreed on most issues. True, he did not know how to deal with women who were not his wife, sister, or mother. But it was not his intention to be abusive; he just was unskilled. When Keele saw this, she stopped bristling every time she encountered him. She took responsibility for dealing with another layer of her painful memories and in this way further integrated the wounded child within into her adult personality. She and her former antagonist never talked about her realization, but he changed too—perhaps because she did. Suddenly they were capable of working together. They even worked successfully on a small committee where they had to spend intense hours designing a new curriculum.

Understanding *projection* can save your job or your marriage! Jim fell madly in love with Jane, an up-and-coming protégée. She admired him so much, and she was so soft and understanding (while his wife seemed more and more critical of him). Jane was complimented by his attentions. He was so knowledgeable and successful. However, she was worried about their getting involved. She knew when such relationships are discovered, often the less senior person (usually the woman) gets fired. Fortunately, Jim was so conflicted about this situation (since he did not want to ruin his marriage or his protégée's career) that he went to a therapist. The therapist talked to him about how falling in love is often an anima or animus projection. (The anima is the feminine part of a man; the animus is the masculine part of a woman.) He might be falling in love with Jane as a way of connecting with his own emerging feminine side.

He and Jane decided to walk the tightrope of admitting

their erotic feelings for one another but not acting on them. Assuming that anima-animus projection was likely, Jim decided to work on developing his own softness, and Jane on becoming more assertive and confident. Although this form of friendship was not without its stresses, they both grew from it. Some years later, Jim's wife passed away and Jane went on to a different firm. They realized at that point that they could have a romantic relationship but decided against it. Far from being deprived, they each had gotten exactly what they needed from the friendship—even if not what they wanted initially. They both gained the capacity for androgyny that is the hallmark of magical leadership.

Jung educated us about how we can project our emerging self onto a role model—a therapist, boss, teacher, or mentor—and learn from this person how to be what we want to be. Many times we feel disillusioned when we discover that he or she is less wonderful than we thought initially. This is a natural process. When our idol's Achilles heel really begins to bother us—or we think, When I'm in a position that powerful, I'll do it differently—we are ready to go our own way.

THE GIFT

Many Jungians have written extensively about how anima or animus projection complicates romantic love. *Less is written about projection in the workplace, but it is equally strong.* As long as we are unaware of our projections, we never will see the world the way it is; we always will be interacting with ourselves! Suffering motivates us to understand and withdraw our projections so that we can genuinely know and appreciate other people. When we do so, we discover that few people, if any, are real villains. They may be wounded or deluded, they may not want what we want, but generally they are crying out for love—just as we are.

It is only when we withdraw what we project onto others that we can recognize those people with whom we have genuine connection. As the magical principle of fire teaches us that each of us is here for a purpose, the magic of water reassures us that each of us also has a magic circle of people with concerns similar to our own: we do not have to do it all alone. We know them by a sudden or gradual sense of camaraderie growing out of similar visions and interests. As with romantic love, however, compatibility is only part of it. The gift of water includes the mystery of good "chemistry."

Outer chemistry reflects inner chemistry: the more we learn to flow with our own authentic responses, rather than controlling and censoring them, the more we experience synergistic interconnections with others. Good chemistry in groups works like jazz improvisation. (Not incidentally, jazz improv has developed out of the strengths of African-American culture, which is more relational than European-based cultures tend to be.) The common mission in a work group is like the basic melody in a jazz performance. Each person in the group needs to play well and to be connected enough with the others so that the music is harmonious. Each person also needs to be spontaneous enough to be able to improvise, and intuitive enough to know when to take the lead. Leadership thus is rotated with ease. The trumpet player knows when to play a solo and when to fade back and allow the drummer to shine. To work from the consciousness of illumination requires a sense of connection—with yourself, your coworkers, and the rhythm of the time and the task.

THE EXERCISES

FOR INDIVIDUALS

- Make a list of several of your key relationships, positive and negative. Which relationships are difficult for you? Which are most rewarding?
- Examine your list. How are the positive relationships alike? In the difficult ones, notice whether the annoying

or frustrating person has qualities you lack or devalue, reminds you of someone else, or elicits feelings you would rather not have. What, in you, needs developing or healing in order to improve the outward relationships?

- With reference to the HMI descriptions (Appendix B)— especially the description of the lower level, or negative side, of the archetype—which archetypes seem most associated with difficult people in your life? These archetypes may be inviting you to learn from them and to integrate their insights into your life. How might you do so?

FOR ORGANIZATIONS

- Make a list of difficult relationships in your organization. Notice whether these relationships form any pattern. Do these involve people with whom everyone has difficulty? If so, what are these people like?
- Make a list of the norms and values of your organization. Are these people operating from different norms and values? How can you help them understand the norms and values of your organization? If their complementary perspective has some value, how can you encourage others to see what they have to offer?

Circle Four: Widening the Circle

THE STORY

Lancelot was raised by the Lady of the Lake and is therefore a child of the goddess, sent by her to Guinevere. Guinevere falls in love with him, moving from an awareness of eros to amore—what Joseph Campbell calls "the meeting of the eyes." She cannot resist Lancelot. Suddenly Guinevere stops simply holding the power of eros for the court; she wants something as an individual, for herself. Amore requires her to assert her own needs and wishes. When she does so, strife erupts in the court, contributing to the eventual demise of Camelot.

THE LESSON

Caitlin and John Matthews see Guinevere as "the eternal May Queen with all the privileges that role entails." The May Queen is chosen for her beauty. She represents the coming of spring, with its proliferation of flowers and green growth. In traditional celebrations, two men fight for her love. This is why the story of the competing love of both Lancelot and Arthur is related to a blossoming of spring within Guinevere herself.[13]

The achievement of individuality by certain knights and Guinevere was a radically new concept in a medieval context. The Camelot story does not resolve competing needs of individuality and community. Creating a community that supports individuality, and therefore allows for amore in the workplace, is a task for our time.

The demise of Camelot begins as key people are excluded from the inner circle. Arthur orders Guinevere to be executed by burning (the only means of killing a goddess, it was believed). Although he allows Lancelot to rescue her, her position in the court is forever undermined. Arthur's sister, the sorceress Morgan le Fay, begins to be perceived as a villainess. Mordred often is described as Arthur's nephew, but modern texts (such as Marion Zimmer Bradley's *The Mists of Avalon*) portray him as the outcome of the incestuous union of Morgan and Arthur in a pagan fertility rite, meant to celebrate the king's marriage to the land. As these native customs went underground, the people who practiced them lost power and eventually were persecuted. Instead of a valued offspring of a religious rite, Mordred is seen as a bastard son.

Medieval Christianity increasingly devalued the flesh, the natural world, sex, and women, and associated darkness with evil. The promise of Camelot, not surprisingly, is the wholeness that can be achieved when mind and body, spirit and matter, men and women, light and dark, are all valued—a potential Bradley sees as resulting from the honoring of both pagan and Judeo-Christian spiritual insights. Much of Judeo-Christian theology today, in one way or another, focuses on reversing this trend—reclaiming both genders, the body, the sacredness of the earth, and the equal worth of both light- and dark-skinned peoples. As theology changes, political, organizational, and psychological theories change as well.

In the workplace today, marginalized workers are unlikely to feel like members of the team or to take psychological ownership of the organization. Moreover, when people feel marginalized, they may not work as hard—seeing work as oppressive rather than as a way to make their cultural contribution. People who cannot get paid for doing work they love feel trapped in their present jobs. When this happens, either they find a way to do their real work outside their forty hours or their creativity turns inward and eats away at them. If they have a great deal of integrity, they still may work very hard, yet their jobs will seem alienating.

Such marginalization operates in the inner as well as the outer world. We might guess that Arthur's denial of his parental feelings not only has alienated Mordred—thus eventually leads to his rebellion—but also must have created a barely repressed civil war within Arthur himself. Undoubtedly that is why he is unable to defeat Mordred. Similarly, Arthur orders Guinevere's execution but cannot carry it out; both his anger and his love are activated. The result is that although Guinevere still lives, she is unavailable to him.

The parts of our psyches that we refuse to acknowledge and express become Shadow selves—then turn on us. Within both the individual psyche and the body politic, the more elements that can be valued, the greater the possibility of peace, prosperity, and ease. Today more and more marginalized people are refusing simply to act in the way they are expected to act. Like Guinevere, they are demanding the right to decide what they really want in life. And, as with Guinevere, these assertions are causing strife. Many people wish everyone would just "behave," so that these problems would disappear. But these problems won't go away. The challenge before us is amore—a love that starts with self-respect and demands truth.

Family systems theory holds that one person can become the "symptom bearer" for the entire family. For this person to get well, the pathology of the family has to be treated. Similarly, when Douglas LaBier worked with "problem" employees, he often found they were carrying symptoms for dysfunctional organizations. These symptoms would not abate until the system was treated, or until they changed jobs and moved into a healthier environment.

Most of us think we can improve our organizations by getting rid of troublemakers, but systems have a way of replicating problems until they are dealt with. A college president at a "Heroes at Work" workshop said to the other participants, "You all are not getting it. Archetypes are real. I used to fire people who were acting out the negative poles of the archetypes, but then other people would just take their place. Until I looked at what was wrong with the system, others would just pop up to take the places of everyone I got rid of." When faculty or staff started "acting out," she stopped trying to get rid of them. Instead, she looked at what energies she was blocking in herself, and then at how she could create a situation where the more positive role of the archetype could be expressed. Seemingly by magic, the faculty then calmed down and did their jobs.

There are many versions of the famous fairy tale in which almost everyone is invited to the princess's birthday party—except for one elderly woman. That woman then casts a spell on the princess, or even on the whole court, causing them to sleep for a hundred years, until a prince cuts through the brambles and awakens them. Whatever or whomever we exclude—in our psyches or in society as a whole—is likely to get angry at being scorned. While the progression from birth to death is natural, the eventual demise of any system is slowed whenever we open it to include more kinds of people, and hence new ideas and energy. (In closed systems, entropy eventually triumphs; open systems are continually rejuvenated by new energy.)

The more homogeneous the mix of people in our organizations, the more comfortable we get—so comfortable, in fact, that more and more parts of our psyche go to sleep. As a result, we become less and less able to respond to new challenges with energy and vigor. We may experience a sense of being jolted awake when we have to work with people who are very different from us. No longer can we assume everything. We have to think all the time—and think in new ways. Suddenly we have to be on our toes, not just going along in the same old ways!

Men's movement leader Warren Farrell (*The Myth of Male Power*) told me that white males feel marginalized and devalued today. Even though their experience appears to define the norm, this does not translate into their feeling fulfilled. In spite of all their seeming advantages, Farrell explained, these men repress their feelings and experience themselves as expendable (dying as soldiers, taking dangerous jobs because they pay more, or, as with high-level executives, working so many hours a day to get ahead that they undermine their health). In their way, he finds them as disadvantaged as women who make lower wages but hold out for cleaner, less dangerous, and more time-delineated work.

Although Farrell's analysis has been used in an unfortunate way—to trivialize and explain away the experience of discrimination ("We all suffer, so we are all equal!")—it has merit when used to increase rather than close off empathy. It tells us that white males cannot be seen in a simpleminded way as the advantaged group. They have issues, too, all the more compelling because they have been taught systematically not to complain.

In the In-Between, everyone feels marginalized and misunderstood. The old ways that still define most organizational and social structures fit no one. Moreover, it is folly to blame one another for what is a systems problem. The issue is not so much who to blame but describing what we now want. The job of the In-Between is to create new systems. Do we want those systems to marginalize and oppress people, or not? The contribution of the water element to the creation of new systems comes from this issue of inclusion: who gets to be part of the new structure? However, if we all feel marginal, we may think we are powerless; changes, we believe, have to come from people who are in the in crowd, at the center of things.

Complexity theorists like Barbara Mossberg would tell us that the very ideas of "center" and "periphery" (and therefore, of "marginality") are anachronistic and hence disempowering. In the modern world, they would say, there is no center. Indeed, in what she calls "round-world thinking," Mossberg argues that every point on the globe has equal claim as the center; similarly, in a world where the fluttering of a butterfly's wing in Tokyo affects the weather in New York, traditional ideas of power and powerlessness may be equally obsolete. In this context, Mossberg differentiates global awareness from internationalism. "Internationalism" emphasizes differences that are construed as problems; "global" emphasizes the whole and the connections that make it up. "The whole" requires interfunctioning of each diverse element. "Actually," she explains, "global awareness requires a new paradigm based on an understanding of the mechanics of interdependence of a 'round world' where 'either/or' polarities and marginality are conceptually illogical. We need to see that diversity is not an antagonist to 'the whole,' and that the relationship of all the elements are crucial. Just as individuals need the different gifts each represents, so too each culture has wisdom humanity needs not only to survive, but thrive."

Mossberg goes on to explain that any viewpoint or curriculum in our newspapers and business books fosters a tragically unnecessary alienation and marginality if it allows the illusion that some peoples are more central and more important to the globe than others. Calling this "flat world thinking," Mossberg cautions that "we cannot formulate realistic policies for a new world if our information excludes the reality of much of the world. If we exclude from our consciousness and study whole segments of people, culture and society—the world itself—we are going to be proceeding on partial data and false premises. We will end up with faulty solutions."

Anthropologist and organizational consultant Gary Ferraro (*The Cultural Dimension of International Business*) gives examples of the catastrophic mistakes American companies make when they try to conduct business worldwide with provincial notions about manners. For example, one group of American businessmen, attempting to put their Japanese hosts at ease, took off their jackets, only to find that what they assumed to be relaxed informality was insulting behavior to the Japanese. In another instance, a North Carolina firm bought a textile machinery company near Birmingham, England. American management was upset because the workers' tea breaks took so long. Noticing that each worker brewed his own tea, management installed a tea vending machine and limited tea breaks to ten minutes. The workers rioted and the plant never went back into production. Think how much more startling the consequences of provincial thinking might be when we are ignorant about weightier matters—like how people find motivation or how they believe people should relate to one another.[14]

Even within our own organizations, cultural differences and feelings of marginality are rampant. Team building and cultural diversity interventions can work to restore community in a pluralistic context (although they can also increase tensions and hurt people if they are not well handled). Consultant Elsie Y. Cross shared with me her technology for team building, with its focus on ameliorating sexism, racism, and other forms of discrimination. Cross explained that injustice to any group has always caused her personal pain. As a child, she learned about the Holocaust and felt acute sadness. As an African American, she has experienced her own problems with discrimination. Asked why she did diversity work, she explained that even when a black female employee has an advanced degree, corporations have difficulty seeing her as executive material. They see a black woman and assume she will do diversity work.

Fortunately, doing such work suits Cross. She finds it miraculous that she can take a diverse group of people away for three days to discuss terribly difficult issues and at the end of the time find not only that they have formed a real community but that each person leaves with higher self-esteem.

Asked how she is able to do this, she said she creates a very safe environment. She believes that discrimination is a by-product of projection. For example, Caucasians have projected onto African Americans the qualities they think are bad and are denying in themselves. To prepare for working with groups, Cross does her inner homework: she recognizes her own less than desirable traits and has compassion for them. Then, not only does she not need to project onto others, but she can have compassion for their less than desirable traits.

In her groups she helps executives identify their company norms and brainstorm about who is advantaged and who is disadvantaged by them. For example, if company norms include 7 A.M. breakfast meetings and 6:30 P.M. wrap-up meetings, what happens to career advancement for working mothers? The male executives find that changing such norms—having meetings at 9 A.M. and 4 P.M.—for the sake of female employees ends up benefiting them too. Then they also can have a family life.

Cross creates a safe environment in which white women, as well as men and women of color, can share their experiences of discrimination with white male executives. Generally, the executives are astounded by the intensity of what they hear. They often do not realize the severity of the harassment and discrimination in their organizations, nor are they aware of how much it disadvantages and wounds employees. Typically, they want to do something about it, but may get hung up on feelings of guilt about being part of a societally favored group or even for acting inadvertently in sexist or racist ways.

Cross has everyone reflect on the messages they have received about what it means to be black or white, male or female. In this context, it becomes clear that we all have been taught to be sexist and racist. It is not our fault that we have these feelings. We are at the cusp of a radical systems change in which we can cast a vote for the future every time we refuse to carry these feelings forward or to act in discriminatory ways. According to Cross, understanding the impact of systems on individuals provides a kind of "secular redemption," so that we do not have to get locked into feeling forever victimized or personally guilty.

She also helps people understand that anytime an individual or a group is marginalized, the organization stops getting their full input. The result is a loss of collective IQ and hence a loss of productivity for the organization. Whether we are dealing with diversity issues or simply group dynamics, the first question anyone typically ponders when entering a group is "Can I be me and fit in?" The more different from others a person feels, the more likely it is that person will repress major parts of his or her personality in order to fit in. Everyone does this to some extent. Good team building helps every group member bring more of his or her abilities and insights to the table, and in this way increases performance.

Cross has worked with teenage gang members who described their experiences in her groups as the first time they ever felt seen and listened to. Some of these tough kids cried as they talked about this. Whether we are concerned with crime in the streets or discrimination in the boardroom, Cross told me, groups, if properly lead, can be magical. For some people, such an experience offers the first (or first workplace) experience of being truly seen as a unique human being.

Needless to say, with this kind of talent Cross has built a large and successful consulting business, specializing in miracles. Her own consulting team practices what they preach, getting to know each other as people, sharing both what is working and what they perceive as hurtful to individual or group performance.

The kind of teamwork Cross is talking about brings amore into the group. In this case, I am not implying the sexual or romantic meaning of amore. Amore also can be a brotherly or sisterly love that involves the meeting of the eyes, where the other's soul is recognized and felt. This means that people bond beyond what it takes to get the job done. They commit not only to doing good work but to knowing other people as complex individuals who live lives as well as earn livings. If you can remember when you last fell in love or even made a good friend, remember how you wanted to know about the other person's life. You felt privileged if he or she was vulnerable enough with you to share hurtful as well as rewarding experiences.

Similarly, when collegial amore enters a work team, members show interest in each other's histories, cultures, and perspectives—irrespective of whether such knowledge is required for the task at hand. When this happens, people stretch so as to empathize with each other's pains as well as celebrate each other's achievements. Whether or not we work in an environment that values individuality in this way, we can open ourselves to an appropriate expression of amore by taking the time to get to know not just what people appear to be but who they really are.

Elsie Cross, looking at me over a table in an elegant restaurant, said pointedly, "Too much emphasis is placed on difference." She and I might look different, she told me, but "we like the same kinds of food, the same kinds of clothes, even the same kinds of jewelry. We most likely enjoy the same movies and books. We are more alike than we are different, if we just take the time to get to know one another."

THE GIFT

Modern team and community building can fulfill the Camelot promise, helping each one of us contribute his or her individuality to the team rather than simply practice "group think." When this occurs, the water element manifests itself not simply as eros but as amore. We then share our unique personal and cultural qualities with others, and welcome the reciprocal learning that results from seeing how they are similar to and different from us.

Margaret Wheatley teaches organizational leaders how to apply the principles of modern science to contemporary management. Many scientists, she notes, have given up the futile search for the ultimate building blocks of matter, concluding that "in the quantum world, relationships are not just interesting . . . they are *all* there is to reality." Just as elemental particles continually change form in relationship to changing conditions and interactions, "none of us exists independent of our relationships with others. Different settings evoke some qualities from us and leave others dormant. In each of these relationships, we are different, new in some way . . . Each of us is a different person in different places. This doesn't make us inauthentic, it merely makes us quantum."[15]

What Wheatley argues here does not deny that we are individuals. It means that we discover the many facets of our individuality only when we allow ourselves to respond to the diversity of relationships possible to us. The more diverse our relationships, the more our own potential is realized and expressed. Diversity in our organizations and in our individual personalities is not a "problem," it is a gift. Without it, we may never question the assumptions and unconscious scripting defined by our socialization and heredity, our gender, our culture, and our particular family of origin. Exposure to cultural diversity at home, like international travel, broadens our own perspectives. As our perspectives expand, we become more magical because we have more options, more ways of thinking and behaving.

Looking at the behavior of water in the natural world, Wheatley asks herself, "What is it, then, streams can teach me about organizations?" As she sits, contemplating a glistening stream by a mountain path in the American Rockies, Wheatley concludes:

This stream has an impressive ability to adapt, to shift the configurations, to let the power balance move, to create new structures . . . Water answers to gravity, to downhill, to the call of the ocean. The forms change, but the mission remains clear. Structures emerge, but only as temporary solutions that facilitate rather than interfere. There is none of the rigid reliance on single forms, on true answers, on past practices that I have learned in business. Streams have more than one response to rocks: otherwise, there'd be no Grand Canyon . . . With sparkling confidence they know that their intense yearning for ocean will be fulfilled, that nature creates not only the call, but the answer.[16]

As Wheatley reminds us, we do not have to cling to a narrow sense of identity ("This is me and I am right"). Quantum physics and the water element invite us to let go and experience multifaceted identities as we allow ourselves to grow and change in a pluralistic, global community.

THE EXERCISES

FOR INDIVIDUALS

- Describe ways or times you have felt marginalized. What was it like? How did you respond?
- In circumstances where you do not feel free to be totally yourself, what positive perspectives or behaviors do you censor? How might such situations improve if you found a way to share what you know?
- With reference to your HMI scores (Appendix B), what archetypes do you censor? What archetypes do you feel free to share? Why?
- Describe positive things you have learned from a person whose culture or race differed from your own? Also note ways you benefit from contributions of groups other than your own. For example, if you are Caucasian, you may have learned meditation from an Asian, or at least from an Asian tradition.
- How might you become more flexible and open to explore other ways to think and behave?

FOR ORGANIZATIONS

- What group sets the norms for your organization? Who seems to benefit from these norms? Who seems disadvantaged by them? What groups or individuals complain of being marginalized, underrepresented, or unheard? What qualities might your organization be missing by the marginalization of these voices? How might these voices be better heard? You might want to bring in a diversity expert to help build a community that values difference and in which no one is marginalized.

- Diagram the organizational influence patterns in your organization. Notice if there are certain groups of people who have less influence—or influence only within their own group. You might have representatives of these groups also draw such charts and compare your findings. Then convene a diverse group to brainstorm solutions.

- Can you recall events when seemingly marginalized groups have had a major effect on the organization— either positively (such as divergent ideas, new perspectives) or negatively (such as low productivity or passive-aggressive behavior)? If the groups affected the organization negatively, low morale as a result of marginality might be a factor to be considered. If positively, what were the preconditions for this success? How were the groups rewarded or reinforced for their contribution?

- How do (or might) your organization's structures and policies be modified to make them more flexible and responsive to human needs?

Circle Five: Claiming Oneness

THE STORY

Mordred wants to marry Guinevere to solidify his reign. For Guinevere, to do this would be a violation of feeling. Therefore, she escapes to a convent, where she devotes the rest of her life to prayer and contemplation. When Lancelot comes to visit her, she convinces him to forswear the active life and become a monk.

Having moved through eros to amore, Guinevere devotes her declining years to agape (altruism, generosity, spiritual love). She atones for the choices she made that hurt others. But her decision is not motivated simply by guilt. Rather, as the British love goddess, she has moved through levels of loving to experience widening spirals of illumination. In her final years her love centers on God and humankind in general, not on any particular person. This is a surprising culmination of her role as May Queen. In identifying with the whole—all people, the cycle of the seasons—Guinevere moves beyond strife, jealousy, and competition to the full flowering of all humanity.

THE LESSON

Magic at Work is not advocating that you join a monastic order to experience agape. Rather, it gives examples of what it means to express consciousness of agape in your everyday life and work. Consciousness of agape shows us that we all are connected and interdependent. What hurts one hurts us all. What helps one helps us all. In fact, if we all are connected, then everyone who is not a success hurts us all! There are no win/lose solutions, only win/win or lose/lose solutions. For example, if some people fail entirely to find and do what they are good at, they may end up on welfare and then the winners pay taxes to support them. Or they may end up on the streets and turn to crime; then the winners live in fear. Or if the most gifted among us are kept from fulfilling their true potential, we may well not have the great art, inventions, and innovations that move society forward. *When each of us gives our gift, we all benefit.*

Magical businesspeople, accordingly, work for win/win options. By helping others, they do well themselves. No one has to lose. In fact, many successful people see their work as a way of caring for people, not besting them; as a way of making a contribution to humankind, not simply as a way of making a living. They do not necessarily call attention to themselves. Most simply take it for granted that any person of integrity would do what they do.

You might not think of real estate as an avenue for higher consciousness. However, real estate agent Liz Winton understands magic, even though she might not talk much about it. Before becoming a real estate agent, she used to help new university faculty members find housing. She did this as a favor to her husband, who was a department chair, but even more so out of a desire to help people. When she decided to go into the real estate business, she kept the same approach she had used when she did it for free. She would get to know the family and match them with the home she thought would make them happiest. Ultimately, her work is about creating community. After she sells you a house, she is likely to introduce you to people she thinks you would like. Of course, people so appreciate her caring, low-key approach to sales that they buy from her. Consequently, she has been able to sell houses consistently, even in the real estate bust of the late 1980s and early '90s.

Love is magical. People are desperate for love. Many individuals in our society are very alone—the only smile they might get during a day comes from a salesperson or coworker. A magical workplace creates more love in the world. If your product or service helps people, it is an act of kindness to make it available to those who need it. This can mean simply selling a product (like a computer or a garden tool) that makes it possible for others to work more efficiently, more quickly, and with more pleasure. It also can mean offering a service (like education or therapy) that develops and empowers people directly. If you are not selling what someone needs, refer them to others. If we all did this, everyone would have plenty of business.

John, an advertising executive, used to write ad copy that sold products by appealing to people's fears—that they would have bad breath or dandruff, miss a deadline or lose their job, or fail to get the girls. He understood that fear is a powerful motivator. He made money, but he did not feel good about himself. When he realized that he was working longer hours than were healthy, and drinking too much coffee in the morning and too many cocktails in the evening, he asked himself why. The answer surprised him. He realized that in spite of his rather cynical demeanor, it bothered him terribly that what he did reinforced people's fears and manipulated them into a cycle of consumerism that eventually decreased the genuine satisfaction of their lives. The gnawing emptiness that grabbed at him from within matched exactly the emptiness he was fostering—by encouraging people to substitute things for genuine experiences.

For a while he thought he needed to change jobs. He considered the ministry but finally realized he could stay in advertising. The issue was not so much what he did but, rather, the level of consciousness that defined how he did it. After a rough jobless period, he began freelancing. Now he writes copy only for products and services he believes in, and he motivates people by appealing to their higher instincts—for example, advertising that promotes good-quality insurance by portraying a man's love for his family, or telephone services by reminding us of the importance of keeping in touch with those we love. He makes enough money (although less than he did before), does community service on the side, and says he would have made the change even if it had required a greater financial sacrifice. His overall level of prosperity now includes not simply what he has in his bank account but, more important, a warm feeling inside where the emptiness had been.

Susan, a high school teacher, once motivated students by lambasting them for their laziness and stupidity. She began every semester by telling them that only a certain percentage could make A's and that some definitely would fail. She thought the more students she failed, the better and more rigorous a teacher she was. She went to a Total Quality Management educator's training course, which caused her to rethink her position. She realized that the idea of scarcity was built into the concept of the bell-shaped curve. Her belief that ability and motivation were scarce *made* them scarce, since the students who got D's and F's inevitably came to believe that they were dumb and inferior. Soon they would cover that belief by pretending to themselves and others that they did not care—and eventually would act out, drop out, or dope out.

Today Susan begins her semesters with a more loving stance—and a commitment to developing all her students. She now sees her primary job as lighting the lamp of each student's love of learning. Actually, she sees herself as "relighting" their lamps, for loving to learn is natural to children. (Even the A and B students lose out in most schools because their natural love of learning is supplanted by a desire to be better than others, to learn for extrinsic, not intrinsic, rewards.) Susan now is happier because she leads with love and because she is more successful (even though she still complains that she is not yet successful with everyone). Her students are happier not only because they are achieving at a level they never thought possible but also because they are turned on to learning again. Finally, both teacher and students are coming to realize that scarcity is not a necessary part of life. Indeed, if every employee and every citizen developed his or her full potential, there would be no problems with national competitiveness—and no real limits to our prosperity.

Consultant and teacher James Gregory Lord shows eager professionals in nonprofit organizations ways to move from a scarcity to a prosperity consciousness in the field of philanthropy. Cautioning against the scarcity thinking encoded in the word "fund-raising," as it is currently used, he tells fundraisers not to erroneously see their jobs as getting money. "When they do, they end up trying to convince someone to give them something either because they are needy and desperate (Orphan archetype) or because they win a battle of wills (Warrior archetype) and talk the donor out of his or her money."

Lord suggests imagining the goal not as raising money but as releasing the philanthropist within people. This means the role of the fund-raiser is to bring out the most altruistic attributes in others. The magic formula for doing so emphasizes reciprocal and interdependent relationships. Too often, Lord says, a potential donor is "seduced and abandoned." The fund-raiser spends infinite time wooing the donor until he or she writes the check—and then disappears until the need for more money arises.

Some fund-raisers say they do not want to have relationships with the kinds of people they feel they have to court for money. Lord emphasizes that "there is plenty of money out there," and advises his clients, "You do not have to seek money from people you do not respect. Seek relationships with people who share your values and whom you would like to spend time with—who also have the financial capability to invest in your project. Seek their counsel before you seek their money. If your mission is consistent with their vision, and they invest their time in an ongoing relationship with you, they are likely to invest their money as well. If you share a dream, and they have the money and you have the expertise to make it happen, synergy occurs."

Says Lord, " 'Investors' want a return, but not a financial one. The return they expect is your fidelity to making your shared dream come true. Moreover, the greater the emotional involvement of the prospective investor, and the longer the duration of that involvement, the larger the investment is likely to be." If relationships with investors are respected and well maintained, he promises, fund-raisers do not even have to ask for the money. When investors see their values, aspirations, and dreams reflected in a vision of the future that benefits the community or society, they often ask, "How much is it going to cost to make this happen?" Then one donor will go on to invite another, first demonstrating his own commitment through making an exemplary pledge.

"It's not a question of telling or selling anyone," suggests Lord, "but simply inviting him or her to join you in doing something you both feel good about—and that you both feel is important. Your own actions speak more eloquently and persuasively than any advice you can give. And so 'invite by example, not advice.' " In this sense, what is commonly called fund-raising becomes a journey of magical and heroic proportions. The donor commits to a philanthropic investment, finds it to be a meaningful experience, and will return to tell another and help the other take the journey. When this heroic donor thus shares the convictions that inspired him or her to make a transformative commitment, a powerful magnetic field of attraction is formed. The first person's rite of passage is an example to others. Lord says, "We want to walk in the door to see the potential donor with the wind at our backs and the ballast in our souls that comes from knowing that we're engaged in something bigger than ourselves—that we're connected to, and part of, a greater idea, a greater good, a greater power than the mere physical body that walks through the doorway."

"Is this about money?" he goes on to ask. "It's about something much larger than money." In this process, we give donors a way to bring their behavior into line with their values and to take a stand and make a public declaration of what they value—"Yes, this is what I want my life to have been about." This is what Lord calls the philanthropic quest—the ethos, even urge, each of us carries inside us that longs to get out and express our "love of humanity" (*phil-anthro-py*).

The opportunity for self-realization and connection that we bring to the donor may be greater than what the donor brings to us, says Lord. "For what the donor receives is the opportunity to speak with you of deep and important things . . . to find meaning . . . to know, in the heart, that he or she is making a difference . . . making magic happen." Philanthropy is about relationships between people and the connection they can have with an idea—a common pursuit that emerges from their hearts and connects them as few human experiences can do.

Raising investment capital for a business is similar to attracting philanthropy, as long as you believe in what you're doing—except investors expect a financial return as well as a sense of making a contribution to something worth doing. Either way, relationships create prosperity.

Magical marketing is similarly client- or customer-centered and relationship-driven. Anytime you feel called to provide a particular product or service, the first question you might answer is "Who needs it?" If no need exists for what you want to do, then you might want to rethink your goals. Prosperity results from anticipating and then satisfying genuine needs—that is, if you also have the self-esteem to tell your own story in a compelling way. Finding ways to get the word out about why your own product or service is critical to your customers and to society is, of course, also important.

An attitude of agape motivates you to provide quality products and services for people—ones that will enrich their lives. It also protects against the temptation to develop and promote products that could harm or exploit them. Agape also may include a love for yourself that is not self-indulgent but, rather, based on an appreciation of your own integrity and value.

Long-term prosperity comes from creating a community of support for yourself and your business. When you care about the quality of your product or service and about your customers, you get repeat business and the ripple effect of referrals from satisfied customers. If you practice worthy values, people respect you, and you respect yourself. You therefore feel more worthy of success.

Everyone these days is telling you to be client-, customer-, or student-centered—but not necessarily sharing the secret for doing so. It is, of course, possible to act as if you care even when you do not, merely for personal gain. That is, you can do so for a while. But to maintain a caring attitude over the long haul, it is best that your concern for others be genuine.

The funny part is that we all do care. Learning agape is simply a matter of unlearning all the blocks to normal, healthy feeling. Therefore, the more we access our own real feelings, the easier it is to be caring. Little children do not naturally walk by someone dying on the street without showing concern. This kind of ability to block out another's pain is a learned behavior, and it also is possible to unlearn it. In fact, doing so is the challenge of our time.

THE GIFT

Agape literally means "a love feast," where there is plenty for everyone. Love helps us prosper as we make the world a better place for everyone. It helps us understand that we are all one. The prosperity we gain, therefore, is multidimensional: the appreciation of those we serve and the self-respect that comes from knowing that what we do and how we do it matter. Once an attitude of agape has been awakened in us, if we were able to make millions from doing something that was harmful to others, we would not feel abundant; in fact, we would feel awful. Moreover, agape helps us care about community and about seeing that everyone is included in some way. Agape helps us understand that everyone has something to contribute that can enhance our collective prosperity. As President Bill Clinton put it, "We do not have a person to waste."

Senior Foreign Service Officer Anne Gurvin of the U.S. Information Agency uses the understanding that agape breeds abundance to meet the ongoing challenges of representing the United States in a new country every three years. As U.S. Cultural Attaché to the Netherlands, for example, she countered limited stereotypes about the United States by turning the embassy into a dynamic exhibit of the best in U.S. art, by bringing in major U.S. speakers for seminars, and by working closely with U.S. and Dutch leaders to double the Fulbright budget and to create prestigious Fulbright chairs, such as the John Adams Visiting Scholar in American Civilization and the George C. Marshall Fellowships in Trade and the Media. In Sweden she worked with Swedish publishers to present a series of U.S. writers such as Toni Morrison, William Styron, E. L. Doctorow, and Joyce Carol Oates, who discussed their creative work. Gurvin believes in bringing people and state-of-the-art knowledge together in order to develop and work toward shared goals. She utilizes the richness of cultural diversity and complexity to stimulate innovation in achieving those goals.

In her managerial style, she incorporates aesthetic principles as well as efficiency in making office layout changes to create an environment that nurtures innovation and excellence, in creating computer templates and macros to customize quality paperwork that speaks to the mind and the heart, and in designing protocols for visiting U.S. speakers and performers that provide memorable experiences—predictably, every time. For her, diplomacy is an art that helps people learn how to understand and trust one another—across cultures—so that they find it easier to cooperate not only as individuals but as nations.

Knowing that substantive results come from integrating the unique talents available in people, she "operates a flat hierarchy workplace, coaching for solid results in partnership with my staff." Gurvin energizes her staff in a team search for excellence and innovation in public service by telling them: "You will work harder than you have ever worked before, but you will look back on this time as a "Golden Age" in your life. You will have the joy of knowing that you are contributing to better mutual understanding between our two countries—and you will blossom as a person while doing it. We will all be moving together in a new direction, stretching our minds, drawing upon all of our talents, utilizing Total Quality Management (TQM). We will not only promote the importance of democracy and human rights in our public programs; we will work in democratic partnership in the office—working together as a team to create, implement, and constantly improve our public service programs. We want to be innovative, efficient, and effective."

Gurvin actively seeks out the most interesting and talented people she can find in each new country to build international program partnerships with her. Through "building informal cross-cultural working teams of interdisciplinary leaders and experts throughout the country," she exponentially increases results by enlarging the talent pool available to her. In doing so, she employs a process that itself increases cross-cultural understanding. As further evidence of abundance rather than scarcity thinking, she considers her embassy budget as seed money only, establishing partnerships with private foundations and corporate CEOs to co-fund and develop her international educational and cultural exchange programs.

Gurvin believes the "butterfly effect" is found not only in chaos theory but also in the field of diplomacy. Peace, she assured me, begins with each of us, and it is by working in concert with others that it can spread worldwide. World peace and economic prosperity result from building better mutual understanding and cooperation in an increasingly interdependent world.

Such awareness combines a respect for different cultural contributions with a recognition of radical interdependence: we all live in one world. We can arrive at this conclusion through a logical, analytical, scientific process, as Gurvin does, or, like mystics and poets more typically do, by a life-changing epiphany.

For some, agape is experienced in a visceral way. In Alice Walker's *The Color Purple*, Shug, the character who most directly expresses the author's vision, describes an experience of oneness with the world during which she felt that "if I cut a tree, my arm would bleed."[17] For many, like Guinevere, this sense of oneness arises from a mystic sense of union with God. Mystic and theologian Julian of Norwich wrote these lines in the fourteenth century:

The Love of God makes such a unity
in us
that when we see this unity
no one is able to separate oneself
from another.[18]

However we describe this understanding, it cannot *not* affect our politics and the way we conduct business. In this century, civil rights leader the Reverend Martin Luther King, Jr., summed up the wisdom of illumination by saying, "It really boils down to this: that all life is interrelated. We are all caught in an inescapable network of mutuality, tied into a single garment of destiny. Whatever affects one directly, affects all indirectly."[19]

THE EXERCISES

FOR INDIVIDUALS

- What are some ways that you contribute to making the world a better place—in your paid work, in work at home, and/or in community service? Are there any ways that your work is harming others? If so, what might be done about that?
- In the work you do, how might you move out of an us/ them, separated mentality to do what you do for the greater good? Describe the us/them, win/lose way to do your work? Then describe the win/win, abundant approach. Pay attention to how this would affect your relationships with other employees and with your customers.
- Have you ever had an experience of oneness with nature, God, or other people? What was that like? How would you act differently if you kept that awareness with you all the time?

FOR ORGANIZATIONS

- How does your organization contribute to the greater good of society? Are there any ways its actions are harmful? If so, what might be done about that?
- Describe what it would be like if you really took seriously the idea that all the people in your organization mattered. How would you communicate to them their importance? How would this affect company policies, training, and structure?
- What does it mean to take a customer-centered approach to your organization's work? How would this affect your policies? Your training? Your advertising? Your structure?

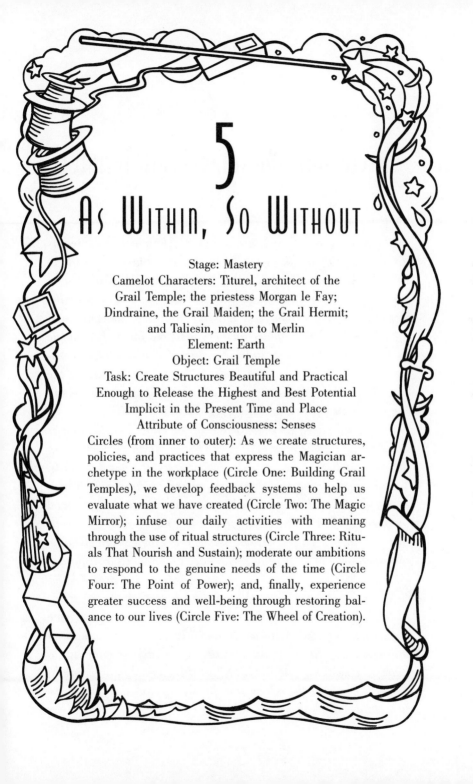

5
As Within, So Without

Stage: Mastery
Camelot Characters: Titurel, architect of the
Grail Temple; the priestess Morgan le Fay;
Dindraine, the Grail Maiden; the Grail Hermit;
and Taliesin, mentor to Merlin
Element: Earth
Object: Grail Temple
Task: Create Structures Beautiful and Practical
Enough to Release the Highest and Best Potential
Implicit in the Present Time and Place
Attribute of Consciousness: Senses

Circles (from inner to outer): As we create structures, policies, and practices that express the Magician archetype in the workplace (Circle One: Building Grail Temples), we develop feedback systems to help us evaluate what we have created (Circle Two: The Magic Mirror); infuse our daily activities with meaning through the use of ritual structures (Circle Three: Rituals That Nourish and Sustain); moderate our ambitions to respond to the genuine needs of the time (Circle Four: The Point of Power); and, finally, experience greater success and well-being through restoring balance to our lives (Circle Five: The Wheel of Creation).

Circle One: Building Grail Temples

THE STORY

At the age of fifty, Titurel, grandfather of Percival, is visited by an angel who tells him to dedicate the remainder of his life to the building of a Grail Temple. As he works, the Grail hovers over the building and magically provides food to sustain the workers. When the temple is finished, the Grail descends and makes its home in the place lovingly prepared for it. The temple incorporates "the circle and the square," symbolic representations of heaven and earth, as well as "archetypal images of the masculine and feminine, so that the circle of the heavens and the square of earth unite in a single image."

The temple itself is a microcosm of the cosmos—the dome is the sky; the crystal floor is decorated with images of swimming fish; the walls are decorated with carvings of trees and birds. Within the building is a miniature replica of the temple, which is where the Grail resides. Built on a mountain and surrounded by deep water, the Grail Temple can be entered only by traveling a sharply edged bridge, known as the Sword Bridge, and then only by individuals who have experienced transformation.

When Titurel completes the building of the temple, he seems to be no more than forty years old, although he really is more than four hundred. His energy and his youth have increased miraculously. In compliance with the Grail's command to marry, he weds the pious and beautiful Richoude, daughter of a Spanish king. In their long and happy life together they have two children, a son and a daughter.[1]

THE LESSON

The stage of the journey associated with the creation of the Grail Temple is mastery—that is, expressing magical consciousness in concrete forms. It is not enough for Guinevere to talk about equality: she has to bring the Round Table to Camelot so that people sitting around it will feel equal. Arthur does not just reassure people that they are safe: the Lady of the Lake must provide Excalibur to ensure his invincibility. Merlin cannot just tell people to seek enlightenment; the Grail has to appear to make the invitation tangible. Similarly, it is not enough for Titurel to yearn for the Grail to descend to earth: he must build a temple beautiful enough for the sacred to inhabit. And it is not enough to find your grail. Mastery is demonstrated when we express magical consciousness in the real-world structures of our own lives and work.

Titurel, who was Percival's grandfather, illustrates the primary attribute of mastery by expressing the wisdom of the Grail in concrete form (Circle One). Other Camelot characters illustrate the supporting circles of mastery. Arthur's sister, the priestess Morgan le Fay, uses the magic mirror of enchantment to provide feedback that helps Camelot characters learn from their mistakes (Circle Two). Dindraine, the Grail Maiden and Percival's sister, employs ritual to imbue their lives with a sense of meaning and value (Circle Three). The Grail Hermit guards the Grail until it is time for Camelot to be created, thus demonstrating the humility, care for detail, and sense of timing necessary to eventual success (Circle Four). And finally, Merlin's mentor, Taliesin, shows Merlin how to use the Wheel of Creation to restore magic to life in the In-Between.

Mastery requires that we be steady, grounded, and practical. Chiropractor Denise Conner talked to me about the importance to her own work of the image of the Magician in the ancient tarot deck. In this classic pose, the Magician holds one hand up and the other down. To Conner, this image is a

THE MAGICIAN

reminder "to open ourselves to inspiration, yet stay grounded in the concrete, manifest in the world." This visual image also sums up the wisdom of mastery, where the Magician reaches up for vision and then "draws the power down" to realize that vision in the world. Magic is not airy-fairy, "pie in the sky." Master Magicians are empiricists, routinely testing theory in everyday practice to see what works. If the outcome is less than magical, they revise or refine the theory until it is.

The most common phrase used by people interviewed for this book was "walk your talk." While most of us know the importance of action congruent with belief, in the In-Between we take many anachronistic structures for granted. We believe in being ecological but simply accept many of the habits of a throwaway society. In business we may believe in the worth of each person but assume the necessity of inflexible, hierarchical structures that tend to treat people as if they were replaceable cogs in a machine.

We are so used to living with separation between our ideals and workplace forms that we take it for granted. Whenever vision and structure come in conflict, structure always wins! For example, in today's research universities lip service is given to teaching, but rewards tend to be tied to publication. What do you think professors will emphasize? Businesspeople talk about developing learning organizations where employees continually expand their horizons and abilities; but when the budget crunch comes, training programs are the first to go.

Many problems in the business world that are viewed as personality clashes, or even as personal incompetence, really are structural at their root. For example, an administrator at a nonprofit organization, Susan, was ecstatic when she was brought on as codirector of a project with a man she admired. Yet George had been there much longer and wanted to be in charge. His superiors told him (to please him) that he was the senior member of the team. Her superiors told her (to please her) that she and George were on an equal footing. Needless to say, in spite of the fact that they liked and respected each other, George and Susan quarreled all the time. He thought she was pushy, unreasonable, and disrespectful. She thought he was sexist and insecure. The board of directors of the organization failed to take responsibility for setting up an ambiguous structure that doomed them to failure. Instead, the board chair told them to work out their personal problems with each other. Fortunately, George and Susan were intelligent people and diagnosed the problem correctly as a structural one. When the board refused to clarify the terms of the codirectorship, they took things in hand and did so themselves, each taking the lead in the area where he or she had particular experience and expertise.

Mastery requires that the forms of our work reflect its spirit. Poetry precedes history. Only now are we able to live out the potential that is expressed poetically in the Camelot stories. The layout of the Grail Temple tells us, in metaphorical language, what magical organizations are like. First of all, they are neither profit- nor customer-driven. The Grail itself supervises the construction of the Grail Temple and nourishes the Templars (those building it). The magical organization is inspiration-driven. Findhorn, a magical community in Scotland, is famous for growing enormous vegetables in sand. The group's social accomplishment—creating a loving and harmonious community—also attracts visitors from around the world. At Findhorn, not only do the residents pray and meditate every day, asking for divine inspiration, but they also commune with the plant spirits, which help them know what the crops need.

If the center of the magical organization is the grail (ether), balance comes from the other four elements: "air" means that the organization is always changing and growing (that it is a learning organization); "fire," that it focuses on flexible and achievable goals; "water," that it responds to the needs of employees, investors, and customers; and "earth," that structures contain and nurture the other elements rather than working against them.

The earth element presides over physical structures as well as workplace systems. In today's workplace we often fail to appreciate the impact on our morale and sense of well-being of our very surroundings. The beauty of the Grail Temple is stressed in these Grail stories. The mountain on which it is built consists of onyx. The vaulting is made of blue sapphires. At the center is an emerald plate. The altar stones are sapphires, and the sun and moon are represented on the ceiling by diamonds and topazes. The sacred, Titurel understood, is attracted by beauty.

Psychoanalyst James Hillman says that people today can be in therapy, go to church, participate in team building at work, and still be incredibly unhappy because our "buildings are anorexic," our "language is schizogenic," and "normalcy is manic." How can we be happy he asks, in rooms with "low ceilings" and "hollow doors," where the settings of our lives are "brutish, ugly, cheap, shoddy, vicious—without soul at all"? He suggests that instead of blaming each other when things go wrong, we see that the structures in which we live have become pathological.[2] If we want to stop crime in the streets, he says, we need to plant gardens. If we want families and relationships to work, we need beautiful homes. If we want a sense of meaning and value in our work, we must make beauty a priority in the workplace.

Psychoanalyst Thomas Moore concurs, arguing that beauty is important to every aspect of our work lives: "When we think of work, we only consider function, and so the soul elements are left to chance. Where there is no artfulness about life, there is a weakening of soul. It seems to me that the problem with modern manufacturing is not a lack of efficiency, it is a loss of soul." Beauty invites soul in.[3]

In many indigenous magical traditions, energy is drawn down from the sky and up from the earth through the creation of a medicine wheel. The medicine man or woman conducts deeply meaningful and beautiful ceremonies, drawing a circle to create sacred space and invoking the elements of air, fire, water, and earth in the corresponding four directions: east, south, west, and north. The center (the place of ether) is where it all comes together—where the sacred is invoked from above and below.[4]

The medicine wheel forms a container in which all the elements can be in balance. Placing the elements in the four directions and the center helps the medicine man or woman get grounded in the natural world—to know where he or she is in space and time.

The attitude inspired by the medicine wheel is one of partnership, not dominance. It helps us recognize that we are not above the natural world, or each other, but in ongoing partnerships. When I was in Sante Fe, New Mexico, on a recent visit, I learned that John Calvin, a prominent Albuquerque builder, made it a practice to sleep on a plot of land before he built a house in order to find out what kind of building the land wanted. If we can imagine ourselves in partnership with the earth, it certainly is possible to imagine partnership ways of relating with one another. Thus, in many contemporary organizations, hierarchical organizational charts are being supplanted by circular ones, as participatory management replaces models of control and dominance.

Global partnerships also lead to breakthrough forms, as the gifts of different cultures synergistically merge to form new and exponentially more advanced structures. Organizational consultant Bob Marshak spoke to me about his interest in Asian five-element systems. Confucian culture, he noted, believed in a cyclical model of change, moving through the Chinese five elements but emphasizing harmony and balance, not progress. Western culture, on the other hand, is progress-oriented and sees change in linear terms, as proceeding from one state, through a transition, into another state. Identifying the Western model as not only masculine but phallic and the Eastern model as feminine and womblike, Marshak noted that an integrative and androgynous form is the spiral. Where progress and balance both are valued, we get a model of truly transformative change.

A CASE STUDY

Leaders who embody the gifts of the earth element are practical and tough-minded. They may enjoy theorizing, but for them the bottom line is "Does it work?" They excel in creating and developing structures that support people in their work. Without this earth element, people can be very ethical, caring, and imaginative, but their efforts dissipate and come to noth-

THE MYSTICAL MARRIAGE

When the Grail Temple is complete, Titurel marries. Why? As with everything else in the Camelot stories, marriage has a symbolic as well as a literal meaning. In *Collection*, family systems therapist Shirley Gehrke Luthman speaks of the intuitive, receptive part of the psyche as the "feminine." The more aggressive "masculine" part, she explains, acts in the service of the feminine—taking the vision and making it a reality.[5] The ancient alchemical image of the androgynous monarch has a feminine side holding a wand (for vision) and a masculine side holding a sword (for action). Images of androgyny recur throughout the Camelot story, with different foci for different elements. The androgyny of air is embodied by Merlin, with his prophetic consciousness of the seer, and by Queen Ganieda, who creates the conditions for nurturing the vision and keeping it safe. The androgyny of fire is represented by the Ship Draped in Silk, the wisdom of Solomon, and the political acuity of his wife. The androgyny of ether is illustrated by Percival's seeking the Grail (striving) and Dindraine's embodying it (being). The androgyny of water is represented by the Round Table, where masculine bonding based on competence within roles is complemented by feminine bonding based on love. The androgyny of earth is shown by the squared circle within the Grail Temple and also by Titurel's marriage. This marriage symbolizes two metaphors for the creative process: Titurel is a builder and Richoude gives birth.

ing. Proper systems are needed to help them implement their good ideas.

Before taking their journeys, leaders who emphasize the practical, commonsense virtues of the earth element tend toward conventionality. Sydney Martin, CEO of Sydron Corporation, is an exemplar of earth. As a young man, he believed what he had been taught: that a man's job was primarily to make money to support his family, and that that was how he expressed love for his wife and children. Martin had an aptitude for figures so he got an MBA from Columbia University and started a financial management company in the real estate business. He did extremely well. In fact, he became quite wealthy—until the real estate bust of the late 1980s.

As he struggled to keep his company afloat, Martin experienced a modern equivalent of the Sword Bridge (where transformation occurs on the way to the Grail Temple). His imagination (air) was stimulated as he diversified his company and, in the process, kept it going much longer than those of his chief competitors. He also increased his people skills, learning from a consultant how to help his team cope with change (water). As a result, his team worked wonderfully together during the business's difficult last years; in fact, Martin looks back at that time with some fondness. Nevertheless, this experience *was* a trial by fire. Although he persisted steadfastly (fire), he lost the business and his marriage at roughly the same time, spawning a complete change in his life and his values. He awakened to a spiritual life (ether) and realized that he wanted real intimacy with family and friends. He was not willing just to play the role of the good provider. Like many others today who have discarded cookie-cutter lives, Martin decided to re-create his life to reflect the truth about who he is.

Martin realized that although he was good at financial management, what he really cared about was people. He therefore returned to school and earned a master's degree in social work. However, people he cared about kept calling on him to use his financial management skills to help them out. He found that he did not want to let them down. He also recognized that many workplace innovations stumble because they do not have the backing of the financial people.

As with many who make an initially drastic midlife change,

in his current work Martin integrates the best of his youthful career decisions with his more mature ones. While he is as realistic as always, he now has a more complex view of what reality is. He helps business leaders understand that change is the only constant. If they do not face this, he says, they are living an illusion. The earth itself is always changing. Mountains exist in former seabeds. Sometimes, as with earthquakes and volcanoes, natural change is even sudden. We fool ourselves if we think workplace structures can be solid and unchanging—especially in the In-Between.

According to Martin, most executives know they have risen to the top because they have fulfilled a particular need. Therefore, they tend to fight change because they believe it might make them obsolete. However, success today cannot be predicated on an illusion. In the In-Between, mastery requires that one be comfortable with constant change—and hence be flexible and open to growth and development. Financial structures, then, must provide support for change, not stasis.

Although enlightened people today understand that change is the only constant, most financial management approaches still control or block innovation. In too many companies, Martin explains, financial planning is centralized and based on history. Units are given a set amount of money and are expected to say how they will spend it and then to stick with the plan. Of course, he adds, "this breeds insanity. As conditions change, people still follow an outdated plan, since they will get a negative evaluation if they depart from it."

Instead, Martin helps companies institute flexible financial planning that grows out of recurring discussions held in the actual offices where the money will be spent—and made. Employees are asked what new opportunities they see on the horizon and how much money they need to respond to them. This gives rise to budget discussions that weigh the relative merits of different proposals and then fund the best of them. Although units are given a budget for the year, they are ex-

pected to depart from their plan when new opportunities are identified. For this reason, budget reviews are held every month to determine how things are going, as well as to celebrate innovative departures from the plan.

The idea that people have separate personal and professional lives, Martin says, is another illusion. People just have lives. When they come to work, they bring their whole selves: their problems and their dreams. They go to work partly for the sake of achievement and earning a living, but also for social life—even to find a date or a mate. Employee assistance programs were the first step in recognizing that we have real individuals in the workplace, but these programs have focused only on people's problems. Martin says that for an organization to be constantly open to change and new opportunities, its leaders should realize that people who bring their evolving dreams and aspirations to work are better equipped to see such opportunities. Instead of trying to keep employees' private and personal lives separate, enlightened managers should be trying to get the whole person back into the workplace.

Recognizing the seamlessness of our personal and professional lives allows managers to anticipate that requiring inhumanly long hours of workers on an ongoing basis (without balancing downtime) will boomerang. Employees are people, not machines. If their health, morale, and families fail, the company will be hit with lower productivity, higher benefits costs, and, eventually, higher taxes (to alleviate the social problems it helped cause).

Martin also sees folly in the illusion of organizational separateness, for example, in the way different parts of an organization tend to be split off from one another as if they were truly distinct. Higher organizational functioning comes from increased information flow. Every department needs to understand overall priorities and have a role in setting them. Moreover, in addition to the evaluative measures that better organizations today have adopted to guarantee the quality of the product and of customer service, Martin sets up feedback loops that help organizations know how their internal customers are faring. For example, most organizations have some kind of employee assistance program, but few ever do anything with the information it provides. Martin helps companies use this feedback (with appropriate protection of confidentiality) to determine whether any training interventions are needed or identify any management problems that should be addressed. For example, if a large number of employees are complaining of harassment or of discrimination, the company can intervene *before* it gets sued!

Although he believes that these are the right actions, Martin does not advocate them merely because they are right. Rather, he knows that doing otherwise is bad business. Mastery in the modern world depends on seeing accurately what is: no one who is in denial can do magic! Martin gets excited as he talks about how magical business can be when people stop fighting reality and work with it: this means working with change, and accepting and even celebrating humanness instead of trying to get people to perform like machines.

THE GIFT

Leaders evidencing mastery create structures that can release the highest potential in individuals, groups, and situations because they reflect powerful archetypal patterns. Rather than following anachronistic control and dominance models of leadership, such leaders get more done by empowering others. Barry Fulton, director of the new Bureau of Information at the United States Information Agency, shared with me an inclusive process of "reinventing government" wherein his bureau was created out of the ashes of the old—even as the budget and personnel were being slashed.

Fulton, a wonderfully humble man, shared his surprise at the way synchronicity (or, as he put it, "coincidences") had shaped his career. Talking with him, it was clear to me that

the magic that informed his life came from within—his curiosity, openness, engagement with people and the task at hand.
When I asked him about his "grail," he said his efforts were
inspired by a deep and abiding concern for fairness and justice. As a leader in the reinventing government effort, he exemplified unself-conscious magic.

To meet the immense challenge he faced, Fulton set up task
forces that determined where cuts were to occur and how the
bureau would be reorganized. In doing so, he threw out old
hierarchical "business as usual" models and with them the
remnants of Cold War (I'd say, Warrior) thinking. Instead of
using information as an ally in a power struggle, agency members now see themselves as spreading the information and
expertise needed to build democratic structures and promote
reform in other countries—including those of the former Soviet Union. Win/win solutions, Fulton explained, strengthen
the world economy and keep the peace.

The process Fulton put in place assumed that the old military, hierarchical organizational paradigm was anachronistic.
His agency broke down us/them expectations by having management and union leaders co-chair its reinventing government teams. Fulton did not try to control the outcome in any
way. As with many magical leaders today, he sculpted the
process of managing change but let go of trying to control its
outcome. Instead, he put his faith in the synergy of task force
groups and in the integrity and intelligence of the people involved. Asked to describe his leadership strengths, he emphasized his trust in people and their tendency to rise to the level
of his expectations.

Experience has shown me that when such processes are put
in place—and when people are trusted to bring their highest
and best instincts to a particular task—magic emerges spontaneously. Therefore, I was prepared for Fulton to tell me that
his task forces had drawn up organizational charts that had
circles emanating from the center rather than ones that
showed the old vertical hierarchical ladders. Even I was taken

aback, however, when Fulton pulled out an organizational chart in the shape of a medicine wheel—in fact, one virtually identical with the magic circle described in *Magic at Work*. In the center his team had placed management. To the north they had placed geographically related projects (earth); to the east, issues-oriented programs (air); to the south, all the programs that kept them on task, such as training, accounting, and evaluation (fire); to the west, resource personnel, that is, those providing products and services to support the rest (water). I told Fulton about medicine wheels and asked him if he or anyone else on the team knew about them. He said no. The members of the team had just come up with this diagram by thinking of what made the most sense for their division.

Magic is natural and archetypal. When the Warrior archetype was dominant, people drew organizational charts hierarchically. Now that the Magician is entering our consciousness, charts tend to be drawn as circles, with management envisioned as in the center, not at the top. The medicine wheel diagram also is being used today because it corresponds to the mandala, a symbol of archetypal wholeness that emerges spontaneously as people begin to become whole. Thus, individuals who have taken their journeys evidence mastery by unselfconsciously revising workplace structures to correspond to their inner realities.

The balance of this chapter elaborates on the ways in which the emergence of the Magician archetype is affecting, or can affect, many of the structures that support our work. Circle One has focused on how we can regain structural alignment with the spiritual and natural truths within us. Circles Two to Five refine our appreciation of structure by teaching us about feedback, ritual, timing, and integration. Unlike the earlier chapters, each of which explores one major character's journey, Chapter Five discusses a series of minor characters, each of whom has an important relationship to the Grail. They are the sorceress Morgan le Fay; Dindraine, the Grail Maiden; the Grail Hermit; and Taliesin, Merlin's teacher. In a chapter devoted to the gift of the humble element, earth, it is appropriate that we focus on characters who are not as visible or as well remembered as Merlin, Arthur, the knights, or Guinevere, but whose quiet mastery make the Camelot story possible.

THE EXERCISES

FOR INDIVIDUALS

- Pay attention to your habits at work. To what degree do they allow you to flow with change?
- How much of yourself do you bring to the workplace? Who or what keeps you from being whole in that setting?
- Is your physical environment comfortable, efficient, and beautiful? Does your soul feel fed by what is around you? If not, what in your environment do you have the power to change?
- In a journal, dialogue with your dominant archetypes from the HMI (Appendix B). How are they, or how would they like to be, expressed in the ways you do your work or structure your environment? Ask them questions and allow them to respond to you in writing. (You can also do this orally by talking to yourself in a mirror, taking, in turn, the parts of the different archetypes.)

FOR ORGANIZATIONS

- Examine the shape of your organizational chart. Is it linear, circular, spiral, or other? What kind of energy flow is encouraged by this shape? Is it congruent with the mission and values of your organization?
- Which organizational structures and policies make work easier? Which ones impede work flow?
- Is your workplace safe, comfortable, efficient, and beautiful? How could the organization allow for more soul in its physical environment?

Circle Two: The Magic Mirror

THE STORY

Morgan le Fay, taught by Merlin and the great priestesses of the magical Isle of Avalon (otherwise known as the Isle of Apples), was a great sorceress. Nevertheless, she often is portrayed as villainess for her role as a tester of aspirants (few of us are willing to recognize our own falseness). Morgan honors the Grail by weaving enchantments to teach people to see through illusions. She tests Arthur by luring him to the Ship Draped in Silk (Circle Three, Chapter II). The Grail quest is a test of valor. Celtic tradition is full of testing cups. The testing cup of Mamannan in Echtra Cormaic, for example, shatters when three lies are said over it, but it reunites when three truths are said. Morgan's tests are designed to see if the Camelot characters are being true to the Grail, or whether their commitment is illusory, shattering when tested.

However, Morgan also is a healer through her commitment to truth. When Arthur is wounded in his final battle, it is Morgan who takes him by barge to her home on the Isle of Avalon to minister to his wounds. Some legends tell us that there she becomes his mate, until it is again time for him to reappear and rule once more. In contrast to Guinevere, who is the May Queen, Morgan is the priestess associated with All Hallows' Eve and its mystical connection with the dead and the otherworld. Her example helps identify and lets go of illusions and behavior unworthy of our best selves.[6]

THE LESSON

Bob Marshak told me that to help him in his organizational consulting, he has studied the attention-managing techniques performing magicians use to divert the audience from what they are doing. Similarly, managers often focus employees' attention on one set of problems to divert them from larger realities. For example, the organization might engage in a flurry of activity around issues of diversity—workshops, signs on the wall, etc.—but nothing really changes. An examination of the company's organizational chart and its reward system might reveal that diversity is not a genuine organizational value—in fact, everything is structured so that the people currently in power keep that power.

Marshak, like Morgan le Fay, helps organizations see through their own and others' illusions by having them notice what is in the background (since most of us focus exclusively on the foreground issues of fire/achievement). To do this, he often has people consider not only what is "on the table" of the organization but also what is "under the table" and "above the table." To use the terms of this book, what is under the table is the Shadow, which needs to be honored; what is over the table is its grail. Ironically, in most organizations people do not hide just their worst selves, they also hide their best selves. They are afraid to reveal their idealism, their values, their hopes and dreams, for fear of being ridiculed or seen as naïve. Being magical requires being whole, and this includes one's best and worst aspects. Marshak's consulting practice and training workshops are designed as processes that allow people to integrate their grails and their Shadows into the workplace by speaking the "magic words" of their own truth.

Marshak cautions other consultants, who often speak of themselves using magical terminology ("my bag of tricks," "secrets of the trade"), about the difference between true magic—which brings transformation—and staged entertain-

TERMINOLOGY

Although Bob Marshak differentiates between the "magician" and the "shaman," I will call them the "trickster" and the "shaman" here to be consistent with the terminology used in this book and to avoid confusion.

ment. Marshak's trickster focuses on whatever the "in" intervention happens to be—not on what the client needs. Tricksters also play to applause, wanting to look good and give the client a good time. Therefore, they allow clients to remain safely in their narrow boxes without having to risk change.

Marshak's shaman, however, "induces a trance-like state, enters the supernatural realm, and executes a therapeutic action. Afterwards, the shaman returns to ordinary consciousness with the hope of beholding a cured client waiting nearby." The examples Marshak offers of structures that move us into the "supernatural realm" include team building, visioning, and other retreat experiences in which the ordinary rules of the work world are suspended, different values are introduced (humanistic ones, for example, in mechanistic environments), and major healing of individuals and the team occurs. The proof of whether someone is being a trickster or a shaman lies in the results. That's why long-term evaluation techniques are so important. Are people more effective and fulfilled after the intervention? Do structures, policies, and habits change? If not, we may have had a good time, but no magic has occurred.

Similarly, in our organizations it is easy to trick ourselves about how well we are doing. W. Edwards Deming's interventions, with their emphasis on systems thinking, quality control, and customer satisfaction, revolutionized first Japanese, then American business. It was not until American companies began to lose their international competitiveness that they were forced to forsake their illusion of invulnerability and realize that they had to learn from feedback just like those in any other country.

Deming's model (popularized under the name Total Quality Management, or TQM) is powerful partly because it emphasizes the proper response to evaluation. People fear they will be blamed if evaluative procedures pick up problems. Deming urged us to "drive fear out of the organization" as well as out of our own minds. If we think structurally, we respond to negative feedback by changing systems. If we trust that everyone has a gift, then he or she is not bad or wrong if feedback is negative. The individual is (1) undersupported by the organizational systems, (2) undertrained for the current challenge, or (3) miscast in his or her position. Each of these situations can be remedied without blame or punishment.[7]

Total Quality Management also reflects the transition from the Warrior to the Magician archetype because it deemphasizes control. Magician managers do not try to control their workers. Once a vision of the desired outcome is in place, they allow people great autonomy in how they achieve those ends. The self-directed teams put together by Barry Fulton of the United States Information Agency structure themselves to produce the desired results. In fact, the entire reinventing government effort eliminates many middle management positions, trusting that people do not need as much direction as previously thought. Enlightened businesses no longer expect workers to function like parts of a well-oiled machine; rather, employees are valued for their intelligence and ability to be reflective members of learning systems. What Total Quality Management and other systems models tell us is that people need feedback on the results of their behavior. Then individuals and teams can self-correct. Of course, having strong training and employee assistance initiatives also helps employees respond creatively to feedback, whether positive or negative.

Morgan le Fay's testing cups symbolize the feedback we

need in order to grow. Psychologist Shirley Luthman (in *Energy and Personal Power*) advocates a circular process of personal growth that begins with intuition and moves immediately to action. When we act on our intuitive awareness, we then experience feedback. Others appreciate us or get angry. We prosper or we fail. Either way, we learn. This learning educates our intuition so that we can trust it more fully the next time. Edie Seashore (interviewed in Chapter Four) believes so strongly in this process that she has written a whole book on feedback: how to give it, how to receive it. Without feedback, we do not grow.

Elsie Cross has taken on feedback as a major issue in her consulting company. Each of her national networks of consultants is rated by a committee of their peers on a list of competencies. The quality of the consultations offered is higher because people are always giving one another feedback. Cross focuses on creating an environment where it is safe to give and receive constructive criticism. So, people are always learning and growing.

In my own consulting, I have been struck by how frequently managers complain about employees without ever having told them exactly what is expected of them, what they are doing right, and how they could improve. Magical results occur time and time again when employees are given this information. The results are even stronger if managers also are open to feedback. They are strongest of all when innovation, competence, and hard work are reinforced consistently by the financial reward structure.

Such feedback helps us to produce higher-quality work and to engage in more effective communication. Quality is not simply a measure of output—of what we produce or do. Rather, the "total quality" a Magician desires is total quality of life.

How can each of us get feedback on the quality of our work lives? Our bodies daily give us valuable input about the structures in our lives—and whether or not they are enhancing our productivity. For example, take the case of an ambitious but iconoclastic young woman who felt alienated at her job. First of all, she was physically uncomfortable wearing conservative suits, hose, and high heels. Her office was sterile, for company policy forbade personal artifacts. The windows did not open, and the office was overheated in winter and overair-conditioned in summer. Further, maintaining a certain image—which included never speaking one's mind—was a major cultural value in her organization. She noticed that when she left work each day, her head hurt, her feet hurt, and her soul hurt. She realized that the physical structures and the policies of this company were a bad match for her—although she noticed that some people did like them. So, she changed not what she did but where she did it. Now, at a different company, with greater latitude for self-expression and with windows that open, she feels supported by the structures around her. She works just as hard or harder, but when she leaves work every day, she still has energy. To her, the change seems magical, especially since, on the surface, the difference between the two workplaces seems so small.

Remember, Titurel does not age or get tired as he supervises the building of the Grail Temple. Why? He is drawing energy from the Grail. When we create from the inside out and are not fighting against our true nature and inspiration, we feel good.

The Grail Temple (like the Round Table, the Grail, and the testing cups) is circular, as is the medicine wheel. It is no accident that companies increasingly are coming up with circular organizational charts, or that their teams are sitting around circular or oblong tables. Old Lodge Skins, the shaman in Thomas Berger's *Little Big Man,* contrasts the nineteenth-century white man's love of angular forms—ladders, squares, and boxes—with the Indian's veneration of the circle; the Indian's circular tepee allows the energy to flow, he points out, while the white man's square house impedes it.[8] The Round

Table's and Grail Temple's circular shapes allow energy to flow between and around people so that it builds rather than dissipates. You do not need to be an Indian medicine man to know the principle at work here. If you ever have experienced the synergy of a group creating harmoniously together, making a circle of energy, you know how energized you feel at the close of the day. Similarly, you undoubtedly know how energy-drained you can feel fifteen minutes into a meeting where people sit across the table from one another or otherwise reflect an adversarial stance—with battling egos, territorial protection, and hidden agendas as the norm.

One of the greatest organizational energy leaks today is Warrior meetings where every communication among people is designed to win points. Truth has no chance in such settings. In fact, the level of discourse typically plunges to the lowest common denominator of intelligence, while all honest grappling with issues—political or otherwise—occurs in the halls or behind closed doors. Moreover, people go home exhausted from having to censor every word they say—since words are seen as ammunition. The result is a loss of energy and a collective decrease in functional intelligence.

You know whether you are building a grail temple at your work by how your body feels. When physical structures and organizational policies, as well as your work habits, adequately hold the energy of your vision, you feel energetic, relaxed, and enthusiastic. When they do not, you may feel lethargic, tense, and unhappy. For many people, body response is the best way to test the fit between a person and a particular job or work process. If the fit is good, your body will feel relaxed and energized. If it doesn't, pay attention to what is wrong. Is it the physical space? Are workplace policies impeding your work? Is the workplace culture out of sync with your own values? Are you honoring your own pace and rhythms in how you do your work?

Most of us want to fit in—and doing so is not a bad thing—

ENERGY AND AUTHENTICITY

Ann McGee-Cooper (in *You Do Not Have to Go Home from Work Exhausted!*) stresses the energizing quality of being able to be true to yourself in the workplace. In addition advocating a healthy lifestyle (nutrition, rest, exercise), she suggests being true to your own ideals (ether); keeping a positive focus on your vision (air); working at your own pace and in your own way (fire); accepting interdependence with others and resisting the superwoman/superman syndrome (water); and arranging your surroundings in ways that nurture you (earth). Depending on your brain dominance patterns, she explains, nurturing surroundings may mean either color, variety, and beauty (for right-brained people) or order and stability (for left-brained people).[9]

so we may ignore physical symptoms that indicate many structures often taken for granted in modern office buildings are not good for us. Sun Bear, a contemporary American Indian medicine man, says that the "most important ingredient for good health is happiness." To put soul in life, expand "on what makes you feel good, continually feeling it, feeding it, nurturing it, and increasing it. At the same time, continue to move away from the things that cause discontent and make you unhappy.[10]

Many of us have reflected on our values, developed a clear sense of vision and mission, and formed close working teams, but we still do not enjoy our work. The sense associated with the earth element is taste. Therefore: The proof of the quality of a meal is in the eating. It does not matter how perfectly you follow a recipe—if the end result does not taste good, the recipe itself is not good. The test that your work is really successful lies in the quality of your working life. If this is not satisfactory, it is back to the drawing board to reconsider what has gone wrong—either in what you are doing or in your attitudes toward it.

Jungian psychoanalyst Marie-Louise von Franz (in *Psyche and Matter*) identifies a loss of energy with separation. She describes ancient alchemical beliefs that the correspondence between the macrocosm and the microcosm is evidenced in the step-down process from God to the universe, to humanity, and to the alchemical stone (that is, matter). In this view, God created the universe and people as an expression of the sacred in matter. Humankind also creates in its own image. Any lack of energy results from a separation from the divine spark.[11] In fact, in the modern world, the pattern has been reversed. In its fascination with technology, humankind has begun to remake itself in the image of the machine. When this happens, spirit is forgotten, and with it our true natures. The result is fatigue, depression, and alienation; we become dispirited.

In the In-Between, people have been transformed faster than the structures in which they work. This creates a separation that is responsible for the ennui of much in modern life. Moreover, although some people yearn for the good old days, the only way to feel whole again is to express who we are *now* in the tangible structures of the workplace. This does not, however, mean that we can forget practicality or the bottom line: money is an important gauge of mastery.

Money is a form of energy that gives us feedback on how we are doing, individually and collectively. Success coach Teri-E Belf told me her name means "earth elf." She helps people make their dreams come true by moving the earth under them in line with their purposes in life. So many people say, "I want to do this or that, but . . ." And then they remain stuck. Often the "but" has to do with money. Belf's experience, however, is that "when people commit to a dream that is right for them, the money comes, often in surprising ways." Clients have committed to taking Belf's success coaching without knowing where the money is coming from. "In one case, the client's parents asked out of the blue whether they could give the client a part of her inheritance while they still were alive. In another case, a client received a call from someone who owed him money. Yet another unexpectedly was offered a research assistant position that paid the exact amount she needed. And so on, and so on."

Notes Belf, "Benjamin Franklin, Alexander Hamilton, and other financiers among the Founding Fathers of our country referred to money as currency because of its two meanings: (1) current as an energy *flow* that serves as a barter system between people, and (2) current as in the *now*. Currency was intended to be kept *in the flow now*."

You cannot eat money. It does not keep you warm or give you a good or meaningful time. In itself, it is not good for anything except a way of keeping count of the ongoing exchange in life as each of us contributes to the common good. Money is a symbol of worth in a cultural negotiation, an internal and external statement of our value choices. We are not necessarily paid what we are worth, we are paid what other people believe we are worth—and that is influenced by and influences our self-valuation.

Belf maintains that "when we have difficulty attracting money to ourselves, there is a block somewhere in the flow of our energy." Currency, she explains, is simply "a physical form of gratitude for supplying a product, service, or experience that someone values." She often finds that low self-esteem is the main block to receiving money. "Some do not feel worthy to have it. Others think it is bad, or will make them bad. Still others feel guilty about having money when others go without it." In all these cases, she helps people reframe their beliefs about themselves and hence their energy, "otherwise known as money."

Blocks to prosperity, however, are not always internal. For example, all forms of prejudice diminish a culture's appropriate valuation and reward of members of disadvantaged groups, undermining the accuracy of feedback systems. All of us are hurt by prejudice because the overall prosperity of any organization, town, or country depends on every person in it being self-actualized enough to contribute his or her gifts to the betterment of the whole enterprise. Individuals in a prosperous country or organization tend to be financially better off than individuals in poorer ones. As we all claim our gifts and make our full contribution, each of us can be wealthier—in terms of money and overall quality of life—than we ever have imagined. And all this can be for the general good, not at anyone's expense.

THE GIFT

Genuine Magicians know they need honest feedback to grow, yet it is human to resist the advice of the contemporary magic mirror—whether it provides statistical or bottom-line feedback. When the wicked queen originally asked, "Mirror, mirror on the wall, who is the fairest one of all?," she did not respond graciously when the mirror said, "Snow White." Neither breaking the mirror nor killing Snow White could really help the queen. Who knows what would have happened had she followed up to ask the mirror about what her own bliss might be now that she was not the fairest one of all.

Morgan le Fay ended up with a bad name because she tested people and often found them wanting. Yet Arthur would not have left Camelot willingly to go on the barge with Morgan had she been a villainess. He knew she was a healer, and her healing came precisely from her ability to see through self-deception to promote true mastery. Today, individual and organizational evaluation systems serve as magic mirrors that hold us accountable for the results of our efforts. Therefore, they are in our interests, even when—or especially when—we do not want to face the truths they reflect.

The ultimate "test" of mastery is the ability to live in the moment, full of gratitude for the daily experiences of one's life. Deferred gratification has its place—as part of the experience of the trial-by-fire stage. Virtually all the people I interviewed for this book love their work and believe they are in

---

THRIVING WITH INTEGRITY AND MASTERY

The integrity check of mastery has two components: (1) to act in ways that are congruent with our values, and (2) to take responsibility for the results of our actions. As Thomas Moore (*Care of the Soul*) argues, quality is not just an economic consideration, it is a matter of integrity. Whatever our job—however humble or exalted—"if what we do or make is not up to our standards and does not reflect attention and care when we stand back to look at it, the soul suffers. The whole society suffers a wound to soul if we allow ourselves to do bad work."[12] We fail the test of integrity if we blame circumstances or other people for our own failure to give our best, or if we make excuses instead of amends when we make mistakes. Integrity in the business world means making things right—with employees and customers. We all make mistakes. People with character do what they can to remedy them.

---

just the right place—for them. They also have a sense of perspective, recognizing that what is right for them may not be right for others. Most also have a sense of life in progress. They know they are living in the In-Between, not in the ideal world of their perfect vision or goal.

They also know that magic does not happen when we are living in the past or future. It happens when we trust the process of our lives enough to let go and find the point of power right in the present. In *What Are You Doing with the Rest of Your Life?*, Paula Payne Hardin tells the story of Laura, a typical woman of today who, balancing the demands of a career with home and family, rushed one day to the grocery store, where she was frustrated and annoyed at its commercialism and stretched by decisions about cost and healthfulness. As she hurried back to her car, the following thought came to her: "Stop, stop! This is the only moment you have

. . . The quality of your life pivots on this moment. How are you living it?" At the same time, she noticed the beauty of the carrots she had purchased, which seemed not so much vegetables as "works of art." In this moment, "gratitude replaced anger. She was thankful for her job, her family, and for having so many wonderful foods available to her. As she stopped obsessing, she felt the wonder of earth—of the physical world. She could appreciate how terrific it is to be alive."[13]

Many people I interviewed are voting with their feet against conspicuous consumption and compulsive achievement, and are choosing instead a kind of voluntary simplicity. They are not doing so because of a fear that there will not be enough for everyone. Rather, they realize that life cannot be savored if we are trying to have, or do, everything at once. An American Shaker folk song puts it:

'Tis the gift to be simple, 'tis the gift to be free,
'Tis the gift to come down where we ought to be.
And when we find ourselves in the place just right,
We will be in the valley of love and delight.

The Exercises

FOR INDIVIDUALS

- Ask three people you work with for feedback on how you are doing. It is good to choose one who ranks above you, one who is your peer, and one who reports to you.
- Look back monthly at your goals for that month. Which ones did you accomplish? Which not? Why? Begin to notice patterns of what is working for you and what is not working. Use the elemental model to notice feedback you are getting on the quality of your ideas, as well as on your persistence, integrity, relationships, and financial prosperity.
- Pay attention to your habits at work. What do you do

when? How do you feel at different times of the day? How could you change your work habits to better honor your natural work preferences and rhythms?

- Compare your stated missions and values with how you actually spend your time in the workplace. To what degree do the details of your day support your own purposes and values? To what degree do they subvert or distract you from them?
- Try using the model in this book as a structure for evaluating your own quality of life. If you are short of ideas or hope for the future, you are being called by air to take the journey of initiation. If you are short of courage to persist in living your dreams, you are being called by fire to embark on a new trial. If you find you are failing to live up to your best self, you are being called by ether to follow your grail, even if it takes you through a waste land. If you do not have the support from others you desire, you are being called by water to experience illumination at a new level. Finally, if you are lacking money or energy, you are being called by earth to restructure the forms and habits of your life.

FOR ORGANIZATIONS

- Describe your organization's strategies for evaluating the quality of its products or services; the satisfaction of its customers or clients; the well-being of its employees; its financial accounting systems.
- How is information from these evaluative strategies used in decision making? How widely is the information disseminated? How frequently is it analyzed and considered?
- What are the organization's illusions about itself? Where does resistance to breaking through these illusions come from? Use the elemental model to evaluate how the organization actually is doing (new ideas, persistence, integrity, relationships, profitability).

- Consider the organization's policies? Which ones release the energy of employees, making them feel supportive and valued? Which ones cause frustration and annoyance? Where does a lack of policy end up with people having to reinvent the wheel, thus wasting valuable time and energy?
- To what degree do organizational structures support the stated mission and values of the organization? To what degree do they subvert them?

Circle Three: Rituals That Nourish and Sustain

THE STORY

Dindraine, the Grail Maiden, presides over a nightly ritual procession in the Grail Castle, a procession including a number of sacred objects: a bleeding lance, a sword, the Grail, and a bowl. The Grail feeds all present the food they most love and invites Percival to ask the sacred Grail questions that eventually heal the Wounded King.

Dindraine tells stories about the Grail's origins to Gawain and the other knights. She also tells how the Ship Draped in Silk came down to them from King Solomon and his wife. In doing so, she invests the knights' lives, as well as her own life, with meaning. After she sacrifices her life to heal the leprous queen (see Chapter Four), her body rests in state in this ship until it takes her to the Holy City of Sarras, where she is buried beneath the Grail. (Sir Gawain has returned the Grail to Sarras by this point in the narrative.)

Dindraine is a living version of the Grail because she knows —through ritual and story—how to make everyday life feel meaningful. She embodies action that is guided by sacred myth, not by the desire for achievement. In this way she provides an important balance to the yang (masculine) energy of the seeking knights. Just before her death, she gives them a symbol that combines yin (feminine) and yang energies, weaving a belt for Gawain's sword made from her hair.[14]

THE LESSON

The soul is nourished by ritual—that is, when ritual is vital and alive. So many people, however, have the mistaken belief that the magic of ritual comes from getting the details right—saying the correct prayer or learning the correct business skill. Betonie, the medicine man in Leslie Marmon Silko's *Ceremony*, observes that people think American Indian ceremonies have to be done exactly right—but that, he says, is not the point. The ceremonies are always changing and evolving to new needs. "Things which don't shift and grow are dead things." He warns that what matters is the consciousness beneath the ceremony and its appropriateness to the time. If the tribe clings to the dead forms, "the people will be no more."[15]

We can add meaning even to routine tasks if we think of work as ritual. All work, says Thomas Moore, is sacred, like a liturgy. When ancient Magicians cast circles to create ritual space, their efforts might take hours or even days. Details were attended to with great care: certain sacred objects were placed "just so"; special herbs or scents might be collected and burned; chants—maybe the same ones handed down over centuries—might be sung. Many of the details of preparing for the ritual might seem mundane, even boring, but they were deeply meaningful to these Magicians because they clearly understood that correctly casting the circle was essential to working magic.

So, too, with all the supposed routine we do in our work—filing, writing memos, attending yet one more meeting. When we are experiencing mastery, we know that "God is in the details." Our being careful and even reverent as we do these tasks opens the doors to magic. In a hierarchical worldview, such routine work often is devalued as beneath people of importance, but to Magicians everything essential to getting the work done is worthy. To become great Rulers or Magicians, we need to give up being princes and princesses, thinking some work is beneath us! All work that contributes to a worthy outcome has dignity.

Moore reminds us of Jung's statement that "the soul is for the most part outside the body"—expressed in the way we live our lives. We can *see the quality of our consciousness by the quality of the work we do, in the quality of our relationships, and in the everyday actions of our lives.*[16] Not only is quality important for personal success and national competitiveness, but it also is critical to self-knowledge and self-esteem. We find out who we are by what we create. Perhaps you have experienced this yourself. You put out less than your best effort—even in the little things—and your sense of yourself suffers. You know it, even if others do not. It also is true that many of us are afraid to take risks because if we do so, we face our own limitations. Yet if you ever have succeeded in doing first-rate work—especially in situations where no one else knows or cares—you know how your self-esteem grows. People who feel justified in doing shoddy work damage not just the economy as a whole but their own spirits as well.

Most of us are sustained—even to the point of being able to face our own mortality—by the hope that the world will be a better place, even if only in small ways, because we have lived. We all are cocreating the world around us by the actions we take, or fail to take. This is a compelling reason to pay our dues. It takes training and hard work to develop the consciousness and the skill necessary to leave a legacy of quality work behind us, so that our accomplishments create ripple effects that improve the world.

We also add meaning to our work when we consciously incorporate elements of ritual into it. JoAn Knight Herren, director of the Head Start Resource and Training Center for the Mid-Atlantic States, shared with me how she does so. Whether she is managing her own office or organizing and facilitating leadership development seminars, she begins by *creating sacred space.* When organizing seminars, she finds

RITUAL, MEANING, AND WORK

Thomas Moore, in *Care of the Soul*, writes: "Workers assume that their tasks, too, are purely secular and functional, but even such ordinary jobs as carpentry, secretarial services, and gardening relate to the soul as much as to function. In the medieval world, these forms of work each had a patron god—Saturn, Mercury, and Venus, respectively—indicating that in each case matters of profound significance to the soul are encountered in daily work. We could learn from our ancestors that the familiar tasks involved in an ordinary job have a presiding god and constitute a liturgy in relation to that god."[17]

attractive hotels in natural settings, then works with trainees to create colorful posters that reflect a vision of the seminar topics. In her office she posts evocative pictures—employees working at their best, for example—as well as letters of appreciation. In both instances she reassures people that they will have what they need to get the job done, and that if they do need anything, she is the person to see. She frequently begins the day by calling everyone together for coffee to celebrate some triumph—even one as seemingly trivial as honoring one employee for being persistent enough to elicit a return call from someone notorious for failing to make them. As I listened to Herren talk about her ways of bringing more soul into an organization, I was struck by the parallels between her strategies and symbolic objects associated with Dindraine.

Creating sacred space in a work environment, for example, involves the expression of an androgynous consciousness. Herren's version of *the belt woven from Dindraine's hair* to hold Gawain's sword (often seen as a symbol of androgyny) has a dual focus on building an intimate community committed to producing consistently high-quality products. This means that community and achievement, relationship and accountability, are held in balance, one feeding the other. In this context, the four sacred objects of the Grail procession can be honored and valued equally.

Herren honors *the bleeding lance* by "wading right in there" where she finds conflict. Whether with her own employees or the 144 Head Start programs with which they work, she practices four magical principles of conflict resolution. First, she and her staff take 100 percent responsibility for everything they say and do. Second, they avoid focusing on people and stay with the issue in question. Third, they avoid escalating that issue by talking to others about it or by bringing in other, unrelated issues; they talk only to the person (or persons) with whom they are having difficulty and avoid letting problems build up. (If you deal with issues as they come, they do not multiply.) Fourth, they use "I" statements, expressing what they feel and think without blaming or accusing others.

The result, Herren told me, is truly magical. She can walk into rooms where people's faces are hard as stone, but as they begin to focus on finding some point of commonality—even about what the problem is—she sees them soften and eventually smile. She also uses the concept of ritual to get people to buy into conflict management techniques *before* an actual conflict emerges. Thus a structure will be in place to resolve discord quickly and easily when it (inevitably) surfaces.

Herren honors *the ritual sword* by a razor-sharp focus on only one task or person at a time. No matter how long her list of things to do might be, she takes time to truly attend to whatever is on her plate at the moment. Similarly, when talking with clients or employees, she gives them her complete, undivided attention. This helps them feel valued, and builds community. More than that, it feeds Herren's soul because "soul loves intimacy."

Herren honors *the grail* by invoking uplifting words and ideas and by sparking people's own creativity. At a recent leadership development seminar, she put inspirational sayings on the walls and changed them every day. She gave Head Start directors who were being asked to envision their future twenty minutes to write songs that encapsulated their vision—and then had them all sing their songs. Not only did people quickly and easily come up with their visions, but they were astounded by how much creativity they had. For this reason, Herren and her staff avoid "off the shelf" leadership seminars, keeping their own creativity alive as they tailor new programs for every group.

Herren honors *the sacred bowl* by creating times and structures to feed people's souls. Working as she does with two huge bureaucracies (the University of Maryland and the federal Department of Health and Human Services), she knows that she cannot expect very much validation from outside her office. Most people in Head Start do the work because they care about children and families. However, it is easy to get burned out without validation. Herren and her staff make it a point to honor themselves, cherish and talk about their accomplishments, and appreciate one another. In Herren's words, they "hold their work dear" and stay "warm about it." Like Dindraine, Herren "tells the story" to imbue work with meaning, spending time reminiscing about accomplishments and what her office has meant to people.

Finally, Herren understands that ritual almost always includes some activity of *invocation* (of what will be) and *exorcism* (letting go of what was). Because of a change in federal policy, Herren and her office had to drop several of their favorite programs and move into new activities they had not chosen. She provided time and reinforcement for "bitching and moaning," as long as people stuck to their own feelings without blaming the bureaucracy or one another. She knew it would take time to grieve and let go of the old focus. Then, although her office was experiencing pressure to get on with its new programs, she told the staff members to take their time. If deadlines were not met, she would take the rap. She knew they could not simply mobilize for these new projects; they needed to move into them slowly until the Magician energy kicked in. Otherwise, they could burn out from the strain of working against their real feelings. Now, she told me, everyone is "rolling along again, enjoying themselves and throwing themselves into the new agenda" just as she hoped they would.

THE GIFT

People use different strategies to imbue their work with meaning and value. I often light a candle in the morning, reinforcing my intent to release the highest and best potential in the day's work. A good friend of mine refers to her appointment calendar as her "Holy Book," because nothing is as sacred to her as how she uses her time.

At work I use ritual principles in planning my own meetings and workshops. To "cast a circle" in order to create sacred space, all one needs to do is create a situation in which everyone is psychologically present and sitting in a circle. Ways to do this include making time for a short meditation or asking everyone to share something brief but from the heart. The sacred is invoked when we remind people of the higher purpose of the meeting and/or encourage them to bring their deeper wisdom to it. As a facilitator, I also find it helpful to maintain elemental balance and harmony in a meeting. Air helps us brainstorm and expand our visions. Fire keeps us on the task or agenda. Ether brings us back to core values or principles. Water fosters honest dialogue. Earth keeps our feet on the ground and demands that we clarify the detailed steps needed to implement decisions. Thinking of meetings or workshops as rituals also reminds me to thank those in attendance (and/or allow time for them to appreciate each other's contributions) and to provide a benediction, sending people forth with a sense of faith, camaraderie, and purpose.

Most organizations have ritualistic events—motivational

meetings, parties, award and retirement dinners, and so forth. If the magic has gone out of such community-building opportunities, the challenge is to think of them as sacred rituals that can remind people of the dignity and value of their work. In planning any such event, it is helpful to remember to make it inspiring (ether), enlightening (air), motivating (fire), bonding (water), and nurturing (earth).

Using elements of ritual in the workplace can remind all of us that our work is a sacred activity. Moreover, rituals that are alive and meaningful feed our souls. This is the real meaning of the Grail that feeds everyone the food he or she most loves. When we are true to who we are and find ways to make the details of our daily lives sacred, our souls are fed.

THE EXERCISES

FOR INDIVIDUALS

- What ritual actions are now part of your work? Do they enliven or deaden it? How might you better use ritual to give greater dignity and meaning to your workday?
- Think about the four objects in the Grail procession and how they play out in your life. How do you handle conflict? How often can you focus on just one thing or person at a time? How much spontaneity and creativity do you allow in your life? To what degree are you able to find ways to contain and give significance and meaning to your work?
- Tell the story of your work as a sacred endeavor. Fill it with grandeur and meaning. What might the ripple effects be if you did shoddy work? What are they when you do your best?
- On a scale of one to ten, what is the value you place on achievement? On innovation? On authenticity? On relationships? On quality of life? Now look at how you spend

your time, considering the percentage of your time devoted to each category.

FOR ORGANIZATIONS

- What rituals and celebrations are part of the life of your organization? What values are they reinforcing? How might principles of ritual be used to make them more magical?
- If you were to describe a typical meeting, what are its ritualistic qualities? What meaning might they hold for people there? If you would like changes in your meetings, describe in ritualistic terms how you might like them to be. (For example, say how you create sacred space and what "gods" are venerated. Say what the sacred objects are and what they represent. How do you let go of the past and move on to the future? What qualities are you invoking? What elements are present? How do you end meetings and what does this "benediction" signify?)
- Tell the sacred story of your organization. Imbue it with dignity and power as you describe what it holds sacred, what it needs to let go of, and what it is invoking. Describe the ripple effects if your organization does shoddy work. Describe them if it consistently does high-quality work.
- What is the relative value for your organization of innovation, integrity, achievement, community, and quality of life (on a scale of one to ten, respectively)? What would you like it to be?

Circle Four: The Point of Power

THE STORY

Perhaps the humblest but most holy and important character in Camelot is the Grail Hermit. As a young man, he took on the task of guarding the Grail and the Sword in a small remote chapel. His whole lifework has been to live in obscurity, protecting these sacred objects. In practice, this does not require battle, just daily maintenance and presence. He keeps the chapel clean and cared for and is there in case anyone tries to steal the objects. Before him, another Grail Hermit did the same thing, and before him, another still. Likely none of them knew that the Grail and the Sword would emerge to give rise to Camelot. Perhaps none even knew that they were, respectively, the symbols of feminine and masculine spiritual power. They did not have to know or understand. They just had to be faithful to their mission. As this Grail Hermit is dying, Merlin appears to claim the Grail and Sword so that he can found Camelot. (Subsequent Grail Hermits humbly minister to the souls of knights seeking the Grail.)[18]

THE LESSON

People with mastery, like the earth element itself, are faithful to their work, even those aspects that are not glamorous or highly visible. Earth is the element of planting and harvesting; of maintaining our buildings, roads, and relationships; and of cleaning up. It relates to tasks that are ongoing, routine, and potentially boring (or steadying) or that support others.

Jill Bogard, director of the Library and Information Services

> ## SOMETIMES THE MAGIC WORKS
>
> Magicians have humility because they know that they do not
> control the universe. Therefore, they can be good-humored
> even when things seem to go wrong. In Thomas Berger's *Little
> Big Man*, the title character goes to the top of the mountain
> with the great Indian medicine man, who has said that this is a
> good day to die. The medicine man, whom Little Big Man
> greatly loves and admires, does a dance. Suddenly thunder and
> lightning appear and he lies down to die. After a long time he
> stands up. It is clear that he has not died. Asked about it, he
> says cheerfully, "Sometimes the magic works, sometimes it
> doesn't."[19]

at the American Council on Education, shared with me how
people find it magical that she can locate very obscure information quickly. She credits experience and, beyond that, synchronicity. "Sometimes, when I am looking up one thing I run
across another—which is then requested the next week." Although people tell her she is a miracle worker, Bogard illustrates the characteristic humility of a Grail Hermit when she
replies, "I'm just doing my job."

People with mastery often are humble, viewing themselves
as servant leaders. Breese White, managing director of North-
Star Partners, Inc., is a high-level example. He is not a servant
of his boss, board, or clients, but of his grail, his spiritual
commitment to a vision of a better world. An artist as well as a
businessman, White creates structures that make organizations both functional and beautiful. He produces visually creative and interesting brochures, workbooks, training materials
—and effective management policies and procedures, using
the same skills he developed as an artist to do so.

White was brought in as a partner in NorthStar to help "ten
brilliant consultants translate their vision into a workable or-

> ## ROLE OF MASTERY: SERVANT LEADERSHIP
>
> When we have gained mastery, it is natural to assume leadership, not for our own career advancement but for the good of the group. Such leaders do not feel above anyone, but, having a sense of real purpose and commitment, they are not afraid to persist in making the world a better place.

ganization." A company dedicated to visions of Camelot, he realized, needed a foundation based on common values. Therefore, he gathered the consultants together and asked them to clarify their values—their grails. Some of these were equality and mutual respect, freedom and independence, appreciation of the environment, the creation of a viable, highly respected enterprise. These core values, White explained, became the "mirror by which we judged everything."

White then helped the team develop structures and policies consistent with their stated values. For example, because the associates care about freedom and independence, people now come and go as they wish and work (for consulting fees) as much or as little as they wish. Because they care about equality, they all charge the same rate.

So that members of the group would not delude themselves, they also decided on tangible measures to validate their fidelity to these values: the commitment to the environment would be demonstrated by using only recyclable paper; respect for the organization, by its reputation; its viability, by its sales; and so on.

The consultants chose White to run NorthStar because they knew he would always think of the company first. Like the Grail Hermit, he understands his role to be a critical supporting one, without which the organization could not be as successful. Indeed, throughout his career, he has identified visionary people and created the conditions under which they could flourish and accomplish their work. While he commands a good salary and great respect from his colleagues, his primary reward is a sense of making a contribution to the greater good.

White and his colleagues consult with other organizations, helping them to clarify their values and then embody them in the tangible structures and policies of their everyday organizational life—that is, to be true to their grails. White stresses the importance of not imposing one's own values on clients but, instead, encouraging their fidelity to their own.

For example, in working with a consulting group that expressed diversity as a value, he was pleased to find a high representation of women and people of color in the firm. However, the group had twice as many women as men. When he asked whether this was a problem, they said no. Men had more power in the world by virtue of their sex (and hence were more confident and assertive), they explained, so having more women than men helped balance the power dynamic; with two women for every man, they actually all felt equal. White did not agree, but he knew it was not important whether he did or not. What was important was that the organization and its members were embodying their own values in a way that provided them with a sense of meaning and congruence.

To White, "an organization's core values are its grail. Mastery requires translating those values into the structures and policies that enable complex adaptive systems to embody what they care most about." White sees himself as a (very sociable) Grail Hermit, guarding whatever is most sacred to the people with whom he works so that their workplaces can be as full of meaning and importance as the Grail Chapel in the Camelot story.

Mastery gives us a sense of security and trust, even when we do not know the future. Let's think for a moment of agriculture. We can plow, and plant, and create the conditions for a good harvest, but we cannot make the plants grow and we cannot change the weather. A children's story I love, called "The Garden," concerns two friends, Toad and Frog. Toad plants a garden. The next morning he is disappointed that the seeds have not sprouted. He decides maybe the seeds are anxious. He begins staying up all night reading to them, playing the violin to them—ignoring the reassurance from Frog that eventually they will sprout all on their own. Finally, when they do sprout, Toad complains what hard work that garden was![20]

Most of us are like Toad. We want what we want and we want it now. In nature, however, things take time. In the middle of winter in a northern clime, if we just looked at the snow around us, we never would believe spring was on its way— except that our experience and that of others tell us spring indeed follows winter, and does so every year. So it is in business. Retail sales, for example, have their own seasons. Only experience can tell us when we are going through a mere seasonal dip and when we are in big trouble. Knowing when to take action and when to wait it out can come only with experience. No matter how hard we are working, if we are planting out of season, our harvest will come to nothing. Even though the Grail Hermit had the Grail and the Sword, he could not create Camelot: the timing was not yet right.

Judy Brown, an educator and consultant in private practice, has an exquisite sense of cultural timing. A former White House Fellow with an impressive history of executive line positions (most recently at the Aspen Institute), she recently decided to trade direct power for broader influence. She sees herself as a modern "troubadour," doing management retreats, delivering keynote addresses, and in other ways traveling around and telling informative and empowering stories. In a time when media consciousness trails behind individual and organizational transformation, Brown told me, modern troubadours are needed to go from "town to town" recounting what they see in ways that spread stories of transformative success.

Her personal reason for the change was a desire for balance and quality of life. Like many others today, she realized she no longer was willing to have anyone else control how she used her time. She now wants to determine the optimal balance between her professional and personal life. Brown also is passionately interested in the state of the culture, reminding me in her interview of the importance of taking the long view to understand what is happening in the In-Between. As she travels, she carries with her a notebook filled with the essays, poems, art, and other artifacts that speak most eloquently to her. She has them ready to seed the discussion if the moment is right, and she adds additional materials as she encounters them. One might think of her as a kind of cultural Johnny Appleseed, spreading the seeds of empowering and transformative thought wherever she goes.

Brown likens society today to the middle of a Shakespearean comedy. Such comedies typically begin with a situation in which social institutions have broken down. So the characters flee to the woods, where the old forms fall away. Women disguise themselves as men so they can travel more freely; people do not recognize one another; and serious aristocrats and clownish peasants engage in important conversations. With the restraints loosened, people have experiences that transform their lives. When they emerge from the woods, a new and healthier order (generally symbolized by the right people pairing up and getting married) has been established.

Brown's retreats are ways of taking people into the woods. Although she uses traditional facilitation techniques, she particularly enjoys strategies that encourage true dialogue. Telling people about the American Indian use of the "talking staff," she constructs playful interactions that help participants speak the truth of their hearts and listen fully to one another. Such times (the in-the-woods times) require that we let the old forms fall away, that we learn to speak and hear in a new way, so that our deeper truths can emerge into the structure of our discourse. When this happens with senior executives, whole organizations can be transformed in the twinkling of an eye. They emerge from the woods and the new forms suddenly are clear.

Brown cautions that the secret of magic in the woods is getting people to be 100 percent present, so that they can disclose what they think and feel and know. Unfortunately, in too many contexts we bring only a part of ourselves to the table. We bring our intelligence but not our doubts. We share our thoughts but not our feelings. In most settings, we bring the perceptions of white males but not those of women, indigenous cultures, or inner city neighborhoods. In virtually every setting, we pretend to think like whatever group is in power in an organization, and we censor whatever about us is associated with less valued people and traits. To solve the problems of today, Brown told me, we need to bring our whole selves, in all our diversity, to our workplace encounters. It's no wonder the world has economic problems when we artificially restrict the wisdom available to us in virtually every collective decision-making process.

When asked what is most magical about her work, Brown mentioned that she never does anything we traditionally think of as marketing. When she decided to be a "troubadour," she simply made a list of the people whose work she really valued, then put the list away. A year later, she had worked with all of them. Instead of marketing, she "turns her head" toward the people and ideas she values, tries to be open and clear in every interaction, and the work that is right for her emerges. On reflection, she realizes that this is what marketing is—at this time when we are culturally "in the woods." The new structures for finding work are not about control or manipulation. Rather, they are about authenticity and openness to life, relationships, and new opportunities.

But what about those who remain in line positions? What are the forms that match the time? Donna Shavlik and Judy

Touchton, director and deputy director of the Office of Women in Higher Education at the American Council on Education, are Grail Hermits extraordinaire. Dedicated to promoting women into major administrative posts, they do not seek visibility for themselves. Indeed, they are always promoting others, finding ways to put them in the spotlight.

Both are masters at redefining structures, believing strongly that form should follow, not control, task. In the late 1970s they (along with Emily Taylor, the previous director of the office) began creating the National Identification Program, a self-sustaining network of female administrators. Although some participants wanted to spend time creating bylaws and otherwise formalizing structures, the Shavlik/Touchton team encouraged them not to do so. Rather, they believed that the network should be fluid enough to change as its needs changed. Knowing that structures can facilitate the process of empowerment—indeed are part of the process—they convened people and trusted them to assess what had to be done. Like Brown, the Shavlik/Touchton team also scanned the environment for groundbreaking ideas and seeded their network by recommending speakers, readings, and strategies.

As more and more women moved into higher administrative ranks, Shavlik and Touchton declared that no longer was it only the women who had to change, but also the institutions in which they worked. Their sense of the right time for things had caused them to emphasize, in the early years of the National Identification Program, that women could compete equally with aspiring male administrators on their own terms, but that some adaptation to existing power structures was needed. As more women moved into top ranks, however, Touchton and Shavlik encouraged a new balance in collective administrative styles, incorporating the best of what women as well as men bring to their roles. What good is it to society, they implicitly asked, if women enter organizations as male clones, leaving behind the perspectives their unique experiences have given them?

In having responded intelligently to the needs of the 1970s and '80s, Shavlik and Touchton see that they have developed processes that are just those needed more widely in the '90s: processes for encouraging self-structuring networks, for promoting nonpolarizing dialogue on controversial subjects, and for empowering individuals to contribute their full potential, even in environments resistant to change. Their broader goal is to use such processes to ensure that women's voices are heard in the larger cultural dialogue about what we, as a society, want to become.

THE GIFT

The gift of the Grail Hermit is a radical trust in process. In the consulting world, Harrison Owen and others are experimenting with "open space technologies," which daringly bring all the employees from an organization into one large room and, with a minimum of structure, allow them to organize themselves. If you remember the discussion in Chapter One of "self-organization systems" in science, you can see that open space technologies translate chaos theory into action.

Owen invites anyone who feels really passionate about an issue to lead a small group discussion on it. Topics are posted on a bulletin board, and people can sign up for as few or as many as they wish. Participants have to promise only that if they are not getting anything out of the session, they will vote with their feet and leave. On the wall, Owen places four basic principles (based on a trust in process and synchronicity in action):

1. Whoever comes is the right people [*sic.*]
2. Whatever happens is the only thing that could have.
3. Whenever it starts is the right time.
4. When it's over, it's over.

Mainstream companies such as Reebok International are trusting this process. Moreover, they are finding that when the wisdom of the group is tapped, structures and policies are changed radically, the outcome being that productivity improves. Open space technologies release the collective intelligence of the work force, wisdom that has been suppressed artificially by outmoded hierarchical, control-oriented management systems.[21]

If hundreds of people can form a self-directing system, certainly any one of us can learn to trust the process of our own lives. Many of the people I interviewed impressed me with their willingness to take risks, knowing full well that no ideal outcome was guaranteed. Some simply did what they had to do and hoped. Others had faith in a synergistic relationship between the larger world and their own lives—that is, they trusted that their own organic growth would be reflected in some way in emerging social structures.

As I reflected on my own life in the light of their example and wisdom, I recognized synchronicity at work. I studied to be a professor before many universities were hiring women. However, just as I was completing my Ph.D., the women's movement erupted, things changed, and I was hired as an assistant professor at a major university. I began doing research in women's studies before women's studies programs existed, even though I was warned that doing so would end my career. Soon colleges and universities were starting such programs, and I was hired to direct one. I followed my interest in Jungian and transpersonal psychologies, even though I was warned that few academic positions were available in these fields. Far from ruining my career, the willingness to take this risk helped it. Suddenly I found myself in demand as a lecturer, consultant, and workshop facilitator, and I had the opportunity to tailor the mission of an academic institute to explore and develop issues of human and organizational development from the perspective of transpersonal psychologies and other innovative contemporary fields of inquiry.

This does not mean, of course, that I have been exempt

from life's traumas and disappointments. Nevertheless, I have learned to trust that institutions and societal attitudes are changing, just as I am. In the In-Between, we often have to make some compromises because a delay may occur between what social pioneers are doing and the creation of markets and jobs for their work. (The earth element changes more slowly than human consciousness.)

However, I also have observed that people who forego their journeys in order to play it safe often lose out. For example, when I was in college, engineering was a popular major even for people who did not enjoy the subject, because it was a growing field. By the time my contemporaries graduated, there was a glut on the market and hence not enough jobs. Today, as then, it is counterproductive to make decisions about the future based on linear projections from the present. Moreover, even if our predictions are accurate, we then are stuck with the seduction of a secure job that is not our bliss. Either we will be unhappy or we eventually will retool. Remember that Camelot is not about finding the permanent slot that makes us safe and defines who we are. Anytime we are doing what we love, we experience a bit of Camelot.

It can be frightening to follow your bliss when you do not see the desired job or contract on the horizon. It may be comforting to remember that many people who have an active inner Magician succeed precisely because they do not mind being scouts for the society. We can either create new structures, compromise with old ones, or trust that other people are developing the structures we eventually will need to make our best contribution to the world. As we follow our own call, we can stay alert for empowering partnerships with individuals, groups, and institutions that are right, if not forever, at least for the time.

Imagine riding through a mist so thick that it obscures your view. You may be inching closer and closer to your personal Camelot (at least the Camelot that can be yours for a while) but not even knowing it. Just as you are about to give up, the mist parts, and there you are.

THE EXERCISES

FOR INDIVIDUALS

- What aspects of your work take timing? What aspects take great patience?
- When have you felt like a Grail Hermit—doing something important because it needed to be done, even though no one knew or seemed to care? What was that like for you?
- How might you honor the more routine part of your work? How might you show more appreciation for the routine work that others do?
- How can the structures of your routine, everyday work be better matched with the needs of the time—in your own life or in the culture as a whole?
- What would you do if you had greater trust in the processes of your own life?
- What could you let go of to create more simplicity and ease in your life? What are you doing, or what do you have, that is extraneous to the quality of your life?

FOR ORGANIZATIONS

- Where is timing most critical in your organization? Does it have ways to teach people how to have better timing? What predictable cycles affect your work? What are the structures that best fit your organization, the people in it, its cultural context, and the needs of the time?
- How does your organization show appreciation and respect for routine work?
- What organizational policies and structures do, or would, encourage people to enjoy the moment? How might your

organization set priorities in ways that allow the extraneous to fall away, creating a voluntary organizational simplicity that enhances the quality of life for everyone?

• Experiment with open space technologies—first in small, then increasingly larger, groups.

Circle Five: The Wheel of Creation

THE STORY

*The Camelot stories are parables about the process of individual
and collective creation. We participate in a sacred activity every
time we take responsibility for directing our lives. The story of
Camelot, then, begins with Taliesin, Merlin's teacher, who in-
structs him how God formed the elements out of nothing, and
out of them, the universe. This process involved dividing things
that were one into categories—light and dark, heaven and
earth, sky and sea—and in that way giving them structure.
Taliesin challenges Merlin to go and do likewise: As God created the universe, so Merlin can create Camelot.[22]*

THE LESSON

The fifth circle of mastery challenges us to put it all together:
consciously to be able to use what we have learned in all five
stages of the Magician's journey. The structures of the earth
element provide the container that can keep all the elements
in balance.

I have learned from several individuals who exhibit mastery
in the informed use of the five elements in the creation process. While researching and writing this book, I was fortunate
to study with Charmaine Lee, director of the Synergy Dance
and Healing Arts Center. Lee teaches people like you and me
to dance the five polarity elements and to experience them as
tangible energies in the body.

Most people are limited in their ability to act on what they
know intellectually because old patterns have crystalized in

their bodies. So, we keep on acting and moving in the same ways. The patterns locked in our bodies make real change difficult. Lee's innovative movements cause the body to release habitual patterns. Her work helps people change at the cellular level—they move through the five elemental energies in a way that not only fosters a strong and flexible body but also frees up consciousness. Her techniques make seemingly abstract—and even ethereal—concepts concrete for everyday people. Lee understands, as Taliesin and Merlin did, that creation occurs in a step-down process from ether to air to fire to water to earth. Once creation is manifest as earth, patterns crystalize and we tend to get stuck. To be fully alive, we need to be re-creating ourselves continually, using the elements to do so.

Lee's own life is a case study in faith and in constant re-creation. Born in South Africa with crippled legs, she healed herself through dancing. One career as a professional dancer was cut short when she was arrested by the South African police and given massive doses of a dangerous truth serum. When she finally was released, she escaped to London, where again she was healed—through learning and utilizing the theories of Dr. Randolph Stone. From these theories she developed the innovative form of dance described above, which teaches people to balance the energies of ether, air, fire, water, and earth in their own bodies as they move. She is quite a magical woman!

Lee understands that although her mission is always clear to her, the structure housing that work needs to change from time to time. Twice in her life she has had to let go of everything she had—once in the move from South Africa to England, and later in a move from England to Washington, D.C. She knows she can survive upheavals that feel as profound as dying. Therefore, for her, letting go of smaller things is simple. Her strength is that she can commit fully to her work without being attached to any particular form.

These principles govern her management style as well as her dance and healing classes. Synergy Dance and Healing Arts was once a for-profit dance center. The work was going wonderfully, but Lee was having a hard time making ends meet. Because she worked with the five elements daily, she could analyze her situation using this tool. The problem was not with the ether element: she knew how to be centered. Nor was it with the air element: she was continually expanding her horizons. The issue clearly did not center around her fire energies: she had a strong sense of her mission and was totally committed to doing her part. The problem certainly was not with the water element: she had wonderful relationships with her dancers and body workers as well as her clients. When conflict erupted, she dealt with it.

She realized that the problem was with the earth element: the for-profit structure did not enable Synergy to utilize the wealth available to it from the water element—the massive goodwill people felt toward the organization. People loved the work she did and respected her for her integrity and perseverance in a difficult challenge. So the form changed. She realized that Synergy should become a nonprofit so that people could donate money to support it. However, to move in this direction, she first had to accept a limitation on how much she could profit personally from her own invention. This required letting go of some piece of her initial vision—the form her reward would take for developing Synergy. At the same time, she began to recognize the need to focus her energy on teaching others, who could then take this work and make it available to more people than she possibly could reach herself.

At this particular moment in history, the earth element—as well as the question of structure—seems difficult for people. Many individuals have shared with me their struggle to find the right form for their work. Philadelphia-based consultant Nancy Post, founder of Systems Energetics, realized early in her career that she wanted to have an impact on social organizations—in the business world and beyond. She worked in organizations that were successful on the surface but pathological at their core. Eventually, she became frustrated because she could see what was wrong but had nothing but instinct to guide her choice of interventions. Her inability to find a solution was due partly to her youth: she was the new kid on the block (a block full of senior managers). But even more, she did not have a clear sense of what strategy would work. Like many people today, she had vision and will, but the form of the work eluded her—until synchronicity (brought through illness) revealed it to her.

One of the organizations she worked for was so dysfunctional that the stress she experienced sapped her strength. When she became ill, a friend referred her to acupuncture. As she learned about the five elements of Chinese medicine—earth, water, fire, wood (air), and metal (ether)—she felt an instant sense of recognition.[23] Here was her form. She knew immediately that she was going to apply the five-element theory to the workplace. But mastery takes time. She already had a degree in economics and had completed training in Gestalt therapy, yet she did not balk at the idea of further study if that was what it took. She wrote a plan that included studying Chinese medicine, developing a workplace intervention model, testing the model with organizations, and learning to run and market a consulting business, as well as getting a Ph.D. in organizational behavior. It took her twelve years of study and practice to achieve mastery in the form of her work.

When Nancy Post works in an organization today, she observes people's movements—the flow of the five elemental energies in the workplace—and views the organization as if it were a living being. She notices where blocks and imbalances occur and treats them. Stressing the need for discernment and accurate observation, Post told me that "magic does not just happen. Intentional magic requires stage setting." She uses her skills as a clown and an actress to keep things fun and to assess a person's or an organization's growth point. But she remains acutely conscious of what she is doing and why—so that she can do transformative work responsibly, doing no harm as the Hippocratic oath demands.

Like many of us, Post still is expanding the form of her work. Having been trained as an economist, she began her career as a consultant. Then she developed a conventional acupuncture practice, treating people with needles. Finally, she started a consulting practice using acupuncture with organizations. She discovered that many people experience physical symptoms caused by elemental imbalances in their workplaces or work groups. For example, Post herself started getting headaches in a company that required too much "in the head" planning. She can diagnose organizational dysfunction by identifying the physical symptoms that have become chronic among employees. In fact, she recently wrote a book, called *Bring Your Body to Work*, that describes the synchronistic interconnection between organizational imbalances and individual ailments.

As we can see with both Lee and Post, elemental theory can be used consciously (1) in the process of creating or re-creating a life, a career, or an organization, and (2) in the evaluation or diagnosis of what underlying imbalances keep individuals or organizations from fulfilling their full potential. You can use it to guide your own activities, and you can also enlist it to assess offered help or intervention. Is the person offering this help considering all five elements, or just fixated on one or two? Does the suggested intervention respond to where the elemental weakness is found, or is it just the flavor of the month?

The most powerful kind of magic, moreover, combines inner and outer work. The elements, as well as the stages of the Magician's journey, have both an inner, introspective aspect

---

MAGIC AND ORGANIZATIONAL DEVELOPMENT

In your workplace you can use magical principles to ennoble your use of very standard organizational development techniques. For example, in strategic planning exercises, as you clarify your values, vision, and mission, you can dedicate this process to the fulfillment of your organization's higher destiny. As you engage in team building and in diversity training, you can understand that you do so in order to express your care and concern in ways others more easily can receive. As you put in place evaluation strategies, you can recognize that you are giving the world permission to be your magic mirror, to teach you —through feedback—higher-level mastery. Using the concept of the Wheel of Creation, you also can appreciate discomfort and unhappiness as calls to new journeys.

---

and an outer, active aspect. The most powerful Magicians consciously work on both levels simultaneously.

Carolina Robertson, a professor at the University of Maryland and former president of the Society for Ethnomusicology, exemplifies the way a single individual in an organizational context can use the five elements as tools for both inner and outer work. Trying to orchestrate the merger of two ethnomusicology programs and, at the same time, expanding the only Ph.D. program in the field, she used the elements in her outer life to develop a vision of this expanded program (air); to clarify its purpose and write a workable plan (fire); to connect that purpose with her values and those of the music department in which she teaches (ether); to network with others, to build consensus around the process (water); and to design practical strategies for its implementation (earth).

Then she went inward. She realized that the chief impediment to the passage of this plan (the music department had to vote on it) was a fear of change. The problem, then, was in the air element. The need was for the airy quality of expansion. Robertson had apprenticed with a shaman in the Andes and knew how to cast a magic circle as a medicine wheel, invoking the four directions and the center. Such ritual structures help ground internal work in an outer structure that reinforces and mirrors consciousness change. In this case, she invoked all five elements for balance, then focused on the air element in her ritual.

In the circle of this medicine wheel Robertson placed seven rocks, symbolizing the current programs in the music department, and gradually moved them apart to make room for the new. She mentally "invited" members of the department (in her imagination) to sit and meditate peacefully, expanding their inner reality without stress or difficulty. In this circle, Robertson chanted ancient Andean chants to invoke *chemoralitum,* a form of "gentle transformation." When she felt that her inner and outer work had been done—when she herself felt peaceful and assured of the outcome on the inner plane—she submitted the proposal. Although people had predicted that the meeting on this controversial program would take hours of heated debate, the proposal passed amicably in seven minutes.

THE GIFT

Mastery requires us to trust ourselves—and to trust life—enough to express our highest and best selves in the everyday world of work. We are fortunate that the Camelot stories can show us how. These ancient recipes for magic really are very simple. Everything I have shared with you thus far boils down to this five-step method for allowing magic to be at work in your life and your organization today:

1. **M**eaning: Like Percival, follow your own grail. Seek out what is sacred or meaningful to you—what calls you. Learn fidelity to your own quest. Be willing to go into

your waste land and find healing for the blocks that keep you from following your own bliss.

2. **Adventure:** Like Merlin, be bold in your imaginings. Understand that life in the In-Between is characterized by constant change. Seize this opportunity as a chance to keep growing. Be willing to face the fear of losing touch with consensual reality, and allow yourself to be initiated into expanded consciousness.

3. **Greatness:** Like Arthur, clarify and commit to your own purpose, and translate that purpose into tangible goals. Then have the courage to take risks to realize these goals. When the going gets tough, focus on where you are headed rather than on what's in your way. Be willing to face your fears of incompetence and defeat, letting go of the outcome, so that you can focus on expressing your highest and best in every moment.

4. **Involvement:** Like Guinevere, allow yourself to get involved—with the world, your coworkers, your customers or clients. Let yourself know them and be known yourself, choosing to listen receptively to others while you speak the truth of your own heart. Be willing to risk heartache and misunderstanding to achieve illumination. Let your work be a love offering—to yourself, others, and the world.

5. **Creativity:** Like Titurel and the other exemplars of earth, be practical enough to manifest your vision in the real world. Craft your dreams into something tangible and useful—a product, a service, a business, the rituals of your everyday habits—being willing to accept the inevitability of imperfection. Learn from feedback so that you develop real mastery.

If you do so, your life can spell "magic," as you release the highest and best potential in every situation and in every moment. If you do so, in the words of medieval mystic Julian of Norwich,

> . . . all will be well,
> And every manner of thing will be well.[24]

THE EXERCISES

FOR INDIVIDUALS

- Refer back to the "Magician's Journey Index for Individuals" in Appendix A to see what stage of the journey may be calling you right now. What is calling from within you organically? Will following the desires that are arising naturally in your heart address the call identified in the index? (Be careful to differentiate emerging desires from ingrained habits, which will tend over time to intensify imbalance.)
- Draw a picture of the five stages of the Magician's journey in your work life. Which elements seem strongest and most balanced? Which ones seem in need of strengthening?
- What would mastery be in your work life? Describe success using all of your senses. Then imagine yourself achieving it fully. This may be the life you are stepping into—right now.

FOR ORGANIZATIONS

- Refer back to the "Magician's Journey Index for Organizations" in Appendix A to identify what stage of the journey may be calling your organization at this time in its development. What seems to be emerging naturally? Is intervention needed, or is the system correcting itself?
- Draw a picture of your organization at each stage of its journey. Identify the elemental gifts as they are ex-

pressed at each stage. What elements seem to be strong?
What elements seem to be weak?

- What would mastery be like for your organization? Describe it using all your senses—in the present tense, as if
  it were happening now. Try to imagine what it would be
  like. Find a way to express your vision for the organization—in a speech, a paper, a model, or any way that
  helps it come alive for you and others.

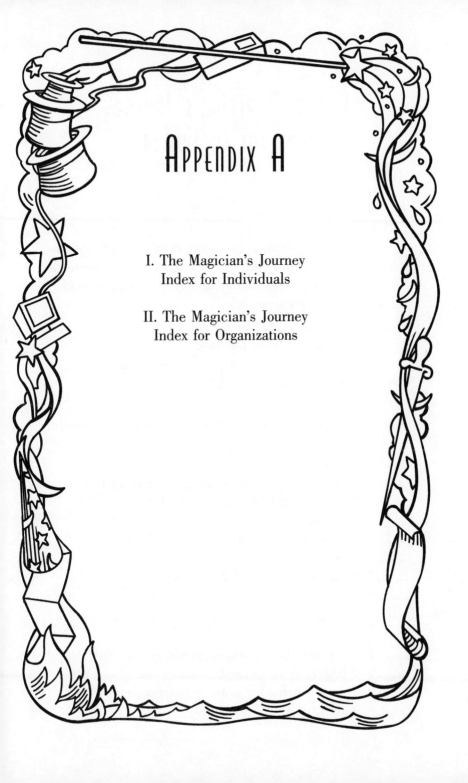

Appendix A

I. The Magician's Journey Index for Individuals

Part One

To find out where you are on your Magician's journey, rate the following on a scale of 1 to 3 as they reflect your concerns at the present time (defined as now and in the past few months). Be sure to use the entire scale.

1 = not important to me at this time
2 = somewhat important to me at this time
3 = very important to me at this time

When you have responded to each item, add up the columns.

A
_____ 1. I develop visions for better ways of doing things.
_____ 2. Dissatisfaction motivates me to dream of better options.
_____ 3. I explore new ideas.
_____ 4. I pay attention to my feelings.
_____ 5. I take notice of everyday miracles.
_____ Total

B
_____ 1. I act to make my dreams come true.
_____ 2. I take risks to succeed.
_____ 3. I am clarifying my sense of purpose or direction.
_____ 4. I set and achieve goals.

_____ 5. I do what needs to be done without worrying too
much about results.
_____ Total

C
_____ 1. I am seeking a deeper sense of meaning in my life.
_____ 2. I am learning to distinguish my bliss from a
distraction.
_____ 3. I am aware of dysfunction and its effect on me.
_____ 4. I feel empathic with those who are suffering.
_____ 5. I have a clear sense of meaning in my life.
_____ Total

D
_____ 1. I create a sense of community around me.
_____ 2. I want to work with people who care about one
another.
_____ 3. I learn from conflicts with others.
_____ 4. I try to better understand others.
_____ 5. I dedicate my work to the betterment of society.
_____ Total

E
_____ 1. I am committed to walking my talk.
_____ 2. I have personal rituals that sustain and nourish me.
_____ 3. I use feedback to grow.
_____ 4. I have good timing.
_____ 5. I strive for balance in my life.
_____ Total

The questions above correspond to the "circles" (or substages)
within each chapter of this book. Each chapter describes one
stage of the journey, corresponding to one element on the
medicine wheel.

A = the stage of initiation (air)
B = the stage of trial by fire (fire)
C = the stage of the call (ether)
D = the stage of illumination (water)
E = the stage of mastery (earth)

You may find it helpful to chart your results on the medicine wheel that follows in order to find the balance of the stages as they are expressed in your life right now. First find the stage. Shade in the concentric circles within each stage. Question 1 corresponds to the center of the circle, with Question 5 as the outermost ring. On any given question, if your score is

1 = do not shade in any part of the circle
2 = shade in one half of the circle
3 = shade in the entire circle.

In filling this in, you can see that the journey is not linear. You undoubtedly will notice that you have differential amounts of your energy and attention going to different stages and sub-stages of the journey at the same time. However, you also may notice one or more of the circles with more shading than others. This would indicate that that stage (or these stages) predominate for you at this time.

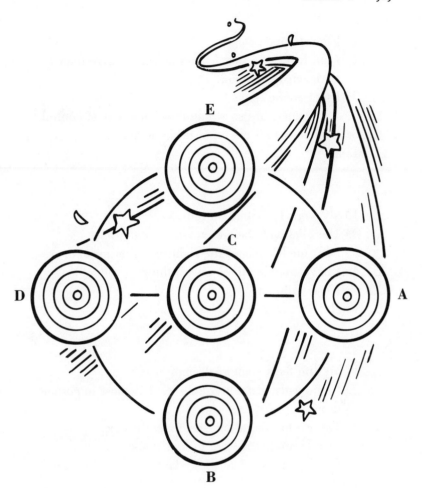

Part Two

We often are called to a journey by problems that plague us till we take it. Part Two allows you to look at your life from the perspective of what is not working for you. Please check all statements that apply. Total the number of checks in each category. Remember, the issue here is not to avoid having problems. Rather, it is to get the message from those problems, learn from them, and grow.

A

_____ 1. I feel trapped.

_____ 2. I am frustrated that I know so much more than I acknowledge I know.

_____ 3. I feel confused.

_____ 4. My feelings are so strong they seem out of control.

_____ 5. Events around me seem mysterious to me.

_____ Total

B

_____ 1. My work feels like an ordeal.

_____ 2. The challenge before me seems daunting.

_____ 3. I am unclear about the right direction to take.

_____ 4. I have trouble sticking with things.

_____ 5. I fear failure.

_____ Total

C

_____ 1. My life feels somewhat empty right now.

_____ 2. I am easily distracted from what is most important to me.

_____ 3. The world around me seems really sick.

_____ 4. People around me are in bad shape.

_____ 5. I feel pretty cynical these days.

_____ Total

D

_____ 1. I'm very alienated from my workplace.

_____ 2. I wish I felt more a part of the team.

_____ 3. I am embroiled in conflict.

_____ 4. I am frustrated working with people I do not respect.

_____ 5. I feel little sense of social responsibility these days.

_____ Total

E

_____ 1. My outer life does not match my inner reality.

_____ 2. I feel very low in energy these days.

_____ 3. I am receiving negative feedback from others.

_____ 4. My timing seems off.

_____ 5. My life does not feel very balanced.

_____ Total

Scores of 1–3 suggest that you are being called to visit or revisit a stage of the journey. Scores of 4–5 suggest that the call is rather urgent. Place your scores on the lines provided below. Circle any that are urgent.

A = the stage of initiation (to achieve the gift of air)
_____ Score

B = the stage of trial by fire (to achieve the gift of fire)
_____ Score

C = the stage of the call (to achieve the gift of ether)
_____ Score

D = the stage of illumination (to achieve the gift of water)
_____ Score

E = the stage of mastery (to achieve the gift of earth)
_____ Score

II. The Magician's Journey Index for Organizations

Part One

To find out where your organization is on its Magician's journey, rate the following on a scale of 1 to 3 as they reflect its emphases at the present time (defined as now and in the past few months). Be sure to use the entire scale.

1 = low priority in the organization
2 = moderate priority in the organization
3 = high priority in the organization

When you have responded to each item, add up the columns.

A

_____ 1. Defining future visions
_____ 2. Recognizing and solving problems
_____ 3. Brainstorming, free sharing of ideas
_____ 4. Learning from hunches/feelings
_____ 5. Calling attention to what is right about the
          organization
_____ Total

B

_____ 1. Working hard to succeed
_____ 2. Persisting in challenging times
_____ 3. Clarifying (or reclarifying) organizational mission
_____ 4. Planning and goal-setting

_____ 5. Working hard for the sake of a higher cause

_____ Total

C

_____ 1. Making work life meaningful and satisfying

_____ 2. Recognizing and assessing new opportunities

_____ 3. Facing up to (or remedying) dysfunction

_____ 4. Responding compassionately to human needs or vulnerabilities

_____ 5. Examining organizational values

_____ Total

D

_____ 1. Establishing (or increasing) participatory management

_____ 2. Team building

_____ 3. Mediating or resolving conflict

_____ 4. Increasing the understanding of individual and group identities (differences)

_____ 5. Responding to customer/client/community needs

_____ Total

E

_____ 1. Reinventing structures or procedures

_____ 2. Learning from (or setting up) feedback/evaluation systems

_____ 3. Creating (or maintaining) nourishing rituals

_____ 4. Responding to the needs of the moment

_____ 5. Assessing (and righting) organizational balance

_____ Total

The questions above roughly correspond to the "circles" (or substages) within each chapter of this book. Each chapter describes one stage of the journey, corresponding to one element on the medicine wheel.

A = the stage of initiation (air)
B = the stage of trial by fire (fire)
C = the stage of the call (ether)
D = the stage of illumination (water)
E = the stage of mastery (earth)

You may find it helpful to chart your organizational results on the Wheel of Creation that follows to find the balance of the stages as they are expressed in your organization's life right now. First, find the circle that corresponds to each stage. Shade in the concentric rings within each circle. Question 1 corresponds to the center of the circle, with question 5 as the outermost ring. On any given question, if the score is

1 = do not shade in any part of the ring
2 = shade in one half of the ring
3 = shade in the entire ring

In filling this in, you undoubtedly will notice that your organization has differential amounts of energy and attention in different stages and substages of the journey at the same time. However, you also may notice one or more of the circles with more shading than others. This would indicate which stage (or stages) predominates for your organization at this time.

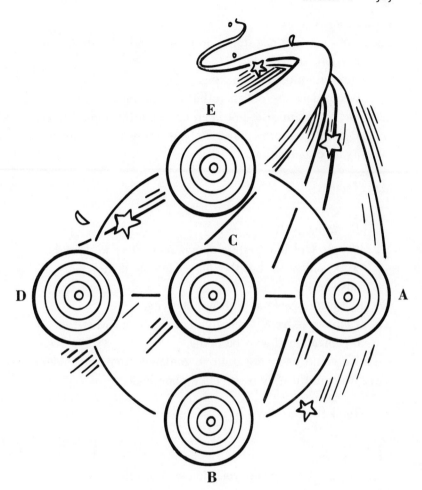

Part Two

What follows is a list of symptoms that may be evident in your organization. Please check all statements that apply. Total the number of checks in each category.

I. Category A

_____ Not everyone has the information needed to do his or her job well.

_____ Innovation often is lacking.

_____ Good ideas are out there but are not picked up on.

_____ We complain a lot but keep on doing the same things.

_____ People often are confused about where we are headed as an organization.

_____ Total A

II. Category B

_____ People feel like gerbils on a wheel. They work and work and work, but they never feel as if they get anywhere.

_____ We have problems with productivity.

_____ Employees have conflicting notions about what the organization should be doing.

_____ We could use more positive guidance from our leaders.

_____ We could use more effective planning.

_____ Total B

III. Category C

_____ Loyalty here means you violate your ethics if necessary to promote organizational success.

_____ Our staff has so many different points of view that we just avoid bringing up controversial issues.

_____ Some employees say we are like a dysfunctional family.

_____ Many employees are in crisis in some way.

_____ Our public pronouncements pretty up the truth of what really is going on.

_____ Total C

IV. Category D

_____ People here really do not know each other very well.

_____ The trust level between individuals and groups is low.

_____ We have complaints of sexism, racism, and/or harassment.

_____ People are territorial and do not cooperate easily.

_____ We have problems with customer relations.

_____ Total D

V. Category E

_____ People seem to be habitually tired or low in energy.

_____ The physical space we work in is sterile or dingy.

_____ Our policies create Catch-22 situations where we cannot get anything done.

_____ We lack reliable ways of knowing how well we are doing.

_____ The quality here is not high.

_____ Total E

Scoring Directions

Archetypal psychologist James Hillman has said that "all our pathologies are calls from the gods" (*Re-Visioning Psychology*). This instrument tells you which magical journey is calling your organization right now.

I. A high score (3–5) in Category A is a call to the journey of initiation and to discover the gifts of air. Read Chapter One for more details.

II. A high score (3–5) in Category B is a call to the journey of trial by fire and to discover the gifts of fire. Read Chapter Two for more details.

III. A high score (3–5) in Category C is a call to the journey of the call and to discover the gifts of ether. Read Chapter Three for more details.

IV. A high score (3–5) in Category D is a call to the journey of illumination and to discover the gifts of water. Read Chapter Four for more details.

V. A high score (3–5) in Category E is a call to the journey of mastery and to discover the gifts of earth. Read Chapter Five for more details.

Any organization that scores 10 or more on this index might seriously consider instituting ongoing leadership development training at all levels, starting at its top.

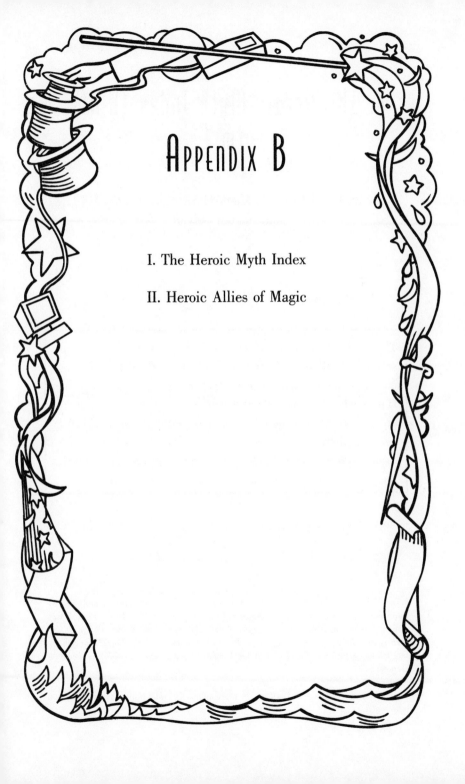

Appendix B

I. The Heroic Myth Index (HMI) Form E*

By Carol Pearson, Hugh Marr, Mary Leonard,
and Sharon Seivert

The HMI is designed to help people better understand themselves and others by identifying the different—and sometimes contradictory—myths (or plots) that shape their lives. On the HMI, each plot is named for its central character and that character's way of interpreting events and acting in the world. All twelve archetypes included in the HMI are valuable, and each brings with it a special gift. None is better or worse. Therefore, there are no right or wrong, or better or worse, answers.

* The HMI was originally based upon an expansion of theories originally published by Carol Pearson in *The Hero Within: Six Archetypes We Live By* (1986, 1989). Form E was designed to be included in Carol Pearson's book *Awakening the Heroes Within: Twelve Archetypes to Help Us Find Ourselves and Transform Our World* (1991). Form D (developed in 1988 for inclusion in Carol Pearson and Sharon Seivert's *Heroes at Work*) includes ten archetypes.

Directions

A. Please indicate how often you agree with each statement below as descriptive of you by writing in the blank beside the statement number:

1 = almost never descriptive of me
2 = rarely descriptive of me
3 = sometimes descriptive of me
4 = usually descriptive of me
5 = almost always descriptive of me

B. Work as quickly as is comfortable; your first reaction often is the best indicator.

C. Please—DO NOT SKIP ANY ITEMS, as this may invalidate your results. If unsure, just make your best determination and go on.

D. As you rate the items, think about your life in the extended present.

1 = almost never descriptive of me	2 = rarely descriptive of me	3 = sometimes descriptive of me	4 = usually descriptive of me	5 = almost always descriptive of me

_____ 1. I collect information without making judgments.

_____ 2. I feel disoriented by so much change in my life.

_____ 3. The process of my own self-healing enables me to help heal others.

_____ 4. I have let myself down.

_____ 5. I feel safe.

_____ 6. I put fear aside and do what needs to be done.

_____ 7. I put the needs of others before my own.

_____ 8. I try to be authentic wherever I am.

_____ 9. When life gets dull, I like to shake things up.

1 = almost never descriptive of me	2 = rarely descriptive of me	3 = sometimes descriptive of me	4 = usually descriptive of me	5 = almost always descriptive of me

_____ 10. I find satisfaction caring for others.

_____ 11. Others see me as fun.

_____ 12. I feel sexy.

_____ 13. I believe that people don't really mean to hurt each other.

_____ 14. As a child, I was neglected or victimized.

_____ 15. Giving makes me happier than receiving.

_____ 16. I agree with the statement "It is better to have loved and lost than never to have loved at all."

_____ 17. I embrace life fully.

_____ 18. I keep a sense of perspective by taking a long-range view.

_____ 19. I am in the process of creating my own life.

_____ 20. I believe there are many good ways to look at the same thing.

_____ 21. I am no longer the person I thought I was.

_____ 22. Life is one heartache after another.

_____ 23. Spiritual help accounts for my effectiveness.

_____ 24. I find it easier to do for others than to do for myself.

_____ 25. I find fulfillment through relationships.

_____ 26. People look to me for direction.

_____ 27. I fear those in authority.

_____ 28. I don't take rules too seriously.

_____ 29. I like to help people connect with one another.

_____ 30. I feel abandoned.

_____ 31. I have times of high accomplishment that feel effortless to me.

_____ 32. I have leadership qualities.

_____ 33. I am searching for ways to improve myself.

_____ 34. I can count on others to take care of me.

1 = almost never descriptive of me	2 = rarely descriptive of me	3 = sometimes descriptive of me	4 = usually descriptive of me	5 = almost always descriptive of me

_____ 35. I prefer to be in charge.

_____ 36. I try to find truths behind illusions.

_____ 37. Changing my inner thoughts changes my outer life.

_____ 38. I develop resources, human or natural.

_____ 39. I am willing to take personal risks in order to defend my beliefs.

_____ 40. I can't sit back and let a wrong go by without challenging it.

_____ 41. I strive for objectivity.

_____ 42. My presence is often a catalyst for change.

_____ 43. I enjoy making people laugh.

_____ 44. I use discipline to achieve goals.

_____ 45. I feel loving toward people in general.

_____ 46. I am good at matching people's abilities with tasks to be done.

_____ 47. It is essential for me to maintain my independence.

_____ 48. I believe everyone and everything in the world are interconnected.

_____ 49. The world is a safe place.

_____ 50. People I've trusted have abandoned me.

_____ 51. I feel restless.

_____ 52. I am letting go of things that do not fit for me anymore.

_____ 53. I like to "lighten up" people who are too serious.

_____ 54. A little chaos is good for the soul.

_____ 55. Sacrificing to help others has made me a better person.

_____ 56. I feel calm.

_____ 57. I stand up to offensive people.

_____ 58. I like to transform situations.

_____ 59. The key to success in all aspects of life is discipline.

_____ 60. Inspiration comes easily to me.

1 = almost	2 = rarely	3 = sometimes	4 = usually	5 = almost
never	descriptive	descriptive	descriptive	always
descriptive	of me	of me	of me	descriptive
of me				of me

_____ 61. I do not live up to my expectations for myself.

_____ 62. I have a sense that a better world awaits me somewhere.

_____ 63. I assume that people I meet are trustworthy.

_____ 64. I am experimenting with turning my dreams into realities.

_____ 65. I know my needs will be provided for.

_____ 66. I feel like breaking something.

_____ 67. I try to manage situations with the good of all in mind.

_____ 68. I have a hard time saying no.

_____ 69. I have a lot more great ideas than I have time to act on them.

_____ 70. I am looking for greener pastures.

_____ 71. Important people in my life have let me down.

_____ 72. The act of looking for something is as important to me as finding it.

Scoring Directions

Move now to the page titled "HMI Score Sheet." Please fill out this form completely, transferring the score of 1–5 you gave on each question to the number that corresponds to that question, then add up the columns to discover how active each archetype is at this time in your life.

After completing the "Score Sheet," graph your HMI scores on the pie chart that follows. This will give you a visual representation of your HMI results.

Scores between 15 and 24 indicate either neutrality or ambivalence about the archetype. If you consistently answer 3 ("sometimes descriptive of me"), it would suggest that the archetype is simply of little interest to you. If conflicting responses of 5's and 1's or 2's and

4's cancel each other out, this indicates ambivalence. Scores of 24 or higher suggest the archetype is active in your life in a conscious way. Scores of 15 or lower suggest either repression of, or aversion to, the archetype (perhaps because you previously overused it).

HMI Score Sheet

Under the name of each archetype below is a column of numbers. The numbers correspond to question numbers on the Heroic Myth Index. On the blank beside each question number, fill in the corresponding answer number from your test. When you have written in your answer numbers for all the questions, total each column. Each of these totals represents your score on the corresponding archetype.

	Innocent	Orphan	Seeker	Lover	Warrior	Caregiver
	5____	14____	33____	12____	6____	7____
	13____	22____	47____	16____	39____	10____
	34____	27____	51____	17____	40____	15____
	49____	30____	62____	25____	44____	24____
	63____	50____	70____	29____	57____	55____
	65____	71____	72____	45____	59____	68____
Totals						

	Destroyer	Creator	Magician	Ruler	Sage	Fool
	2____	8____	3____	26____	1____	9____
	4____	19____	23____	32____	18____	11____
	21____	31____	37____	35____	20____	28____
	52____	60____	42____	38____	36____	43____
	61____	64____	48____	46____	41____	53____
	66____	69____	58____	67____	56____	54____
Totals						

Pie Chart

Mark on each axis your degree of identification with that archetype. Then shade in toward the center of the circle. Then add up your scores for the subcategories of air (Seeker, Sage, Creator); fire (Warrior, Destroyer, Magician); water (Orphan, Lover, Fool); earth (Innocent, Caregiver, Ruler). Place the totals in the boxes provided to see the relative weights of air, fire, water, and earth in your life.

Earth [   ]   Air [   ]

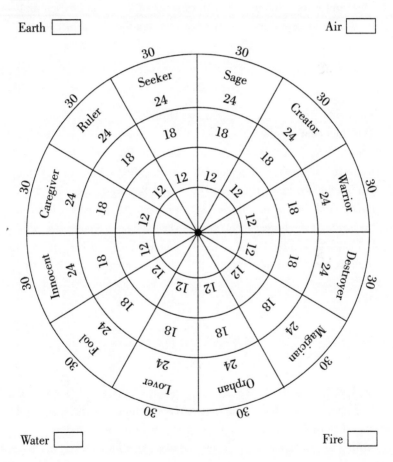

Water [   ]   Fire [   ]

HMI Type Descriptions

The following descriptions are designed to help you understand your HMI scores. Your score in each category indicates your degree of identification with each type (6/low–30/high). Remember, no type is better or worse. Each has an important contribution to make to our lives and work. You may want to transfer your scores for each archetype here to determine which archetype leads for you in each category.

SECURITY

Innocent: Score: _____

The Innocent is the pre-fallen person who lives—or tries to live—in Eden. The Innocent's gift to the world is trust, optimism, and belief in things as they are. At the lowest level, belief is preserved by denial; at the highest level, by transcendence.

Orphan: Score: _____

The Orphan has the same wish as the Innocent—to live in a safe world—but the Orphan feels betrayed, abandoned, victimized. At the lowest level, the Orphan is a confirmed victim and cynic. At a high level, the Orphan simply reminds us of human vulnerability and interdependence.

IDENTITY

Seeker: Score: _____

The Seeker explores internal and external realities and is willing to give up security, community, and intimacy to achieve autonomy. Seekers find out who they are by differentiating them-

Lover: Score: _____

Lovers find out who they are by discovering who and what they love. At a lower level, the Lover may love only a few people, activities, or things. At a higher level, Lovers expand that love to

selves from others. At worst, they are just outsiders. At best, they find their unique identities and vocations.

enjoy and respect all of life's diversity.

RESPONSIBILITY

Warrior: Score: _____

The Warrior defeats the villain and rescues the victim. Warriors are courageous and disciplined, imposing high standards on themselves. At worst, they run roughshod over others. At best, they assert themselves appropriately to make the world a better place.

Caregiver: Score: _____

Caregivers take care of others even when doing so requires sacrifice. They give to make the world a better place for others. At worst, the Caregiver's sacrifice is maiming or manipulative. At best, the Caregiver's giving is compassionate, genuine, and of great help to others.

AUTHENTICITY

Destroyer: Score: _____

When the Destroyer is active within a person, what we see is the effects of tragedy and loss. At best, this initiatory loss leads to a greater receptivity to new ideas, empathy and compassion for others, and a deeper knowledge of their own identity and strength. At worst, it simply decimates a personality, and we see before us only a ruin of what was.

Creator: Score: _____

When the Creator is active within a person, she/he is in the process of discovering or creating a more adequate sense of self. At best, this new identity is transformative and leads to a more fulfilling and effective life. At worst, it is simply an experiment, and the person retreats or goes back to the drawing board to start over.

POWER

Magician: Score: _____

Magicians create new realities, transform old ones, serve as catalysts for change, and "name" and thereby create reality. At worst, their efforts can be disempowering "evil sorcery." At best, they discover empowering, win/win solutions.

Ruler: Score: _____

The Ruler in each of us understands that we are responsible for our inner and outer lives: the buck stops here. At worst, the Ruler is a despot. At best, the Ruler's order is inclusive, creating inner wholeness and a peaceful and prosperous outer community.

FREEDOM

Sage: Score: _____

Sages find freedom through understanding the big picture (global or cosmic) and a capacity for detachment. At the lowest level, the Sage may have little interest in the ordinary, mundane pleasures of life. At the highest level, however, the Sage combines detachment with love, wisdom with joy in life.

Fool: Score: _____

The Fool finds freedom through unconventionality and a capacity to enjoy every moment. The Fool lightens us up, finds clever, innovative, and fun ways around obstacles—intellectual or physical. At worst, the Fool is irresponsible. At best, Fools live lives of joy because they live fully every moment.

II. Heroic Allies of Magic

The twelve heroic allies that follow connect concepts in *Magic at Work* with those in my earlier work, *Awakening the Heroes Within: Twelve Archetypes to Help Us Find Ourselves and Transform Our World.*

Heroic Allies of Initiation (Air)

THE SEEKER explores options, seeking his or her own truth. Seekers learn to critique accepted ideas, and they explore new and divergent thinking. Merlin is strongly influenced by the Seeker archetype in the forest where he begins to find his own way and his own perspective. Like many Seekers before and after him, Merlin often feels like an outsider, and only late in his life does he find ways to reconcile being true to himself with being at home in the world. Today the Seeker archetype helps develop magical ability by motivating our desire to improve ourselves and to think or act independently.

Your Seeker Score: _____

THE SAGE seeks wisdom, striving to align with truth and to live in keeping with its mandates. Merlin's major accomplishments come because of his dispassionate commitment to truth. That is why he is a scientist and philosopher as well as a seer. The challenge of his madness requires sorting out true vision from hallucinations. Wisdom is essential to magic, for without wisdom, power easily can be used for ill. Today the Sage may move us through confusion to clarity.

Your Sage Score: _____

THE CREATOR employs imagination to express his or her wisdom in the world in creative ways—art, inventions, developing innovative ideas or products. Merlin expresses the Creator in building and inventing things, as well as in singing and writing. Often the objects he invents are magical. His magic singing moves Stonehenge to England. Today the Creator expresses itself in any form of creativity or innovation.

Your Creator Score: _____

Allies of Illumination Total: _____

Heroic Allies of Trial by Fire

THE WARRIOR provides focus, discipline, courage, and the ability to persevere when things get tough. Arthur uses the Warrior as an ally in defeating the kings and dukes who have refused to honor his leadership. The Warrior in the service of magic removes the blocks to the expression of the miracles that always are ready to emerge in our lives. Today the Warrior can be expressed as the ability to clarify goals, stick to them, and assert our needs and rights.

Your Warrior Score: _____

THE DESTROYER is the archetype of letting go, clearing out, weeding, providing space. Arthur has to let go of the old order to create Camelot. He also has to sacrifice his earlier self-image as the bastard son to rise to the occasion and be king. The Destroyer serves magic as the archetype of banishing and exorcism. Today the Destroyer may be expressed in housecleaning—clearing out of habits, relationships, or activities that no longer serve our journeys.

Your Destroyer Score: _____

THE MAGICIAN is, of course, the archetype for this entire book. *Magic at Work* describes how the Magician operates when in touch with all five stages of the journey. The archetype's home base, however, is the stage of trial by fire and the element of fire, because magic is active and makes things happen. Today the Magician may express itself as an ability to "pull rabbits out of hats," or to do anything that strikes others as miraculous.

Your Magician Score: _____

Allies of Trial by Fire Total: _____

Heroic Allies of Illumination (Water)

THE ORPHAN helps us recognize when we are being abandoned, victimized, or betrayed by others so that we can decide what to do about it. It helps us to be realistic about others, to feel and express our pain in situations where it is safe to do so, and to ask for help or rescue when we need it. Guinevere frequently is abducted and rescued by others. She is abandoned when the court turns on her because of her relationship with Lancelot. The Orphan supports magic by showing what needs to be transformed. Today the Orphan archetype expresses itself anytime we feel like motherless children.

Your Orphan Score: _____

THE LOVER helps us bond, connect, and be intimate with others. As a love goddess and as the protagonist of a love story, Guinevere is the epitome of this archetype. The Lover archetype supports the Magician by creating a field of connection between people that allows them to let go of narrow self-interest to act in concert to make dreams come true. Today the Lover archetype helps us experience intimacy, passion, and commitment.

Your Lover Score: _____

THE FOOL knows how to be with others in a spirit of lightness and play. If others are combative, the Fool can play at war. If they are hurtful, the Fool moves on to something more enjoyable. The Fool lightens people up so they can have a good time. Guinevere is known for being the gracious hostess who helps make court life light and fun. The Fool, as Trickster, supports magic as a master of illusion. Today the Fool may be expressed anytime we enjoy ourselves.

Your Fool Score: _____

Allies of Illumination Total: _____

Heroic Allies of Mastery (Earth)

THE INNOCENT is simple and trusting and good, often seeking guidance and truth from others. Dindraine, dedicating her life to the Grail procession, is known as a virgin. In at least some versions of the Grail myth, virginity is presented as purity of mind and heart rather than as a physical condition. The Innocent supports magic because it allows us to be receptive and to learn from others. The Innocent also helps us have the simplicity and loyalty to allow fidelity to a simple task (like caring for the Grail or leading the ritual procession). Today the Innocent may be expressed by an optimism that transcends the apparent facts of the situation.

Your Innocent Score: _____

THE CAREGIVER nurtures others and tends or maintains the natural world (cleaning, repairing, cooking, etc.). The Grail knight demonstrates qualities of the Caregiver by taking care of the Grail. He also demonstrates the sacrificial quality associated with the Caregiver, sacrificing his own pleasure and ambition to his responsibilities. The Caregiver supports magic by creating or maintaining sacred or nurturing environments where magic can happen. Today the Caregiver may be expressed in the joy of caring for children, developing a protégé, planting a garden, or maintaining orderly and attractive environments.

Your Caregiver Score: _____

THE RULER is master of the physical world, taking control of, and responsibility for, the creation of forms, systems, and policies in order to maintain a just, orderly, and prosperous kingdom. Titurel takes on leadership, supervising the building of the Grail Temple and organizing the work plans and the workmen so the plan is executed in an orderly way. The Ruler supports magic by commissioning it; for example, the king is a patron of the court Magician. Arthur, of course, is strong on the Ruler archetype as well as the Warrior—otherwise, he would not be king. Today the Ruler archetype is expressed when we take on leadership or other responsibilities.

Your Ruler Score: _____

Allies of Mastery Total: _____

Note: Instead of heroic allies, the stage of the call and the element of ether preside over the aspects of the psyche: ego, soul, and self. (Ego refers to our everyday sense of who we are. Soul is our deeper authenticity. Self includes both, plus access to the richness of the unconscious. Ether helps us find a uniqueness beyond heroic archetypes.)

Notes

PREFACE: FROM WARRIOR TO MAGICIAN

1. Albert Einstein, quoted in numerous sources with no citation.

2. Robert Johnson, *Inner Work: Using Dreams and Active Imagination for Personal Growth* (San Francisco: Harper & Row, 1986), pp. 27–35.

3. See also C. G. Jung, *Four Archetypes: Mother/Rebirth/Spirit/Trickster*, trans. R. F. C. Hull from *The Collected Works of C. G. Jung*, Vol. 9, Part 1, Bollingen Series XX (Princeton: Princeton University Press, 1969).

4. Carol S. Pearson, *The Hero Within: Six Archetypes We Live By* (San Francisco: HarperCollins, 1986); Carol S. Pearson, *Awakening the Heroes Within: Twelve Archetypes to Help Us Find Ourselves and Transform Our World* (San Francisco: HarperCollins, 1991); and Sharon Seivert and Carol S. Pearson, *Heroes at Work*, privately published. (For more information about the workbook, contact Ms. Seivert, 10 Magazine Street, Cambridge, Mass., or Dr. Pearson, Mount Vernon Institute, 2100 Foxhall Road, N.W., Washington, D.C. 20007.)

INTRODUCTION: CREATING CAMELOT IN THE IN-BETWEEN

1. Charles Handy, *The Age of Unreason* (Boston: Harvard Business School Press, 1989), p. 5.

2. Joseph Campbell with Bill Moyers, *The Power of Myth* (New York: Doubleday, 1988), p. 151.

3. R. J. Stewart, *The Mystic Life of Merlin* (New York: Arkana, 1986), p. 16. Stewart makes the point that "the central thesis of the Western Mysteries is that the primal spirit creates outer reality through imagination." This observation provides the inspiration for the central thesis of *Magic at Work*.

4. Jessie L. Weston, *From Ritual to Romance: An Account of the Holy Grail from Ancient Ritual to Christian Symbol* (New York: Doubleday, 1957).

5. H. A. Guerber, *Legends of the Middle Ages* (New York: American Book Co., 1924).

6. Richard Cavendish, *Legends of the World* (New York: Crescent Books, 1989), p. 273.

7. Robert Ellwood, "Shamanism and Theosophy," in *Shamanism: An Expanded View of Reality*, ed. Shirley Nicholson (Wheaton, Ill.: Theosophical Publishing House, 1987), pp. 253–66.

8. Stewart, *Mystic Life,* pp. 113–30. See also Stewart's *The Elements of Creation Myth* (Longmead, Shaftesbury, Dorset: Element Books, 1989), pp. 103–11.

9. Franklin Sills, *The Polarity Process: Energy as a Healing Art* (London: Element Books, 1989), p. 24. The correlation between the senses and the elemental energies used in this book is based upon polarity theory with two exceptions. I have used taste for earth and touch for water, reversing the usual polarity correlations.

CHAPTER ONE: WHAT THE CRYSTAL BALL REQUIRES

1. The stages of Merlin's initiation described in this chapter and all the stories that open the circles come from R. J. Stewart, *The Mystic Life of Merlin* (New York: Arkana, 1986).

2. Brian A. Hall, *The Genesis Effect: Personal and Organizational Transformations* (New York: Paulist Press, 1986), p. 11.

3. T. H. White, *The Once and Future King* (New York: Berkeley), p. 34.

4. John Matthews and Marian Green, *The Grail Seeker's Companion: A Guide to the Grail Quest in the Aquarian Age* (Wellingborough, Northhamptonshire: Aquarian Press, 1986), p. 52.

5. Thomas S. Kuhn, *The Structure of Scientific Revolutions* (Chicago: University of Chicago, 1962).

6. Peter Senge, *The Fifth Discipline: The Art and Practice of the Learning Organization* (New York: Doubleday, 1990), p. 73.

7. Stephen R. Covey, *The Seven Habits of Highly Effective People* (New York: Simon and Schuster, 1989), p. 23.

8. Arthur Rubinstein, *My Young Years* (New York: Alfred A. Knopf, 1973), p. 255.

9. Michael Ray and Rochelle Myers, *Creativity in Business* (New York: Doubleday, 1986), p. 142.

10. Evelyn Keller, *Reflections on Gender and Science* (New Haven: Yale University Press, 1985).

11. Nevill Drury, *The Shaman and the Magician* (New York: Arkana, 1982), p. 17.

12. Lynn Andrews, *Medicine Woman* (San Francisco: Harper & Row, 1981), p. 107.

13. Starhawk, *Dreaming the Dark: Magic, Sex and Politics* (Boston: Beacon Press, 1982), p. 13.

14. Jeremiah 31:33–34. *The New Oxford Annotated Bible,* Revised Standard Version (New York: Oxford University Press, 1973), p. 955.

15. Stewart, *Mystic Life,* pp. 220–21.

16. Ibid., p. 131.

17. Senge, *Fifth Discipline,* pp. 95–104.

18. R. Buckminster Fuller, *Operating Manual for Spaceship Earth* (New York: Pocket Books, 1970), p. 85.

19. Carlos Castaneda, *The Teaching of Don Juan: A Yaqui Way of Knowledge* (Berkeley: University of California Press, 1973), pp. 14–19.

20. Stewart, *Mystic Life*, p. 148.

21. K. C. Cole, *Sympathetic Vibrations: Reflections on Physics as a Way of Life* (New York: Bantam Books, 1985), p. 38.

22. Margaret J. Wheatley, *Leadership and the New Science: Learning About Organization from an Orderly Universe* (San Francisco: Berrett-Koehler, 1992), p. 99.

23. Hugh Prather, *A Book of Games: A Course in Spiritual Play* (New York: Doubleday, 1981), p. 61.

24. Gareth Knight, "Merlin and the Grail," in *At the Table of the Grail: Magic and the Use of Imagination*, ed. John Matthews (New York: Arkana, 1984), p. 63.

25. Suresh Srivastva and David L. Cooperrider, *Appreciative Management and Leadership: The Power of Positive Thought in Organizations* (San Francisco: Jossey-Bass, 1990), p. 119–24. The quote in the text is from a study by the Dutch sociologist Fred Polak (1973) cited by Cooperrider.

CHAPTER TWO: THE CHALLENGE OF THE MAGIC SWORD

1. *King Arthur and His Knights: Selected Tales by Sir Thomas Malory*, ed. Eugene Vinaver (New York: Oxford University Press, 1980), p. 9. The stories that provide the opening matter for this chapter are taken from various translations of Malory's work, including the above and: *Tales of King Arthur*, trans. Michael Senior (New York: Schocken Books, 1980), and Chrétien de Troyes, *The Quest of the Holy Grail*, trans. P. M. Matarasso (New York: Penguin Books, 1969).

2. Robert Ellwood, "Shamanism and Theosophy," in *Shamanism: An Expanded View of Reality*, ed. Shirley Nicholson (Wheaton, Ill.: Theosophical Publishing House, 1987), p. 260.

3. Pablo Casals, *Joys and Sorrows: Reflections by Pablo Casals* (New York: Simon and Schuster, 1970), p. 76.

4. Kaleel Jamison, *The Nibble Theory and the Kernel of Power* (New York: Paulist Press, 1984), pp. 40–66.

5. This point is also made by Michael Ray and Rochelle Myers in *Creativity in Business* (New York: Doubleday, 1986), pp. 26–27.

6. Marsha Sinetar, *Do What You Love, the Money Will Follow: Finding Your Right Livelihood* (New York: Paulist Press, 1987), pp. 73–74.

7. Peter Block, *The Empowered Manager: Positive Political Skills at Work* (San Francisco: Jossey-Bass, 1991), pp. 105–34, offers a useful guide to vision and mission formulation. See W. Warner Burke, *Organizational Development: A Nor-*

mative View (Reading, Mass.: Addison-Wesley, 1987), for more information on strategic planning.

8. Shakti Gawain, *Creative Visualization* (New York: Bantam Books, 1985), p. 2.

9. Robert Johnson, *Inner Work: Using Dreams and Active Imagination for Personal Growth* (San Francisco: Harper & Row, 1986), pp. 213–14.

10. Henry Gradillas, Keynote Speech, Calvary Board of Education Conference, May 1992.

11. Swami Durgananda, "The Way of the Warrior," in *Darshan: In the Company of the Saints* (South Fallsburg, N.Y.: SYDA Foundation, 1987), pp. 32–34.

12. Parker Palmer, "The Woodcarver," in *The Active Life: A Spirituality of Work, Creativity, and Caring* (San Francisco: HarperCollins, 1991).

13. Roger von Oech, *A Whack on the Side of the Head: How You Can Be More Creative* (Stamford, Conn.: U.S. Games Systems, 1983), p. 155.

14. Vaclav Havel, *Disturbing the Peace* (New York: Alfred A. Knopf), p. 32.

15. Parker Palmer, *Leading from Within: Reflections on Spirituality and Leadership* (Washington, D.C.: Servant Leadership School, 1990), p. 4.

16. David Whyte, "The Faces at Braga," in *Where Many Rivers Meet* (Langley, Wash.: Many Rivers Press, 1990), pp. 25–26.

17. Ursula K. Le Guin, *A Wizard of Earthsea* (New York: Bantam Books, 1968), p. 71.

CHAPTER THREE: THE CALL OF THE GRAIL

1. Chrétien de Troyes, *The Quest of the Holy Grail*, trans. P. M. Matarasso (New York: Penguin Books, 1969), pp. 43–44.

2. Joseph Campbell with Bill Moyers, *The Power of Myth* (New York: Doubleday, 1988), p. 151.

3. I am particularly indebted to Joseph Campbell's *Transformation of Myth Through Time* (New York: Harper & Row, 1990), Campbell's *Myths to Live By* (New York: Bantam Books, 1973), Robert Johnson's *He: Understanding Masculine Psychology* (New York: Harper & Row, 1989), and Emma Jung and Marie-Louise von Franz's *The Grail Legend* (Boston: Sigo Press, 1986) for the interpretation of the Percival story contained herein and to Chrétien de Troyes's *The Quest of the Holy Grail*. The stories included in this chapter come from these sources.

4. Campbell, *Power*, pp. 217–18.

5. Chrétien de Troyes, *Quest*, p. 281.

6. Dolores Ashcroft-Nowicki, "The Path to the Grail," in *At the Table of the Grail: Magic and the Use of Imagination*, ed. John Matthews (New York: Arkana, 1984), pp. 198–99.

7. Ibid., p. 200.

8. Ibid., pp. 198–99.

9. Brian Hall, *The Genesis Effect* (New York: Paulist Press, 1986), p. 9.

10. David Bohm, *Wholeness and Implicate Order* (London: Ark Paperbacks, 1980).

11. Jan Halper, *Quiet Desperation: The Truth About Successful Men* (New York: Warner Books, 1988), pp. 27–30.

12. Judith Duerk, *A Circle of Stones: Woman's Journey to Herself* (San Diego: Lura Media, 1989), pp. 24–27.

13. Arthur W. Frank, *At the Will of the Body* (Boston: Houghton Mifflin, 1991), p. 134.

14. John Matthews and Marian Green, *The Grail Seeker's Companion: A Guide to the Grail Quest in the Aquarian Age* (Wellingborough, Northhamptonshire: Aquarian Press, 1986), p. 51.

15. Robert Johnson, *Owning Your Own Shadow* (San Francisco: HarperCollins, 1971), pp. 4–6.

16. Adolf Guggenbuhl-Craig, *Power in the Helping Professions* (Dallas: Spring Publications, 1971), p. 96.

17. Ursula K. Le Guin, *A Wizard of Earthsea* (New York: Bantam Books, 1968), p. 179.

18. Campbell, *Transformation*, p. 260.

19. Doug Boyd, *Magicians, Shamans, and Medicine People* (New York: Paragon House, 1989), p. 20.

20. Jessie L. Weston, *From Ritual to Romance: An Account of the Holy Grail from Ancient Ritual to Christian Symbol* (New York: Doubleday, 1957), p. 141.

21. Margaret Wheatley, *Leadership and the New Science: Learning about Organization from an Orderly Universe* (San Francisco: Berrett-Koehler, 1992), pp. 56–57.

22. John Scherer, *Work and the Human Spirit* (Spokane, Wash.: John Scherer and Associates, 1992), p. 127.

23. Joseph Campbell, *Power*, pp. 217–18.

24. Serge King, "The Way of the Adventurer," in *Shamanism: An Expanded View of Reality*, ed. Shirley Nicholson (Wheaton, Ill.: Theosophical Publishing House, 1987), p. 193.

25. Chrétien de Troyes, *Quest*, p. 283.

26. Caitlin Matthews, "Sophia: Companion on the Quest," in *At the Table of the Grail: Magic and the Use of Imagination*, ed. John Matthews (New York: Arkana, 1984), p. 127.

CHAPTER FOUR: THE GIFT OF THE ROUND TABLE

1. Caitlin Matthews and John Matthews, *Ladies of the Lake* (San Francisco: Aquarian Press, 1992), pp. 2–55. All the stories and information in this chapter about Guinevere come from this rich source. The Matthewses' work, moreover, is critical to the central ideas in this chapter as well.

2. Thaddeus Golas, *The Lazy Man's Guide to Enlightenment* (New York: Bantam Books, 1980).

3. Hyler Bracey, Jack Rosenblum, Aubrey Sanford, and Roy Trueblood, *Managing from the Heart* (New York: Delacourt, 1990).

4. Caitlin Matthews and John Matthews, *Ladies*, pp. 47–51.

5. Audre Lorde, "The Uses of the Erotic," in *Sister Outsider: Essay and Speeches by Audre Lorde* (Trumansburg, N.Y.: The Crossing Press, 1984), pp. 53–59.

6. Chrétien de Troyes, *The Quest of the Holy Grail*, trans. by P. M. Matarasso (New York: Penguin Books, 1969), pp. 207–21.

7. Christopher Matthews, *Hardball, How Politics Is Played by One Who Knows the Game* (New York: Harper & Row, 1988), pp. 21–22.

8. Sally Helgesen, *The Female Advantage: Women's Ways of Leadership* (New York: Doubleday, 1990), pp. 10–14.

9. Peter Senge, *The Fifth Discipline: The Art and Practice of the Learning Organization* (New York: Doubleday, 1990), p. 248.

10. Caitlin Matthews and John Matthews, *Ladies*, p. 41.

11. Ibid., p. 44.

12. Readers may remember a similar, and more familiar, version of this tale, known as "Sir Gawain and the Green Knight." I use this lesser-known story because it highlights Guinevere's role as the head of the Court of Women.

13. Caitlin Matthews and John Matthews, *Ladies*, p. 39.

14. Gary P. Ferraro, *The Cultural Dimension of International Business* (Englewood Cliffs, N.J.: Prentice Hall, 1990), pp. 7–9.

15. Margaret Wheatley, *Leadership and the New Science: Learning About Organization from an Orderly Universe* (San Francisco: Berrett-Koehler, 1992), p. 34.

16. Ibid., pp. 15–16.

17. Alice Walker, *The Color Purple* (New York: Simon and Schuster, 1982), p. 178.

18. Julian of Norwich, *Meditations with Julian of Norwich*, trans. Brendan Doyle (Santa Fe, N.Mex., Bear and Company, 1983), p. 113.

19. Martin Luther King, Jr., *The Trumpet of Conscience* (New York: Harper & Row, 1967), p. 69.

CHAPTER FIVE: AS WITHIN, SO WITHOUT

1. H. A. Guerber, *Legends of the Middle Ages* (New York: American Book Co., 1924).

2. James Hillman, *Interviews* (San Francisco: Harper Colophon Books, 1983), p. 137.

3. Thomas Moore, *Care of the Soul: A Guide for Cultivating Depth and Sacredness in Everyday Life* (San Francisco: Harper & Row, 1967), p. 183.

4. The placement of the elements in the four directions differs from tradition to tradition. The placement given here, and used throughout this book, comes from Starhawk, *The Spiral Dance* (San Francisco: Harper & Row, 1979). I use Starhawk's system because she is tracing an indigenous tradition that began in northern Europe, one that venerates goddesses as well as gods. The traditions Starhawk describes appear, based on locality of origin and their androgynous focus, to have common roots to the Grail stories.

5. Shirley Gehrke Luthman, *Collection: A Continuation of "Intimacy—"* (San Rafael, Calif.: Mehetabel, 1980), pp. 28–45.

6. Caitlin Matthews and John Matthews, *Ladies of the Lake* (San Francisco: Aquarian Press, 1992), pp. 57–80. The reference to the Mamannan in Echtra Cormaic comes from T. P. Cross and C. H. Slover, *Ancient Irish Tales* (Dublin: Figgis, 1936).

7. Rafael Aguayo, *Dr. Deming: The American Who Taught the Japanese About Quality* (New York: Simon and Schuster, 1990). See also Andrea Gabor, *The Man Who Discovered Quality* (New York: Penguin Books, 1990).

8. Thomas Berger, *Little Big Man* (Greenwich, Conn.: Fawcett, 1964), pp. 113 and 441–42.

9. Ann McGee-Cooper, *You Do Not Have to Go Home from Work Exhausted* (New York: Bantam Books, 1992), pp. 85–102.

10. Sun Bear, *Walk in Balance* (New York: Prentice Hall Press, 1989), pp. 16–17.

11. Marie-Louise von Franz, *Psyche and Matter* (Boston: Shambhala Publications, 1988), pp. 169–84.

12. Moore, *Care*, p. 185.

13. Paula Payne Hardin, *What Are You Doing with the Rest of Your Life? Choices in Midlife* (San Rafael, Calif.: New World Library, 1992), pp. 46–47.

14. Caitlin Matthews and John Matthews, *Ladies*, pp. 182–98.

15. Leslie Marmon Silko, *Ceremony* (New York: New American Library), p. 133.

16. Moore, *Care*, p. 182.

17. Ibid., p. 186.

18. Mary Stewart, *The Hollow Hills* (New York: Fawcett, 1973), pp. 264–67.

19. Berger, *Little Big Man*, p. 445. The scene described here occurs in the movie version of the novel. In the novel, Old Lodge Skins' magic works. He just lays down and dies.

20. Arnold Lobel, "The Garden," in *Frog and Toad Together* (New York: Harper & Row, 1979), pp. 18–29.

21. Srikumar S. Rao, "Welcome to Open Space," *Training* (April 1992), pp. 52–56.

22. R. J. Stewart, *The Mystic Life of Merlin* (New York: Arkana, 1986), pp. 113–30.

23. The Chinese five-element system is similar in its dynamics and intent to the five-element polarity system used by Lee and in this book. Because I am treating the elements as archetypes, the rough equivalents I have sketched in the text work well enough. However, as the elements in each system refer to energy systems in the body, they are quite distinct. One can use both systems.

24. Julian of Norwich, *Meditations with Julian of Norwich*, trans. Brendan Doyle (Santa Fe, N.Mex.: Bear and Company, 1983), p. 48.

About the Authors

Carol S. Pearson, Ph.D., is the dean of, and a Distinguished Human and Organizational Development Research Scholar at, the Mount Vernon Institute at Mount Vernon College and the author of *The Hero Within: Six Archetypes We Live By; Awakening the Heroes Within: Twelve Archetypes to Help Us Find Ourselves and Transform Our World; The Female Hero in American and British Literature* (coauthor Katherine Pope); and *Educating the Majority: Women Challenge Tradition in Higher Education* (coauthors Donna Shavlik and Judith Touchton). At the Mount Vernon Institute and in her own consulting practice, Pearson uses the theories described in this and her other books in speeches, personal growth workshops, success and executive coaching, team building, and whole-organization systems interventions. She also trains psychologists, educators, consultants, managers, and others in professional applications of these concepts.

She can be contacted at the Mount Vernon Institute, Mount Vernon College, 2100 Foxhall Road, Washington, D.C. 20007. Phone 202-625-4506; fax 202-338-4261.

Sharon Seivert is the president of GREAT WORK, a management consulting firm based in Cambridge, Massachusetts. Her collaboration with Carol S. Pearson since 1985 has resulted in the development of *Heroes at Work*, the Heroic Myth Index, the Organizational Myth Index, and now *Magic at Work*. Before that time, Seivert served as CEO of the Central Minnesota Group Health Plan and was a board member of the Group Health Association of America. Today she is a workplace teacher, advisor, and writer who infuses organizational change efforts and leadership development with the vital concepts of the magic circle, the five elements, and the Magician's journey, as well as those contained in *Heroes at Work.* Moreover, Seivert has first-hand experience of the stages of the Magician's journey: as an apprentice in the authentic Usui healing tradition of Reiki. Recently she was initiated as one of six hundred such Reiki Masters in the world.

She can be contacted at GREAT WORK, Inc., 10 Magazine Street, #1004, Cambridge, Mass., 02139. Phone 617-547-8014; fax 617-547-6720.